D0847967

# Espionage and Enslavement in the Revolution

*The True Story of Robert Townsend and Elizabeth*

## Claire Bellerjeau and

## Tiffany Yecke Brooks

LYONS
PRESS

*Guilford, Connecticut*

An imprint of The Rowman & Littlefield Publishing Group, Inc.
4501 Forbes Blvd., Ste. 200
Lanham, MD 20706
www.rowman.com

Distributed by NATIONAL BOOK NETWORK

British Library Cataloguing in Publication Information available

Library of Congress Control Number: 2021930922

ISBN 978-1-4930-5247-9 (cloth : alk. paper)
ISBN 978-1-4930-5248-6 (e-book)

♾™ The paper used in this publication meets the minimum requirements of American National Standard for Information Sciences—Permanence of Paper for Printed Library Materials, ANSI/NISO Z39.48-1992.

# CONTENTS

# Foreword

I FIRST MET AUTHOR CLAIRE BELLERJEAU AT THE OYSTER BAY HIStorical Society on a beautiful autumn Sunday for a very special event. The reception we were attending involved my ancestors who have lived in this tiny close-knit community on the north shore of Long Island since the early 1800s—most notably, my great-great grandfather, David Carll, who was born in 1842 in nearby Cold Spring Harbor and raised his family in Oyster Bay after he fought in the Civil War. His body, plus those of many of my relatives, are laid to rest on a hill in an all-Black cemetery called Pine Hollow, which on that autumn day, November 4, 2018, became recognized as a historical landmark. The graveyard is only steps away from the house that David Carll bought to raise his family with the enlistment bounty money he received as a Union soldier and where my father Milton A. Williams Jr. was born years later in 1935. Though David Carll first arrived in Oyster Bay in the 1840s, the neighborhood called Pine Hollow had been home to free Black families since the 1680s, when the first slave freed on Long Island, Tom Gall, made the sandy hill his home.

The Carll/Williams Family is proud of their Oyster Bay roots, and I had the wonderful opportunity to explore them when I appeared on the TV research show *Who Do You Think You Are?* in 2010. Claire was able to help trace my lineage back to the 1830s and 1820s, to include David's father, Lewis Carll, a man named Stephen Carll, and even earlier, a young man named Stephen who was purchased in 1795 by a white man named Gilbert Carll—offering a possible link all the way back to a time when my enslaved ancestors did not have a last name.

Besides my Oyster Bay lineage, Claire wondered if I had ever heard of the story of the Townsend family whose son was a spy for George Washington and whose family enslaved upwards of twelve African Americans.

I asked local Oyster Bay historian John Hammond, who had also helped me do the research for the show, if he had heard of any connection of my family to the Townsends. Though he couldn't find a direct connection, I was hooked after Claire described the story of a brave young woman of color from Oyster Bay who started life as a slave, became involved with the spy Robert Townsend (and may even have been a spy herself), and finally achieved her freedom all in the same area where my roots as an American go back hundreds of years. At a time when historically marginalized voices and stories are at last being brought to the forefront, it's exciting to learn about a true story explaining details of the Revolutionary War on Long Island, African American history in New York, and the valiant fight for independence in a world full of loss, heartache, and eventual triumph. Claire's research, collaborative writing with Tiffany, and commitment bring history to life and reveal a new African American female hero . . . Liss. Enjoy!

—Vanessa Williams

# Introduction

## January 1785

The deck of the *Lucretia* swayed dizzyingly as the gray, frigid waters of New York Harbor swirled, barely darker than the January sky. Below decks and down a narrow flight of stairs, a woman sat locked in a windowless hold, crowded between barrels of cherry rum, English oats, and crates of hyson tea.

The woman may have breathed in her baby's smell as she clung to a tiny curl, clipped from her son's head. Above her, the footsteps of her fellow passengers sounded almost cheerful—a man with two little boys, an elderly husband and wife, the reverend she had looked at pleadingly as they boarded, with his stiff white collar and indifferent expression—and why not? They were headed to Charleston; surely the South Carolina coast was more hospitable this time of year than New York. But for the young woman, no sunny skies awaited her at the destination. She had been loaded aboard with dry goods and counted among the inventory as just another piece of cargo ("one negro wench: Elizabeth") by the ship's captain and a man named Hopkins.

Elizabeth, called Liss, had never seen Hopkins before today, when he had torn her screaming baby son from her arms, dragged her from the house, and thrown her into the wagon that brought her to where the brig lay anchored in New York Harbor. Just two years ago her worst fear had been moving to the wilds of Nova Scotia with a newborn. Now she had just been sold south to Charleston, to a master she had never met, alone.

Liss had no way of knowing that, just a few blocks away from where the *Lucretia* was now docked, a group of men would gather for the first meeting of the New York Manumission Society (NYMS) in eight days— at the exact same moment Liss would be disembarking in Charleston.

The society's primary aim was to bring an end to the evils of slavery, the trading in human lives, and the tearing apart of families. With John Jay as its president and Alexander Hamilton as its vice president, the NYMS included some of the most prominent intellectuals of the day, and among their numbers would soon appear the name of Robert Townsend.

As the ship lurched and began slicing through the waters, pushing southward to Charleston, it was clear there would be no eleventh-hour rescue for Liss. If only Robert had known, he would have moved heaven and earth to save her from this fate. He had smuggled messages to General George Washington as a spy in occupied New York during the war; surely he would have managed the impossible again. Of that Liss was certain—Robert had done so before on her behalf.

But this deal had been done in secret, and now, as she settled in for her first night without her baby, she wondered who would care for Harry, where he would live, and whether she would ever see him again.

# Part I

# The Times That Try Men's Souls

## CHAPTER ONE

# Merchants and Masters

THE FIRST AFRICAN MAN TO SET FOOT IN NORTH AMERICA, JUAN GAR-
rido, arrived in Florida as a freeman—a conquistador alongside Juan
Ponce de Leon on his quest for the mythical fountain of youth in 1513.
When he died sometime after 1540, he had traveled extensively through
Mexico, managing gold mines, and along Baja California with Hernán
Cortés, serving as a trusted and respected aide. The first enslaved person came to Florida in 1526, followed several years afterward by a man
named Esteban, considered the first slave whose name was recorded in
the New World.[1] In Virginia, the first Africans were transported to the
colony against their will in 1619, but they were viewed as indentured
servants who could eventually gain their freedom. When the Dutch
West India Company brought eleven African men to New Amsterdam in
1626, they were classified as employees of the company, not slaves. True,
they had been purchased from those who practiced the human trade, but
the price was paid for the labor the captive men could provide, not for
their actual persons.[2]

Then, in 1641, a Puritan law, ironically titled the "Body of Liberties,"
established Massachusetts as the first colony to legalize slavery. When
the British assumed control of New Amsterdam and renamed the colony
New York in 1664, British common law came with it, stipulating that the
terms of slavery did not extend beyond a person's natural life. But a few
years later, in 1670, an amendment to the "Body of Liberties" added that
all children born in Massachusetts whose mothers were slaves would also
be legally enslaved at birth.[3]

Within just a few generations, the laws in this provincial backwater across the Atlantic changed until people from Africa or of African descent who were imported or born into slavery anywhere in the colonies were deemed the exclusive property of the highest bidder, in perpetuity extending to the enslaved person's children.

In 1700, estimates show there may have been more than 2,250 slaves in New York, with over 40 percent residing on rural Long Island, and the numbers were about to explode. By 1703, close to 40 percent of homes in New York City had slaves, and still the slave ships made the dreaded Middle Passage to keep up with the demand for labor and servitude in the new colony. And, of course, babies were born daily into the system from which they now had no hope of escape. From the close of the seventeenth century to the start of the American Revolution—a span of barely seventy-five years—the number of enslaved people in the colony of New York grew by 900 percent, until New York had more slaves than not only any other colony north of Maryland but all of New England combined.[4]

Any notions of northern slavery being more humane than its southern counterpart should be dismissed. Although smaller estates, family farms, and growing cities, rather than large plantations, dominated the landscape, the work was no less backbreaking and the punishments no less medieval. Contemporary records indicate that beyond whipping, branding, and time spent in the stocks, slaves committing major offences could be hanged, burned at the stake, hung in iron cages until they starved, and even "broken upon the wheel"—an ancient torture device with roots as far back as the sixth century, which relied on physical mutilation for a slow and agonizing death.[5] Additionally, in 1730, every town in the colony of New York was required to have an official "slave whipper" in its employ,[6] though some had already had one on the books for decades.[7]

Since it was here that the most fervent abolitionist movements eventually took root, it may be tempting to imagine that the northern colonies somehow rectified the horrors of slavery rather quickly. But the truth is that chattel slavery was alive and well throughout British North America for the greater part of two centuries, and New York, with its busy ports and auction houses, was the northern epicenter. Universal emancipation did not become a cultural imperative *anywhere* in the United States until several decades after the Revolution and not in New York until 1827.

It was into this world that a white child named Robert Townsend and a black child named Elizabeth were born in the middle of the eighteenth century, within the same house in Oyster Bay, on Long Island. And it was this world that these two would eventually seek to change.

———

The fledgling village of Oyster Bay was part of a sprawling township of the same name that extended from the north shore, on Long Island Sound, to the south side, on the Atlantic. Although it did not receive its charter from the British government until 1667, the site had been occupied by homesteaders and a few small farms for some thirty years prior.

In the 1640s, when European settlers were scratching out six-acre homesteads in "the Town Spot" of Oyster Bay, three brothers emigrated from Norwich, England, to New Amsterdam. John Townsend, who was listed on the original patent of Flushing, along with his brothers Henry and Richard, did not immediately find the New World welcoming and frequently butted heads with the Dutch magistrates over local law and governance. They were particularly persecuted by Governor Peter Stuyvesant for allowing Quakers to meet in their homes for religious gatherings, called "conventicles." After more than a decade of settling and resettling at least three separate times in both New Amsterdam and Rhode Island, the Townsend brothers finally purchased property in Oyster Bay in 1661.[8] Later, perhaps because of their willingness to aid the Quakers, there was a belief that the original Townsends were Quakers themselves, but there is no evidence of this. The many Townsend descendants—and there were hundreds—belonged to different denominations in and around Oyster Bay, including Baptist, Anglican, and even, occasionally, Quaker. Others appear to have had no religious affiliation at all.

Especially significant about the Townsend brothers' frequent clashes with the authorities was how they demonstrated their commitment to civil rights. At least two of the brothers were progressive freethinkers, willing to risk their own well-being to protect the rights of others. Whether

Richard held less enlightened views on the rights of man than his brothers or was simply less demonstrative in his political and philosophical views is unclear, but prior to their final move to Oyster Bay, John and Henry both signed the Flushing Remonstrance (which is further evidence they were not Quakers, as no Friends signed the edict).[9] The Remonstrance, which has since been regarded as a precursor of the Bill of Rights, was a petition signed by roughly thirty settlers in the village of Flushing, sparked by Governor Stuyvesant's ban on Quakers in New Amsterdam. The document was the first to assert the human right to worship in the manner of one's choosing, whatever form that faith takes. Its language was remarkably enlightened for its time. In support of "those people called Quakers," the signatories vowed "not to judge least we be judged, neither to condemn least we be condemned, but rather let every man stand or fall to his own Master." The document also included eloquent statements in defense of several other marginalized groups, declaring, "Wee are bounde by the law to do good unto all men, especially to those of the household of faith. . . . The law of love, peace and liberty in the states extending to Jews, Turks and Egyptians, as they are considered sonnes of Adam."[10, 11]

The Townsends' political and humanitarian impulses were not extinguished when they moved to Oyster Bay a few years afterward. Within a year of their arrival in the village, John and Henry, along with ten others, signed their names on March 25, 1662, to another declaration of individual rights, this one unique and virtually unknown. Henry's name appears first on the document, set apart from the others, indicating he was the author. This early declaration was bound in a book with several other significant records and later described as "a few sheets of small foolscap sewed in a canvas cover, many of the last leaves of which are either cut out or mutilated by handling & age." Though the original document has been lost to history, a single transcription remains in the unpublished writings of Dr. Peter Townsend, dating to the middle of the nineteenth century. This obscure yet significant declaration asserted the citizens' commitment to "defending or Freeing anyone . . . that may be arrested or Troubled" by figures in authority, to "Promise & Engage in a Just and Right way to stand by one another," and asserted collectively "our desire of doing right to all men."[12]

As Oyster Bay was actively promoting the ideals of independence for freeholders from unfair laws, it was nevertheless a very typical New York town in its oppression of enslaved African Americans and had appointed a man named William Howard as the official Town Negro Whipper in 1714—sixteen years before such a position became a colony-wide requirement.[13] A ledger from 1756 records the town's paying the blacksmith for repairs to the whipping post, which indicates it was used with at least some degree of regularity.[14] As late as 1802 another blacksmith named Daniel McCoun was paid for "putting a band & a bolt on a Black" and selling "3 waring [*sic*] irons and a ring." Six years later the same man was hired for "strapping a Black for a welt to a wagon tire" and "12 nails and putting on."[15]

The earliest enslaved people arrived in the area soon after Oyster Bay's founding. One of the first was a young boy who was bought by a woman named Alice Crabb, a "founding mother" of the hamlet.[16]

Born in England around 1614, Alice was a Quaker. At age twenty-one, she sailed to Virginia on the ship *Thomas* before traveling northward to Massachusetts the following year, where she married her first husband, Peter Wright. By the time she was thirty-nine, Alice had given birth to twelve children, seven of whom survived infancy. In 1653, she and her large family sailed to Long Island on the vessel *Desire*, and her husband, along with two other men, purchased a large tract of land "scituate[d] upon Oyster Bay" from leaders of the Matinecock tribe. In exchange, the native peoples received "six Indian coates, six kettles, six fathom of wampum, sixe hoes, sixe hatchetts, three pr of stockings, thirty aule blades or axes, twenty knives, three shirts, and as much peage [shell beads] as will amount to foure pounds of Stirling." Peter is credited as the original founder of the village, as he was the first to put down permanent stakes in the new settlement. When he passed away in 1661, Alice, now a wealthy widow, soon remarried a man named Richard Crabb.[17]

Despite her Quaker faith, and presumably to help manage her extensive landholdings (which now included property from her deceased brother-in-law), Alice obtained an enslaved boy named Owah from Lewis Morris in 1673. Morris, an elderly gentleman, had himself just inherited over five hundred acres in the Bronx (later named Morrisania) as well as an island off the coast of Oyster Bay called Hog Island (now Centre Island) and a tract in nearby Glen Cove called "Morris Run." One of the most prominent and largest landholders in the northern colonies, Morris was also one of the largest slave owners in New York. He owned these enslaved people despite being a follower of George Fox, the founder of Quakerism.

Crabb's contract with Morris, while it bound Owah into continuous "survuss and labour," also promised that he would "bee sett free, as a free man for him selfe" either by age thirty-one or when his mistress died, whichever came first. Alice died in 1685, when the young man was twenty-four years old, making him the first known slave freed anywhere on Long Island. At the time of his emancipation, he was given a calf, a mare, and an iron skillet with which to make his way in the world. By then, Owah's original African name had been changed to "Tom," and as a freeman he chose the last name "Gall."[18] Tom Gall made his home in Pine Hollow, on a sandy hill next to the main road leading into the village. Tom was clearly a determined and ambitious person, as he managed to build a successful life for himself: records show he eventually owned several properties, a small herd of cattle, and an orchard.

He married a free African American woman named Mary, and together they had a daughter. Tom was able to save enough money to purchase his daughter's future husband, an enslaved man named Obed, in 1717, but the laws of the colony stipulated slaves could not simply be freed.[19] An enormous bond of £200 was required to do so, and it took another four years before Tom was able to pay the fee required to emancipate his own son-in-law. This money was supposedly intended to provide care for freed slaves should they become indigent, but the sum was so onerous that only one other man was legally freed in the town of Oyster Bay by these means over the next one hundred years. Descendants of Tom and Mary Gall's family continued to live in Oyster Bay for over 250 years, appearing in the store ledgers of the Townsend family from the 1750s to the 1820s, with last names spelled both Gall and Gaul. Two different homeowners, Naomi Gaul and Plato Gall (who also spelled his name Gale), were listed on lots of land in Pine Hollow as late as 1959, along the same sandy stretch of road on the outskirts of town.[20]

Subsequent generations of enslaved people in the area had their own notable members. In 1711, on a nearby island called Queen's Village, a boy named Jupiter was born into slavery to the wealthy Lloyd family, shipping merchants who owned the entire island and many other slaves, including Jupiter's likely parents, named Opium and Rose. Surprisingly, young Jupiter, who took the last name Hammon, was given a formal education, taught alongside the Lloyd children by their live-in tutor. With his high level of literacy, his work as an adult slave included assisting in the Lloyd family business. He also wrote for pleasure, and with the support of his masters, some of his works were published as broadsides, including four religious poems and three essays. The first known poem, titled "An Evening Thought," was written in 1760, when he was forty-nine, and printed and distributed a year later, predating Phillis Wheatley's first book by a dozen years, making Jupiter the first published African American author in the New World.[21]

Though the poems his masters chose for publication never criticized slavery, an unpublished poem, discovered in 2011 at Yale University, told a different story. This 1786 poem, titled "An Essay on Slavery," included the lines "Dark and dismal was the day when slavery began / All humble thoughts were put away; then slaves were made by Man."[22] A second unpublished poem that touched on early-American religious history was discovered in 2014, hiding in plain sight among the Townsend Family Papers at the New York Historical Society.[23] Jupiter Hammon, through his poems and broadsides, attained a degree of local celebrity that was unheard of among those who were enslaved.[24]

Given each man's prominence in his own way, it is not particularly surprising that Tom Gall and Jupiter Hammon should have crossed paths as neighbors on Long Island's north shore. What is remarkable, though, is that a firsthand account exists of one such incident in 1728, which centers on Tom's propensity to poach deer on the Lloyds' land and Henry Lloyd's outraged reaction. Since Lloyd had been trying unsuccessfully to catch Tom (who was then sixty-seven) in the act for at least seven months, he did the next best thing—he captured Tom's dog during another illegal hunting trip in September. The two men appear to have struck a deal wherein Tom agreed to give the dog (apparently a well-trained sporting companion) as a "gift" to Lloyd's son in lieu of Lloyd's killing the poor animal as punishment for the trespasses.

One can't help but wonder what Jupiter's reaction was to what came next in the feud, given that his duties would have meant he was managing the Lloyd house when Tom carried out his revenge. As Henry Lloyd wrote later in a formal complaint, after he left his house only a week later,

> *I have been plagued . . . by Tom Gall, a free Negro of Oysterbay, who comes by stealth to Hunt Deer on this place: since last february in the great snow I Discovered him but could not till Saturday last find evidence enough to prosecute him, & had in a manner given over the thought of it, but in my Absence from home last week he or somebody for him broak into my house and Stole a Dog from under a table where it was tyed.*
>
> *The Dog was formerly his, but when he was Discovered hunting, I took the Dog from him.*[25]

There is no evidence that Tom was ever arrested or jailed for taking back his dog, but the Lloyd family remained aggressively committed to prosecuting deer poachers on their three-thousand-acre island for the next century.

Along with the Lloyd, Floyd, Buchanan, and Jones families, the Townsends were among the most prominent merchants and civic leaders in the area. A century after the first Townsends arrived in America, Samuel Townsend, now a fifth-generation Long Islander, willingly stepped into the role as head of his branch of the family tree. Born in nearby Jericho, with the merchant trade all around him, Samuel was raised in a world that revolved entirely around shipping. His father, Jacob, was a merchant with a large store and coastal sloops that sailed from New York up the Connecticut coast.[26] In 1738, at the age of twenty-two, Samuel moved to Oyster Bay with his wife and purchased a house in the middle of town on one of the plots owned by Alice Crabb seventy years earlier, where young Owah had labored as a slave. Samuel went into business with his brother Jacob Jr., who purchased the house next door, and the two established a large shipping business, eventually building five large transatlantic vessels in Oyster Bay. The first vessel, the sloop *Prosperity*, had a fitting name, as the brothers' partnership was thriving. The other four bore names of family members: the sloop *Solomon*, named for Samuel's oldest son; the brig *Sarah*, for his wife; the brig *Audrey*, for his oldest daughter; and the brig *Sally*, for another of his girls.[27]

Samuel invested his wealth wisely, building up his estate to include 350 acres in seven large tracts of land outside the village, as well as much of the land between his house and the bay. Despite his best efforts, however, Samuel's extensive holdings were nothing compared to those of his forebears. An enormous tract of six thousand acres in South Oyster Bay had once belonged to the second generation of Long Island Townsends but was now owned under the Jones family name. The male Townsend heir had no interest in the undeveloped wilderness, complaining, "Does my father want me to go out of the world?" when it was offered to him, so the massive parcel was instead given as a wedding gift to the next in line, a daughter named Freelove Townsend, when she married Thomas Jones in the 1690s.[28] In the subsequent decades, the once-unwanted estate had proven tremendously valuable for timber, farming, and the sheer power of landholdings. The Jones family had since become one of the wealthiest dynasties on Long Island, but the loss of the land stuck in the Townsends' collective craw. Still, Samuel did quite well for himself and the Townsend family name all the same. He had a large apple orchard, many barns and outbuildings, forty sheep, twenty-five hogs, oxen, horses, a second house in Oyster Bay, a storehouse for his products, and at least nineteen enslaved people. The family home is described as a "commodious 2 story house, with 4 rooms on a floor, near the center of a village, on the main road to the mill, 60 rods 330 yards from the harbor." The property also boasted "a well at the door" and a spring running nearby.[29]

In short, Samuel could not have established a more comfortable or profitable homestead for a man in his position, and he was well aware of his good fortune; he did not shirk from the noblesse oblige that being a Townsend in Oyster Bay brought. For decades Samuel served as both justice of the peace and town clerk and, in 1758, made his own stand for the rights of a persecuted minority group—not the Quakers, as his ancestors had done, but the "Neutral French."

Three years earlier, the British colonial government had forcibly deported almost seven thousand French-speaking Catholic Acadians from Nova Scotia and systematically sent them to live in small groups throughout North America.[30] Their only crime was refusing to take an oath of allegiance to the king, preferring to remain neutral in the conflicts between France and England. Families were cruelly torn apart, forced into the holds of vessels, and turned over to local governments throughout the colonies. Some of these Neutral French families were sent to Oyster Bay, and Samuel Townsend, in his role as justice of the peace, had to find places for them to live, on the guarantee that any expenses incurred would be paid back by the government. In March 1758, Samuel sent an urgent appeal to the colonial administrators to better provide for these desperate refugees, but his letter to the assembly, now lost, apparently contained strong language that was deemed "indecent and insolent," and the petition was denied.[31] What was more, David Jones, the Speaker of the assembly and current owner of the six-thousand-acre tract of land that had once belonged to the Townsends, declared Samuel guilty of "High Misdemeanor and a most Daring Insult" and threw him in jail in New York City for having the audacity to "write and send a letter" on behalf of the unfortunate Acadians.[32]

The Oyster Bay schoolmaster, Zachariah Weekes, wrote in his diary about the incident, news of which had no doubt spread through the town like wildfire. "Last Monday," he noted, "was a report about Town that Justice Townsend was sent for . . . to be brought forthwith dead or alive." Samuel was taken into custody overnight and the next day had to plead for forgiveness and "humbly to express his Uneasiness and Sorrow, for having wrote the said Letter." After promising he would never again lodge such a complaint against the regime, he was released and allowed to return home. The schoolmaster observed, "He returned and since it has been as still as a mouse in a cheese."[33]

While to modern observers the inherent disconnect between the Townsend family tradition of fighting for basic human rights and supporting the slave trade is apparent, the fact is that the Townsends were still very much people of their time. Slavery was regarded as a normal and expected part of running the household and business of a successful merchant, and no one seems to have questioned the stark philosophical inconsistencies. Family records note the names of eighteen enslaved individuals who served in the Townsend home between 1749 and 1827: Amos, Catherine, Elizabeth, Gabriel, Hannah, Harry, Jacob, Jane, Jeffrey, John, Lilly, Nicholas, Priscilla, Rachel, Susan, Susannah, Violet, and William.[34] The nineteenth record, chronologically the earliest-known slave purchase by Samuel, is perhaps the most evocative of them all: an unnamed man purchased for £37 at an auction for goods and slaves from the privateer ship *Hester*, which was essentially a pirate vessel operating with royal permission.[35, 36] New York newspapers often published details of the *Hester*'s daring adventures, as her crew (called "brave Britons") set out on "a Cruizing Voyage against his Majesty's Enemies," during which they would attack and board ships and seize all their goods.[37] The public could then purchase these spoils at bargain prices on the *Hester*'s return. It is impossible to know the name of the man Samuel bought in the spring of 1749 or what language he spoke—perhaps Spanish, French, or Portuguese or an African language like Kingwana (Congo) or Mende (West Africa), which were the most common among enslaved people in the Americas. There is no way to know if he was a free person when the *Hester*'s crew forced him into their hold or already facing a life of enslavement. But no matter where his ship was headed or what the original purpose of his voyage, he ended up in the port of New York and eventually in the Townsend home.

This intriguing anonymous individual aside, the rest of the Townsend slaves were procured by a variety of the more typical means: private sales, gifts, and procreation. John was a gift to Sarah from her father, William Stoddard; Jacob was purchased in a private sale in 1767 for £95 from one of Samuel's neighbors, Thomas Seaman. Many more slaves were added to Samuel's rolls through birth.[38] For example, one of Samuel's slaves bore Liss around the year 1763 and another daughter named Hannah around 1765. Susannah gave birth to a son named Jeffery in 1769. Catherine, born in 1772, and Lilly, born in 1774, were daughters of his slave named Susan. In 1787 Hannah gave birth to a girl named Violet. One of his enslaved women, Jane, had seven children. All drew their first breath in a life of slavery.

Several newspaper advertisements in the 1760s show that Samuel's brother Jacob sometimes sold slaves alongside his other merchandise. One 1765 ad promised "a few healthy young negro slaves to be sold very cheap."[39] No records exist that indicate that Samuel himself sold slaves in this way or that he was an abnormally cruel or demanding master; in fact, considering his concern about the fair treatment of others, he may have been liberal in both the care and treatment of his slaves. Little is known beyond a few purchases of coarse fabric ("We was induced to buy the Duffel from a supposition that you would want something of the kind for your Negroes")[40] and another instance when he purchased "two Garments for the Blacks."[41] In fact, one unusual document shows that Samuel permitted local slaves to engage in at least some degree of personal commerce. Though it does not include the names of his own slaves, his "Negro Ledger" recorded the purchases of other local families' slaves.

The account book, spanning twenty-seven years between 1761 and 1788, seems to have been something of an exercise in bookkeeping for the younger Townsend children, including David, William, Sally, and Phebe, who signed their names in some of the margins and noted each transaction, with penmanship exercises filling the front and back endpapers. This unique record tracks the purchases and running tabs of thirty-four African American customers, most of whom were enslaved, with their owner's names listed beside their own, like "Lew, that belongs to Daniel McCoun" and "Henry Ludlum's Jem." Several free people of color are listed as well, including a man named "Jack Broken Tooth" and another named Obet. Most notably, the ledger offers an insight into the private lives and everyday concerns of the African American population of Oyster Bay. Listed are a variety of items, which were paid for both in kind—potatoes, beets, turnips, and cucumbers are specifically noted— and in cash, though it is unclear if the purchases were charged to the family account or the enslaved people had money of their own. Some entries include basic grocery items, like sugar, molasses, rum, wheat flour, coffee, and tea, but others trended toward the more luxurious. In one undated entry, an enslaved man named Tom purchased an earthenware plate, perfume, and a gilt teapot, paying with a combination of cash and flaxseed. Others of his contemporaries bought handkerchiefs, shoes, gloves, stockings, textiles, "sundrys," and even, on two occasions, spelling books. One of those who purchased a spelling book was a slave named Betty, owned by Daniel Youngs, and the other was a man named Jack, owned by the Birdsall family.[42] Certainly, as Jupiter Hammon could attest, literacy among enslaved people was not unheard of, but it was certainly not the norm. In the southern colonies it was often illegal to teach slaves to read or write for fear, in part, that they would then create counterfeit freedom certificates or travel papers. In fact, in 1771, just a few years after the spelling book was sold to Jack, an advertisement seeking an escaped slave named Jack from Oyster Bay notes that he "may forge a pass."[43]

When the earliest entries were made in the "Negro Ledger," Samuel Townsend's third son Robert was eight years old; about two years later, Liss was born as a slave in the Townsend home. While Robert was studying the ins and outs of shipping, tariffs, inventory, and trade deals as a teenager, Liss was a young girl learning everything from cooking and cleaning to the basics of being a lady's maid to the Townsend daughters, Audrey, Sally, and Phebe—a role she would have been expected to grow into with time. Although she was around ten years younger than Robert, the two would have been very well known to each other, given Liss's position in the family home; he may have even teased and pestered her, as he certainly did his youngest sister, Phebe, who was the same age as Liss.

As a bright and ambitious young man, however, Robert would not have had much time to spend within the comfortable walls of his family home. Samuel Townsend understood the social expectation that he would raise the members of his household to be industrious and civic-minded individuals, and he began training his children (and those enslaved by his family) early for the roles they were destined to fill. The first Townsend son, Solomon, died at four months, and the next child was given the same name. The subsequent Solomon began serving aboard the family ships as a cabin boy at age thirteen on both domestic and international voyages ranging from the West Indies and South America to Europe. By 1769, at the age of twenty-two, he was captaining his own vessel for the family, the newly built brig *Sally*.

With Solomon at sea, the second surviving son, Samuel Jr., took the lead in the Townsends' next generation of merchants. In 1772 and 1773, he recorded sales of cotton, flour, pork, and tea, trading up and down the eastern seaboard and also organizing "adventures" to Jamaica and Hispaniola with the sloop *Betsy*, captained by James Farley, who would later marry his sister Audrey.[44]

A large proportion of Samuel Jr.'s business involved purchasing rum and sugar from his maternal uncle Robert Stoddard. While there is no record of the Townsends transporting enslaved Africans on their merchant vessels, Stoddard, based in Newport, Rhode Island, had made his fortune in the slave trade. Stoddard led at least three yearlong voyages to the coast of Africa between 1754 and 1766, where he and his crew forcibly transported hundreds of Africans to the Caribbean ports of Jamaica, Saint Kitts, and Antigua and sold them into slavery.[45] One Newport newspaper ad from 1766 boasts, "Captain Robert Stoddard, of this port, is arrived at Antigua, with a fine cargo of slaves."[46] During these voyages, records show Captain Stoddard and his crew forced 429 people onboard but delivered only 365. During the Middle Passage from Africa to the Caribbean, a total of sixty-five men, women, and children died in the disease-ridden and crowded holds of his ships, where the enslaved were chained down and packed so tightly that there was hardly enough room to sit upright.[47] While some were transported to North America to be resold, the majority stayed in the Caribbean, laboring on sugar plantations. Samuel Jr.'s many purchases of sugar and rum from his Uncle Robert are a stark reminder of the close family and economic ties that connected the Townsends to the African slave trade.

Tragedy struck the family in early 1773, when Samuel Jr. caught a fever and died at the age of twenty-four while on a business venture for his father in Wilmington, North Carolina.[48] Due to the nature of his death from a contagious disease and the limited means of sanitary transport available at the time, his body was never brought home. His wife and two-year-old son, Penn, were living in Oyster Bay when they received news of his sudden death. Then, only a few months after Esther learned she was a widow, baby Penn also died. The devastated family buried young Penn in their ancestral graveyard on a hill a short walk from the house and did their best to recover from the shock of their losses.

With Samuel Jr.'s death, the third Townsend son, Robert, came into his own. He had already proven himself a hard and willing worker when, at eighteen, he left Oyster Bay, traveling to Manhattan to apprentice with Templeton & Stewart, a clearinghouse and auction company in New York City. For two years, Robert oversaw not only the sale of everything from barrels of limes to mahogany furniture but the auctioning off of children—some close to Liss's age, as evidenced by a Templeton & Stewart ad featuring the sale of "a likely, handy Negro girl, about 9 years of age."[49] Seeing slaves regularly sold alongside looking glasses and earthenware plates would have exposed a teenaged Robert to the brutality of the slave trade, which he might not have witnessed growing up in Oyster Bay, where he was shielded from the separation of families on the auction block.

In April 1773, Robert Townsend left his position at Templeton & Stewart to step into his deceased brother's place as owner of the sloop *Betsy* and buyer for his father's coastal trade. With Solomon gone for long stretches on shipping expeditions and the mantle of second son now on his shoulders, Robert's role as a merchant-in-training carried more weight as the family's fortunes—and the fate of the American colonies— looked more and more uncertain.

## CHAPTER TWO

# Congressman and Commissary

As 1775 DAWNED TO THE RUMBLINGS OF REVOLUTION THROUGHOUT the colonies, New York remained fixedly loyal to King George. All around—in Pennsylvania, in New Jersey, in Connecticut, and especially in Massachusetts—patriotic fervor was growing daily. But New York was still considered a less consequential city than Philadelphia or Boston, and the more rural areas surrounding it, like Long Island, were especially conservative.

The American colonies had been in open rebellion since at least March 1770, when five Massachusetts men were killed in an altercation with British infantrymen in what came to be known as the Boston Massacre. Richard Palmes, a stout young apothecary with a reputation for having a short fuse, took part in the mob scene and became a key witness at the soldiers' trials. "I saw apice of Ice fall among the Soldgers. Ameadiately upon this the Soldger at his right hand fired his Gun," he wrote, describing the taunts and snowballs from the American civilians that allegedly sparked the melee. "That Instant I herd the word fire but who said it I know Not; the Soldgers at his Left fired Next, and the others as fast as they Could one after the other, I turned my Self as Soon as I could & Saw one Lawy Dead at my Left, upon wich I struck at the Soldger that fired the first Gun."[1]

The weapon Palmes used to strike the soldier was described as a "cudgel," a short, blunt club; he hit the other man's hands with such force that he dropped his gun. As other soldiers continued to fire, Palmes rushed forward, swinging his club at the British captain's head, which missed the mark but landed a heavy blow to his arm. The rest of the assembled Bostonians followed Palmes's example, but their sticks were no match for gunfire and bayonets. Crispus Attucks, a dockworker of African and Native American descent, was killed by the initial round of British bullets, making him the first casualty in the American Revolution.[2]

The incident in Boston set into motion a series of increasingly bold acts of insurrection. In December 1773, the Sons of Liberty (who counted Richard Palmes among their number) consigned ninety-two thousand pounds of tea to Boston Harbor, immediately securing themselves a place in the American mythos.[3] The Crown responded swiftly, bringing an iron fist crashing down on Massachusetts in the form of the so-called Intolerable Acts: even further taxation, increased military presence, and a revocation of the colony's royal charter. Intended to send a warning to the other colonies not to fall into step with their mutinous sibling, the acts only served as fuel. Civil disruptions were no longer bonfires of discontent; they were funeral pyres for British rule.

In the fall of 1774, the First Continental Congress assembled in Philadelphia to discuss, among other things, how to react to Britain's draconian response to the Boston Tea Party. Every colony, with the exception of Georgia, sent delegates. Despite making a decent showing of a united front to outsiders, the Congress actually resolved very little, and the colonies themselves bickered over their objectives.

In the months that followed and into early 1775, a series of further disturbances and small riots broke out in Boston, including one that pitted two young men and four members of the city's night watch against approximately twenty British officers and a few Loyalist citizens. Some soldiers were harassing the young men, goading them into a scuffle after accusing them of being "stiff Americans"; one officer even drew his sword. The resulting fracas ended in the arrest of eight of the officers and a Tory saddle maker named Richard Sharwin, who threw some punches on behalf of the British.[4] Tensions in Massachusetts had reached a boiling point.

New York could no longer turn a blind eye to the situation of its more radical neighbor, so a convention date of April 20, 1775, was set to debate the pressing question of independence, and every city and village was to select its representative (or "deputy") for the assembled congress. Out in Oyster Bay on Long Island, town clerk Samuel Townsend held a meeting in late December 1774, urging a group of ninety townsmen to appoint a delegate immediately, but the group decided to wait several months for the annual town meeting on April 4 before electing their deputy. In March, Samuel published and circulated a notice encouraging all freeholders—that is, men who owned property, which gave them the right to vote—to consider the resolves of the Continental Congress. The men of the town seem to have had a very decided opinion on the matter, but it was not the one for which Samuel hoped. At the April meeting, not only did the men of the town not choose to name a delegate in favor of challenging the Crown, but they voted 205 to 42 not to send any delegate at all.

Undaunted, Samuel called another meeting of the Patriot minority, who named their own deputy, one Zebulon Williams, and addressed a letter to the Provincial Convention, stating, "Whereas, the unhappy disputes between the mother country and the American colonies, we humbly conceive, has arisen from power, claimed by the British Parliament, to pass laws binding on us in all cases whatsoever, hath given us great uneasiness . . . unanimity among the inhabitants of the colonies is the only means under Providence to secure the essential rights and liberties of Englishmen." In such a spirit of unanimity, the letter continued, the Patriots of Oyster Bay chose to follow the decree from the colony of New York and send a delegate anyway, despite the stubborn refusal of the majority of their neighbors to comply with the request. The letter was signed by forty-three men (apparently at least one person joined the forty-two original dissenters), of whom more than 20 percent bore the surname Townsend.[5]

Twenty-two-year-old Robert Townsend, however, was not one of them. He remained in Manhattan, well removed from Oyster Bay's internal politics—and all for the better. New York's Congress did not even have a chance to debate the question of how best to address the taxation and rebellion crisis. The day before they were appointed to meet, skirmishes broke out between British troops and colonial Minute Men two hundred miles away in Massachusetts, in the towns of Lexington and

Concord. Word spread like scattershot up and down the eastern seaboard, and the debates about independence were no longer hypothetical. The colonies were at war.

On June 14, 1775, only three days before the pyrrhic victory was handed to the British at the Battle of Bunker Hill, the Second Continental Congress approved measures to establish the Continental Army, the first national defense force. Previously, colonists had relied on local militias and British regiments for protection. Now, all able-bodied men over the age of sixteen were expected, though not required, to enlist. In some cases, men over the age of fifty were so engorged with patriotic fervor that they too joined up. Robert would have been a prime candidate, not only because of his age and apparent health but also because he came from such a prominently pro-independence family. But Robert was deeply invested in the family business, having fully embraced his new role as second son and stepping into his brother's vacated spot. The Townsend family ledgers beautifully capture the transition as Samuel Jr.'s "Waste Book" records his entries in heavy, inky script, while Samuel Sr.'s hurried scrawl fills in his daily account book. Samuel Jr.'s final volume is followed by a new ledger, this time filled neatly with Robert's careful, almost lacy handwriting.[6]

By 1775, Robert was very capably managing his family's business, organizing voyages to the Carolinas, Ireland, and England, and handling the affairs of the *Betsy*. It was a fortunate thing, too; in the previous decade, Samuel and his brother Jacob were doing extraordinarily well for themselves as merchants, but business dropped off steeply as new taxes and tariffs hampered trade. The outbreak of war threatened to sink the business even further just as the next generation of Townsend men stood poised to take over operations. Robert, however, proved quite adept at managing the complications and obstacles the conflict presented, and his father did not fail to notice his level head and natural proclivity for organization.

This role of family savior might normally have been filled by the oldest son, but Solomon was engaged full-time as a ship captain in partnership with the Buchanan family, another extremely wealthy and well-connected Long Island dynasty. Unlike the Townsends, however, who (thanks to Samuel) were well-known Patriots, the Buchanans kept their political cards much closer to the vest, flirting and demurring with both sides of the conflict, waiting to see which way things would eventually shake out. The wait was an anxious one for all sides.

Frustrated with the determined loyalism in Oyster Bay, Samuel and another of his brothers, James Townsend, attended a meeting in Jamaica, Queens, in May 1775, which was organized to help mobilize local Patriots. Both Townsend brothers were named as deputies for Queens County, a title that granted them an official voice in colony legislation. After three failed attempts to organize the Patriot cause in his hometown, Samuel had finally found a circuitous path to his seat at the Second New York Continental Congress.[7, 8]

The congressmen assembled regularly in New York City, meeting with ship captains to ascertain the current state of trade and reading letters from key figures like General George Washington, John Hancock, and John Adams.[9] They even debated whether they should run a massive iron chain across the mouth of the Hudson to block British ships from penetrating inland.[10] On August 23, 1775, Samuel took an oath of secrecy alongside a number of other delegates, committing their proceedings and resolutions to confidentiality. What they were doing, after all, was tantamount to treason, and they had little reason to believe that they would emerge victorious. The same day that Samuel took his oath, the Congress read aloud a letter from Benjamin Franklin detailing the lack of gunpowder available and the desperate need for sympathetic private citizens to make more.[11] Whatever their spirit, the Patriots were sorely lacking in resources.

While these meetings were taking place, Samuel took up temporary residence in town, most likely staying with Robert so they could review business records by candlelight in the evenings. The thirty-five-mile trip from Manhattan to Oyster Bay was no small feat—one had to travel through the city, across the East River before traversing nearly twenty miles of unpaved country roads on Long Island. Samuel and Robert both still maintained a presence in Oyster Bay, however, checking in on the household periodically and making sure the neighbors knew Samuel had not abandoned his property and fled to more

Patriot-friendly areas like New Jersey, as was becoming an increasingly common practice. Samuel, now chairman of the Queens delegation, was also receiving intelligence on shipping patterns and troop movements from General Washington and urging those on the east end of Long Island to form militias and remove forage and livestock.[12] To what degree Robert was aware of his father's intelligence activities at this point is unclear, but the Townsend family certainly showed enthusiasm early on for covert proclivities.

But even a pot stirrer like Samuel had his limits, and his came just as the reality of war was gaining traction. On January 2, 1776, the Continental Congress passed the Tory Act, which enjoined Patriots to educate the "honest and well-meaning, but uninformed people" who remained loyal to Britain on the "origin, nature and extent of the present controversy. . . . [T]he more our right to the enjoyment of our ancient liberties and privileges is examined, the more just and necessary our present opposition to ministerial tyranny will appear."

The Congress further asserted that anyone remaining loyal to the Crown should be stripped of weapons and "the more dangerous among them either kept in safe custody" or at least compelled to pledge on their honor that they would not conduct themselves in any manner that could undercut the American cause. In fact, the Tory Act even went so far as to permit local Patriot bodies to respond to perceived threats "whenever retaliation may be necessary."

Samuel campaigned against the act, urging other lawmakers to recognize that most Loyalists were reacting out of fear and uncertainty rather than malicious intent or a desire for "ignominious rewards," as the Tory Act charged. The act, he feared, would be inflammatory and pit already divided communities against one another. But Samuel's warnings went unheeded, and his attempt at building bridges went nowhere.

In May, the New York Provincial Congress sent Samuel to the wealthy Lloyd family estate on Queen's Village (now called Lloyd's Neck), roughly ten miles from Oyster Bay, to take inventory of the goods, livestock, and raw materials available should the need arise to commandeer resources for the war effort.[13] Jupiter Hammon, now well into his sixties and a published author, though still enslaved, most likely assisted

Samuel in his work on the Lloyd property. Perhaps the relationship between the two men was amicable, as a copy of an unpublished poem Hammon had penned in 1770 made its way to Samuel's youngest daughter Phebe, who carefully wrote out her own copy—the only surviving one. The three-page poem is an ode to seventeenth-century Boston resident, Puritan heroine, and champion of civil disobedience Anne Hutchinson. "In Wisdoms ways She always went," Phebe's practiced hand carefully copied onto the page. "He gave her grace that set her free."[14] One can only imagine what her servant and confidant, Liss, thought of such bold lines penned by an enslaved person, who knew not only how to read and write but glorified the history of a woman who was persecuted for defying the rules of men.

That same summer, Samuel and the New York Congress received and ratified the Declaration of Independence, five days after the Continental Congress in Philadelphia signed it. Samuel was present in White Plains when the declaration was first read aloud, then eagerly stood in line with his fellow delegates to add his signature to New York's copy.[15] This act by Samuel and his cohorts aligned the colony with what was, essentially, a sixteen-hundred-mile coup d'état stretching from Savannah, Georgia, to the Canadian border. The Loyalists were, of course, displeased by this act of rebellion, but most found solace in the fact that there was little chance the colonists could succeed in shaking off the Crown. They also took for granted that the cause would dissolve at the first sign of pushback from King George's expertly trained and equipped troops, and life would return to normal as soon as the silly fervor for independence passed.

New York appointed thirteen men to draft a new state constitution, and Samuel was among that number; first, however, he had to return home to conduct an evaluation of how to move livestock from the east end of Long Island to the western end to prevent them from falling into the hands of the British.[16] The island was bound to come under attack; it was too rich in resources for either side to ignore. It was merely a question of how soon.

War was already much more than an abstract threat to the Townsend family, though. At the urging of the politically neutral Buchanan family (and against his own better judgment and protestations), Solomon had made a voyage on the *Glasgow* the previous autumn to Scotland for the purpose of transporting a shipload of Highland refugees to America. Upon docking in New York Harbor, however, the *Glasgow* was immediately boarded by the British warship *Asia*, and all the male passengers were impressed into service.[17] Solomon, too, was forced to run the British flag up the mast. His ship was fitted with cannons and officially declared part of the Royal Navy.[18] Solomon Townsend, eldest son of ardent Patriot Samuel Townsend, was now captaining an official transport ship for King George.

Though he may have been the first Townsend son to find himself suddenly facing military service, he was not the last. Despite later historians' portrayal of Robert as a passive presence in the family, his service record paints a far more nuanced picture. On August 26, 1776, Robert's civilian business dealings came to an abrupt halt when the New York Provincial Congress—almost certainly working on Samuel's recommendation—appointed him as commissary. His skills and knowledge of managing a storehouse and organizing sales were admittedly well suited for the role, and Robert was abruptly charged with procuring provisions for no one less than the president of the New York Congress and brigadier general of the Queen's County Militia, Nathaniel Woodhull.

It was a short-lived commission.

For more than a week, General Woodhull and the New York Congress had been writing to General Washington, begging for reinforcements—specifically, two regiments from Long Island whom Woodhull had personally helped to raise. The letters were conveyed by Samuel, but they were met with an unclear response from Washington. On the one hand, he would agree to send the force of five hundred men, but in the same letter he replied that "he was afraid it was too late." Washington remained convinced that the British were going to land on Manhattan; as a result, he left Long Island shockingly unprotected. Woodhull and his small unit of untrained militia men, stationed in the Long Island town of Jamaica, watched the ever-growing presence of British and Hessian ships assemble in the waters to the south while Woodhull's already barebones ranks diminished daily as men deserted in the face of certain defeat.

On August 27, just one day after Robert Townsend's appointment as commissary to Woodhull was approved, the Battle of Long Island crushed the American forces and General Washington's hopes of securing all of lower New York Bay as a naval command. Robert had not yet even reported for duty when General William Howe split his amassed thirty-two thousand British troops on Staten Island just across The Narrows from the Continental Army in Brooklyn. With one short ferry across Upper New York Bay, nearly twenty thousand troops moved onto Long Island, and three hundred Redcoats made a feint attack on the right end of the Continental Army line while the bulk of the troops flanked the Patriots on the other end of their fortifications. Woodhull wrote, "I am now at Jamaica with less than 100 men. . . . The enemy I am informed is entrenching in the heights. . . . I have now received yours, with several resolutions, which I wish was in my power to put in execution; but unless Col. Smith and Remsen . . . join me with their regiments, or some other assistance, immediately, I shall not be able. . . . I shall continue here as long as I can, in hopes of a reinforcement."

Already woefully outnumbered by almost two to one, the untested American troops panicked. Fully one-fifth were killed or captured, with many more wounded men limping back to basecamp in Brooklyn Heights to face what looked like certain retreat or slaughter. The British, meanwhile, settled in for a siege, while torrential fall storms thundered overhead.

As swift as the defeat had been, the Americans refused to capitulate easily, continuously firing their cannons into the British lines until well after dark on August 28. That day, Woodhull sent a final, defeated message to Washington, telling him not to send any reinforcements after all; his men were already surrounded by the enemy. Washington's response acknowledged the sentiment and rendered Woodhull's plight even more hopeless: he was ordering a retreat and abandoning Long Island.

Samuel Townsend was tasked with the job of delivering the fateful news to Woodhull in person, since Washington did not want to risk a written message falling into enemy hands and tipping them off too soon to the plan to evacuate the remaining forces.[19] On August 29, Samuel made his way on horseback through the dense forests and oyster-shell-paved roads to reach Woodhull's last known headquarters near Jamaica Pass on Long Island—a point now behind enemy lines. The long-familiar paths were rendered completely foreign as a thick fog had settled on the area, remnants of the downpours that added insult to injury for the bedraggled and war-weary Americans. As he struggled to find his way in the misty darkness, Samuel must have felt dread mingled with urgency.

At this point, the narrative becomes unclear. Samuel never recorded whether he reached Woodhull in time to share Washington's devastating verdict, but it wouldn't have mattered. Woodhull's meager troops were already doomed. Surrounded, the general and many of his remaining men were captured. According to tradition, Woodhull replied, "God save us all," rather than "God save the King," when challenged by a British officer, an act of defiance that resulted in savage sword wounds to Woodhull's head and arm.[20]

On the night of August 29–30, the same day that Samuel was scrambling to reach Woodhull, who was resigning himself to his fate, General Washington was plotting a way to salvage what little was left of American men, supplies, and morale. In one of the finest examples of military leadership in the early years of the war, Washington denied General Howe the satisfaction of a drawn-out siege by orchestrating a mass withdrawal of nine thousand men across the East River to Manhattan. Under the cover of that same thick fog that frustrated Samuel, Washington evacuated troops, horses, cannons, and supplies on barges and boats supplied by local watermen—all without losing a single man. The Battle of Long Island had been an ignominious defeat for the Continental Army, but there was, perhaps, some small and ironic consolation that the retreat had been a resounding success.

The minutes of the New York Continental Congress reveal one final duty given to Samuel on August 29, after his delivery of the terrible news to Woodhull. He was ordered back to Manhattan, to the American enclave of Horn Hook, located on the present site of Gracie Mansion, with instructions to make sure the same five hundred men originally promised to defend Long Island were transported safely away from the city. He was authorized to impress any horses, wagons, boats, or vessels needed to do so and allocated a sum of £100 to make any arrangements.

No records remain of how this was accomplished; we know only that the men of Colonel Josiah Smith and Colonel Henry Remsen's regiments dispersed.[21] How Samuel himself escaped capture and made his way home to Oyster Bay, which lay well behind enemy lines, also remains a mystery.

In the weeks that followed, the American troops withdrew from New York City entirely, but war hates a vacuum almost as much as nature does. Washington and his generals looked on helplessly from Westchester as the British army immediately swarmed in and quickly established Manhattan as a key strategic headquarters with access not only to deep-water ports but also to an almost limitless supply of food, fabric, female companionship, and other essentials for maintaining the welfare and morale of a fighting force.

Unfortunately, the damages to the American cause were not limited to material losses. General Nathaniel Woodhull, Robert Townsend's would-be commander and one of Washington's most trusted leaders in New York, languished for three weeks before finally succumbing to his injuries, which became infected while he lay in the filth of a British prison ship. He died on September 20.

Any hope and promise the future seemed to hold for the Americans in the summer of 1776 had all but evaporated by the start of September. Perhaps Samuel had plans to rejoin his compatriots to begin drafting the new state constitution under the leadership of John Jay, the brilliant legal mind from Manhattan. Unfortunately, he never got the chance. One week after Washington's retreat, a British unit thundered into town and surrounded the Townsend homestead. Oliver De Lancey's 17th Light Infantry was an elite regiment of local Loyalist men—American-born boys from Long Island, many of whose names and faces Samuel knew well. These were also the same soldiers who had viciously attacked General Woodhull in Jamaica. They already had two men with them under arrest: George Townsend, a distant cousin who was active in raising local militias, and John Kirk, one of the leaders of the Patriot movement in nearby Jericho.

A large group of villagers, as well as the Townsend household, gathered outside the large Dutch door of the family's house. A soldier stepped forward asking for "Sam Townsend"—the nickname intended to belittle the man local Patriots considered great—to which Samuel replied, "I am the man."

"Get yourself ready to accompany us to the provost at New York," the solider ordered. A shudder ran through the waiting family; the British prison ships were notorious for disease and privation. Over the course of the war, an estimated eleven thousand men would perish within the holds of prison ships like the HMS *Jersey* as she lay anchored in Wallabout Bay off of Brooklyn—more than twice as many as died in combat in the entire conflict.

The British did not leave with their inmate immediately, however. According to family records, while Samuel sent a household slave to an out-lot for his riding horse, soldiers entered the house and smashed a game fowling musket, charging that "a rebel" should not have even a hunting weapon in his possession. Then one officer's eyes fell on a portrait of Solomon, which he had had commissioned on a voyage to Portugal in 1772. When the redcoat demanded the whereabouts of that young man, he was informed that Solomon was at sea. "I regret it is not within my powers to wreak the vengeance of my superiors upon him also," the officer sneered.

Allowed only a single change of clothing, Samuel was marched off with the other two prisoners before the unsympathetic eyes of his Loyalist neighbors. The residents of Oyster Bay may have forgotten Samuel's protests against the Tory Act but not the sentiments behind its damning measures.

As Delancey's 17th Light Infantry marched up the hill out of town, the brigade passed a traveling party consisting of Audrey (Samuel's oldest daughter), Almy (Samuel's niece), and Thomas Buchanan (Almy's husband). A few brief words revealed the gravity of the situation, and it was here that the Buchanan family's neutrality served them well. Thomas, who had been riding in a phaeton carriage with his wife, took Audrey's horse and galloped off to collect £2,000 of his personal fortune to pay the bribe required to free Samuel.

Thomas Buchanan succeeded, and Samuel was released on Buchanan's bond that the ardent Patriot would step away from his political rabble-rousing, which was punctuated by a signed oath of allegiance to King George. Stumbling back to Oyster Bay, Samuel couldn't help but observe that his home, land, and family were all now inescapably situated in the heart of enemy territory—and he couldn't raise a finger in protest.

George Townsend and John Kirk, however, did not enjoy nearly so speedy or painless a release. Though both were eventually freed thanks to the efforts of friends a few months later, they were not without their scars. Kirk paid most dearly; he contracted smallpox aboard the *Jersey* and had to be carted home in a wagon. Although he eventually recovered, his wife and young daughter both caught the disease and died shortly after his return.[22, 23] His son, John Kirk Jr., looked on helplessly as his family seemed to receive a double share of the suffering the Townsends had managed to escape. Death may be the great equalizer, but war can highlight the inequalities of life.

Liss was about thirteen when she stood in the bright sunlight of a September afternoon and watched the enemy frog-march her master away. Her world was only as big as Oyster Bay—the water that constrained her to the north, the fields and forests that hemmed her in to the south, east, and west, and the laws that bound her for all intents and purposes to the Townsend homestead. She had certainly heard of, but probably never witnessed, the bold blue uniforms of the Continental Army and the great men on horseback who commanded armies and made a far more impressive showing than they had recently done in the bungled defense of New York. What Liss knew at that moment was that the men in red coats and gleaming brass buttons bespoke power: power over her world—maybe even the entire globe—and certainly power over her master. It is not an exaggeration to say that she may have even regarded them as demigods, had it not been blasphemous both by Christian and by Townsend standards to think so.

When Long Island fell, the occasion would have been at once completely undetectable and earthshaking for a young woman like Liss. Very little about her day-to-day routine would have changed. The Townsend household still needed meals; the family still required laundry; stockings and petticoats still needed mending. The girls, who were Liss's closest companions, would still have wanted their hair brushed up into the latest fashion and their gowns pressed neatly before church each Sunday morning. King George had been the distant but sovereign ruler of Oyster Bay before the Battle of Long Island, and he remained so now. Any rumblings of revolution had always been louder in the Townsend home than probably anywhere else in the area, so a more firmly established presence of British troops did not mark any kind of a drastic shift in the way things ran.

At the same time, however, the presence of the British portended the possibility of a very different future for enslaved people. The Crown had already begun to pass small but significant restrictions on the slave trade, with more than ten thousand domestic slaves legally emancipated in England and Wales in 1772. Although both the British and American sides eventually came to promise freedom to slaves who enlisted, the British army made the offer first, and its government seemed the most committed to the cause. In short, the fate of an entire people might just rest in the hands of the eventual victor of the current conflict. Very few enslaved people allowed themselves to feel too much excitement at the possibility, but it was certainly a topic one could not completely disregard. Robert, meanwhile, returned to his work in the city never having had to carry out his service as military commissary after all, and Solomon, sailing under the Union Jack, continued in reluctant service to King George. Their father's forced oath of loyalty to the Crown seemed to have muted his patriotic zeal, at least for the time. The Townsends of Oyster Bay laid low, going about their business quietly so as not to attract any more unwanted attention and waiting to see which way the winds blew. If they could just make it through the war with their family and property largely intact, it would be enough. Trade continued in the town, just as it did in the city, and the younger Townsend siblings continued to keep records in the Negro Ledger. For a few months, life continued much as it always had in Oyster Bay, but everyone knew that could all change in an instant. Late in the autumn of 1776, it did.

# CHAPTER THREE

# Oyster Bay Occupied

SOLOMON TOWNSEND WAS RESTLESS AND MORE THAN A LITTLE DIS-gusted. After his recent debacle delivering the Scottish refugees, the *Glasgow* had been called back to New York. To Solomon's relief, another captain, Robert Craig, was tapped for the new assignment: serving as a prisoner transport. While Solomon spent a sweltering Christmas ashore in the British colony of Jamaica, Captain Robert Craig picked up 225 near-dead American soldiers in New York to exchange under a flag of truce on December 25.[1] But after only a few miles, while passing through Hell Gate in the East River, the *Glasgow* struck a rock. The damaged ship drifted and sat at anchor under repair for eleven days before crossing Long Island Sound, with little or no provisions aboard for the weak and ailing soldiers, many of whom had smallpox. Twenty-eight died and were thrown overboard while the rest were dumped on the frigid beach of Milford, Connecticut. Shocked townspeople brought the emaciated and sickly men ashore and fed them corn, potatoes, and boiled beef, causing nineteen more to die from overeating. Using the town hall as a makeshift hospital, the well-intentioned locals attempted to save as many as possible, but twenty-seven more of the men perished.[2]

When he resumed his captaincy of the *Glasgow* in March 1777, following that grim mission, Solomon voyaged with the fleet to England and now, back in Quebec, found himself stalled on the Saint Lawrence River while attempting to sail up to Montreal. The water level was more suited for a flatboat than this three-masted vessel now burdened with the extra weight of cannons on her deck, and there was little wind to assist Solomon in what was quickly proving to be a Sisyphean task.

Failing bilge pumps and a leaking barrel of tar had damaged a quantity of the cargo from London he was hauling under British orders. As his crew removed the sticky, sodden mess and brought onboard new boatloads of barrels and crates, Solomon's mind wandered, carefully planning his next move. When at last the *Garland*, a twenty-gun ship, arrived in October to lead the convoy back to London, he gladly hoisted his sails, not only to escape the scrutiny of the British troops stationed in Canada but also to put his plan into action.[3]

Landing in London in early December, Solomon set about repairing and replacing the *Glasgow*'s badly damaged sails and rigging and offloading and selling the cargo. Over the next few months, he settled all outstanding disbursements, payrolls, and accounts, including his brother Robert's £100 bill for goods. Solomon would not tolerate any sloppiness or unfinished business. He even made note of the value of his brass hanging compass, two mirrors, and a spy glass, which he planned to leave on board. Then, with everything properly squared away, Solomon ended his decade-long career as a sea captain, resigned his position, and left his ship. He purchased a trunk, had his hair styled, bought an atlas of America, and armed with letters of introduction from his father, made his way across the channel to France.[4]

Motivated by a singular mission, Solomon reached Paris and sought out Benjamin Franklin, who knew his father as a fellow Continental congressman.[5] At the time, Franklin was also reluctantly hosting his socially awkward fellow diplomat John Adams, who was escorted by his own personal bodyguard with a tough reputation: Richard Palmes. It had been Palmes's testimony regarding the Boston Massacre that had proved a key aspect in the trial of the accused British officers—for whom, ironically, Adams served as defense council.[6, 7] Solomon could not help but feel a bit awed in the presence of both Franklin and Adams whose roles in debating, drafting, and disseminating the Declaration of Independence had already secured their status as great men in the American mythos.

Solomon later spoke fondly of his time in Paris, describing Franklin as an unassuming and unpretentious gentleman. In fact, one of Solomon's sons recalled a favorite family story wherein Solomon stopped by

Franklin's quarters "rather early one morning, [and] Dr. Franklin came out of his room *en déshabillé* (in his breeches in fact) & apologized to my father bidding him at the same time not to go as he would join him in a few moments."[8]

Whether on that day or another, Franklin certainly was wearing more than just his underwear when Solomon petitioned him for a certification of loyalty, which the young man could take back to America to prove that any service he carried out for King George was done under physical duress and threat of imprisonment. Satisfied with Solomon's character and the veracity of his claims, which were no doubt aided by Samuel's reputation as an ardent Patriot, Franklin agreed to vouch for the erstwhile captain. On June 27, 1778, the great Patriot hero signed the following declaration: "I certify to whom it may concern that Captain Solomon Townsend of New York, mariner, hath this day appeared voluntarily before me, and taken the oath of allegiance to the United States of America, according to the resolution of Congress, thereby acknowledging himself a subject of the United States."[9]

Franklin also commissioned Solomon a lieutenant in the Continental Navy, providing him with a uniform and sword. In August, with his hard-won proof of patriotism in hand, Solomon boarded the frigate *Providence*, part of an American convoy traversing the Atlantic. Richard Palmes, having safely delivered John Adams to Paris, also returned with this fleet, resuming his position as a captain of the Continental Marines aboard the frigate *Boston*, traveling in the same fleet. Commodore Abraham Whipple, commander of the *Providence*, also provided Solomon with a written testimony of his character, declaring, "[D]uring the whole of the passage [he] behaved himself as a good & faithful citizen of the United States."[10, 11] Together, Solomon hoped, the two declarations of his fidelity to the American struggle would carry enough weight to undo any damage to his reputation done by his period of forced service to the Crown.

Both frigates landed in Portsmouth on October 15, 1778, whence Solomon made his way to Orange County, New York, where he located his cousin, Peter Townsend, who willingly took him in.[12] Peter owned an ironworks that had greatly contributed to the Patriot cause the year before by forging the "Great Chain" to prevent the British from sailing up the Hudson River at the fort at West Point; he agreed to bring his newly repatriated cousin into the business. Solomon would have liked to return to Oyster Bay straightaway, but circumstances had changed at the Townsend homestead, and it was hardly a place for a man who was now a sworn Patriot of America. Sending a letter to Robert in British-held Manhattan via a "flag of truce," Solomon wrote, "I am in this part of the country, and very well in health. If you have any opportunity to write to me, shall be very glad to hear from you. A letter directed to Peter Townsend, near Goshen, will likely come to hand. Please remember me to all friends."[13]

Robert carefully copied the good news and sent it on to Oyster Bay. Though his family had not laid eyes on their oldest son since the war began, knowing Solomon was safe, and now on the preferred side of the conflict and the Atlantic, was a huge relief. But their own situation was not nearly so simple as before.

———

John Simcoe's eyes swept across the village, quickly surveying the spot that was to be his home for the next six months: a few shops, a few houses (some were rather handsome, he had to admit), a smithy or two, a mill, and a rather large stretch of apple orchard that swept up the surrounding hills, right from the center of town. At the waterfront, some well-situated docks punctuated a hundred yards of salt marshes, and in the bay, several surprisingly large merchant vessels were currently at anchor. It was humbler than many other cities he had ridden through, but rather larger than most of the provincial towns that were springing up all over the colonies. The people seemed—well, perhaps not outright welcoming, but not altogether hostile to a British presence, at least. Some of the citizens even seemed downright sophisticated . . . by American standards. He had certainly billeted in worse settings, that much was certain, like his stay at the somewhat seedy Cucklestown Inn on Staten Island.[14] Yes, Oyster Bay would do, he decided. And who knew? If it proved especially sufficient, he just might invite his old friend John André to join him from the Hamptons for a visit, if General Sir Henry Clinton decided he could spare his aide-de-camp for a few weeks.

When the Queen's Rangers rode into Oyster Bay in November 1778, their forest green uniforms cut a striking contrast to the ubiquitous red coats of most British units. But the uniforms weren't the only thing that set apart the Queen's Rangers.[15] Commanding officer Colonel John Graves Simcoe, at only twenty-six, was already a veteran of the American campaign, having made a name for himself as a soldier of unusual restraint as befitted his gentlemanly bearing and his education at Eton and Oxford. He saw action in some of the British army's earliest victories at Boston, New York, New Jersey, and Pennsylvania and distinguished himself at the Battle of Brandywine, outside Philadelphia, in the 40th Regiment of Foot. During the bloody battle he fought alongside the Queen's Rangers and, along with over half their officers, was severely wounded. After he recovered, he was given command of that unit and immediately put into place strict rules of moral conduct.[16] For example, when on patrol, his Rangers were to avoid unnecessary bloodshed and to capture rather than kill rebels. Although plundering the dead and wounded was common practice, Simcoe forbade any such behavior, going one step further to issue special orders against the robbery of enemy prisoners as well. He even once spared a lone American sentinel, sending him a warning that he was in danger rather than picking him off with rifle fire. Simcoe recalled the incident in his military journal: "A patrolling party of the Rangers approached undiscovered so close to a rebel sentinel, posted upon the bridge, that it would have been easy to have killed him. A boy, whom he had just examined, was sent back to inform him of this, and to direct him immediately to quit his post or that he should be shot; he ran off."[17]

Even more unusual, however, were Simcoe's progressive views on the contributions of African Americans to the war effort. While many regiments traveled with people of African descent—either individuals enslaved by members of the unit or escaped slaves who joined the encampment for shelter and protection—Simcoe believed a great deal of potential was being wasted in consigning those individuals to drudgery and service work. An ardent abolitionist, he recognized that slaves might be emboldened to run away if promised an opportunity to join up with the British and live as free men in the army. Prior to assuming command of the Queen's Rangers, Simcoe used his considerable influence to advocate for raising just such a regiment under his command.[18] His ambition was denied, but Simcoe enjoyed the ear of British commander in chief Sir Henry Clinton and persistently petitioned him to consider opening the ranks to people of color.

---

In the fall of 1778, however, Simcoe found himself preparing to winter over in the comfortable lodgings of one Mr. Samuel Townsend of Oyster Bay, New York.[19] True, Simcoe's host had a reputation as a patriotic firebrand, but the man he encountered seemed subdued and begrudgingly accepting of the orders Simcoe presented that permitted him to quarter in the Townsend home for the next six months. The house was handsomely appointed, if significantly smaller than the country estates Simcoe was used to back in England, but wealth was measured differently in the colonies—not by one's forebears but by the sweat of one's own brow. A highly successful merchant here lived more like a prosperous farmer back in England; but, after all, colonists were starting with far less in the Americas. Generational wealth had barely had time to gain a foothold. Besides, however modest the habitations, they were still vastly superior to a tent and a bedroll in the field—and certainly more comfortable than that abomination of a winter camp that General George Washington had subjected the Continental Army to out in Valley Forge earlier in the year.

The Townsend home promised more than just shelter and a warm hearth too. Mrs. Sarah Townsend was a gracious hostess who offered a generous table and adequate silver and china. And the Townsend children still living at home—Audrey (twenty-three), David (nineteen), Sally (seventeen), and Phebe (fifteen)—were lively and amusing.[20] The girls, especially, were a welcome feature of the household. Simcoe was still a young man, after all, and he was well aware of the glittering social life of banquets and balls he had left behind in England to serve in this rebellious backwater. The Townsend daughters may not have been London ladies of good backgrounds, fine titles, and inheritances padded by pedigree, but they could still provide clever conversation and a civilizing influence, both of which he desperately needed after months at a time surrounded only by common soldiers.

Simcoe also found himself intrigued by the dozen or so enslaved people who completed his hosts' household, which included a young couple named Gabriel and Jane; a middle-aged woman named Susannah and her son Jeffrey (nine); a woman named Susan, with her two daughters, Lilly (five) and Catherine (seven); and two teenaged girls, Hannah (about thirteen) and Elizabeth (about sixteen), whom everyone called "Liss." It seemed like quite a large number until he learned that besides the orchards in town, the family also owned 350 acres in large tracts outside the village, where oats, wheat, flax, corn, potatoes, and other crops were cultivated both for the family's use and for sale. Add to that forty sheep, twenty hogs, a herd of cattle, several pairs of oxen, and a sizable shipping business, and the Townsend estate was a model of industry.[21] While nothing in comparison with the vast plantations that sprawled for miles across America's southern colonies, it was an impressive holding for New York, and the enslaved men, women, and children labored from dawn to dusk both in the house and fields. Simcoe saw their skill, intelligence, and ingenuity and regretted yet again the limited vision of his superiors, who failed to support his efforts to mobilize the large number of people he knew would escape their masters to take up arms for Britain if presented with the chance. Maybe one day, if he got that commission up in Canada he was hoping for. . . . But for now, Simcoe resolved to focus on making the most of his current position, and that meant situating himself and his men properly in a town that greeted them with mixed emotions.

The arrival of the Queen's Rangers was heralded with a fit of excitement at the promise of new faces and fatigue at the demands of yet another regiment descending upon the town, swelling its ranks by over 350 additional soldiers. Oyster Bay was beginning to recognize its value to the British as a garrison, a site of forage collection and transport, and a stopover for troops to rest, train, and bide their time until they received orders for the next campaign. Situated near Long Island Sound, the village was close to both British-held New York and Patriot-held Connecticut, which was clearly visible from nearby Pine Island; yet it was still remote enough to offer the advantages of ample crops and livestock for food and land for forage, and wood for fuel. There was adequate housing for the officers in private homes, and the enlisted men were quickly put to work improving and enlarging a sizable fort on a hill near the center of town that could accommodate seventy-five soldiers, providing a clear view of both harbor and village. The remaining troops commandeered local church buildings and barns as barracks, occupying every available space with either men, horses, or equipment belonging to the regiment.[22]

Simcoe vigilantly maintained law and order. Two sergeants-of-the-horse convicted of stealing from locals were flogged. When the rations provided by the quartermaster proved insufficient or spoiled, Simcoe encouraged his men to be resourceful rather than disruptive by taking advantage of the plentiful oysters in the nearby waters, from which the village took its name. In short, Simcoe worked hard to show respect to the reluctant hosts of the town.[23] After all, Oyster Bay's well of hospitality had already been tainted by previous regiments.

The first unit to come through had been De Lancey's Brigade, in November 1776, just two months after the capture of General Nathaniel Woodhull at the Battle of Long Island by its 17th Light Infantry. Also called the New York Loyalists, this band of fifteen hundred was the largest force of local men ("provincials") raised in the colony. The 3rd Battalion consisted of five hundred soldiers, who were divided between Huntington, Brookhaven, and Oyster Bay for "wintering over" into the spring of 1777. Even with a third of the men, Oyster Bay was clearly stretched beyond capacity. The brigade's orderly book from February notes that lunch had to be served in two shifts owing to a lack of available cutlery. Wood was also scarce; on February 25, an order was issued to prevent soldiers from dismantling residents' fences to burn the rails for heat.[24] Major Joseph Greene, commander of the 1st Battalion, seems to have made every effort to keep the men in check. He had, after all, learned a thing or two about maintaining law and order from his father, high sheriff of County Kilkenny, back home in Ireland.[25] But a bored army with nothing to do will always find a way to create amusement—and trouble. Greene warned that "unwarrantable acts, such as Maroding & etc shall be Severely checked & he [Greene] Expects that the good

Soldiers will inform should they see any Acts so shameful which brings disrespect upon the Body at large."[26]

In April, Greene also enacted a strict prohibition on the sale of rum to soldiers, followed by a cessation of all gambling among the troops. But despite his efforts to keep his men in check, DeLancey's Brigade seems to have worn thin their welcome—even from staunchly Loyalist Oyster Bay.

Though the citizenry endured some hardship, not all interactions with the military were hostile. The officers often became fixtures in the households and deeply enmeshed in the lives of their hosts, despite any political differences that might make such matches seem unlikely. Since the Townsend home was among the largest and most comfortably outfitted, it naturally hosted the highest-ranking officers and became headquarters, which, in the case of DeLancey's Brigade, situated Major Greene in the immediate company of the Townsend girls and their teenaged cousins Martha and Hannah, who lived next door. The gentleman was, by all accounts, a generous and well-respected officer while he resided at the Townsend homestead during his battalion's stay. Already familiar with the village before the war (his name appears in Oyster Bay shop records as far back as 1768),[27] Greene was rumored to have been instrumental in helping Thomas Buchanan secure Samuel Townsend's release from British custody earlier that autumn. Buchanan's wife, Almy, was Martha and Hannah's older sister, and it seems that Hannah had already caught Major Greene's eye.

During the winter, whatever flirting had previously occurred between the officer and Hannah grew into a whirlwind courtship that saw the couple beating a regular path between the adjacent houses for social calls. Despite being on opposite sides of the conflict, the two were married on January 7, 1777.[28] Greene purchased a lavish assortment of foods for the wedding celebration from the bride's uncle Samuel, including ham, turkey, mutton, a bushel of corn, butter, sugar, tea, and cider.[29] The wives and daughters and especially the enslaved people from both families would have been involved in the preparations for the banquet and the excitement of preparing Hannah's trousseau. The soldiers may not always have been welcomed and politics in this instance were certainly not aligned, but a British officer made a good match by anyone's estimation.

Oyster Bay enjoyed barely one month's reprieve between the departure of DeLancey's Brigade and the arrival of the next regiment in June: the King's American Rangers, led by Colonel Edmund Fanning and his second in command, Major James Grant.[30] During this unit's brief stay that summer, Samuel Townsend and his family again hosted the officers in their home-turned-headquarters, and these guests seem to have been far less welcome than their predecessors. Described as "rude and ill-behaved," the soldiers imposed draconian restrictions on the townspeople, erected sentry boxes in the streets, established strict curfews, and enforced daily signs and countersigns that the citizenry were expected to memorize. One evening, "a respectable young man" named John Weeks failed to produce the latest password when he was challenged by a sentry. The boy tried to run but was quickly "seized, tried, and sentenced to be whipped." As the Townsends' home had been established as headquarters, Weeks was tied to the tree in front of the house while his mother and sister yelled and cried, begging for mercy. The entire household came pouring out to investigate the clamor on their doorstep before the British finally relented and released the boy.[31] No one was sorry to see the backs of the King's American Rangers as they rode out of town a few weeks later.

It is little wonder that the villagers were already fatigued by the war and its inconveniences when the next wave of occupation brought Oyster Bay some better-behaved guests in November. Simcoe recognized quickly that the previous year of mandatory billeting had already stretched the hospitality and provisions of the town, and he resolved to make himself as agreeable and accommodating as he reasonably could. The Townsend account book reveals Simcoe to have been a loyal patron of his host's store, regularly purchasing fowl, beef, and other meats as well as fabrics, candles, and a remarkable number of nails.[32]

The colonel's efforts to ingratiate himself and his men to the Townsend family appear to have been successful by nearly every account. Samuel and Sarah seem to have recorded no grievances, and the children—especially Sally—had even less to complain of. Evidence of mutual admiration between the exotic officers and the teenaged Townsend daughters is abundant. "The adorable Miss ~~Sally~~ Sarah Townsend," Captain John McGill etched into one windowpane on the front of the house. "Miss A.T.—The Most accomplished Young lady in Oyster Bay," read a dedication to Audrey on another pane. A third simply bore the name of a Townsend cousin: "Sally Coles."[33] Close to everyone's mind, of course, was the advantageous match cousin Hannah had made with Major Greene the previous year, which brought with it a modest estate and country home on the Irish coast, in addition to whatever land in the colonies or Canada the Crown might grant the major in return for his service in the war. Patriotic ideals were important, but so were respectable inheritances.

Colonel Simcoe himself indulged in a flirtation with one of his host's daughters. On February 14, 1779, he addressed a poem to Sally, opening, "Fairest Maid, where all is fair, Beauty's pride and Nature's care. To you my heart I must resign, O choose me for your Valentine!" For twenty-six lines, Simcoe extolled her charms and beauty (also remembering to compliment her mother), before ending with advice from Cupid:

> *Shall no fair maid with equal fire awake the flames of soft desire:*
> *My bosom born, for transport, burn and raise my thoughts from Delia's urn?*
> *"Fond Youth," the God of Love replies, "Your answer take from Sarah's eyes."*[34]

Never mind that he had addressed a startlingly similar poem to a young lady in Boston in 1775[35] and just a few years later would write more of the same to the future Mrs. Simcoe, one Miss Elizabeth Gwillum; the verse to Sally nevertheless stands as the earliest-known valentine in America and certainly impressed the addressee.

The etching of the name "Sally Coles" into the windowpane might have been due to the arrival of the Townsends' Rhode Island cousin, Bob Stoddard Jr., who moved to town during the Queen's Rangers' stay and began helping out in the family store. Bob's father, Captain Robert Stoddard, had been a slave trader who made frequent trips to Africa before dying suddenly on September 28, 1776.[36] During his brief stint in the British navy at the start of the war, Bob's vessel sank in Newport Harbor, and swimming to shore, the teenager took advantage of his presumed death to switch sides, coming to live with his patriotic aunt's branch of the Townsend family in Oyster Bay.[37]

What Robert thought about all the goings-on in his family home is unclear. Simcoe was, by no means, universally adored in the town. He permitted his men to harass several prominent local Patriots and oversaw the decimation of the Townsends' large apple orchard to form an abattis, or field fortification, around a fort built uncomfortably close to the family graveyard. But whatever feelings Robert had about the colonel's behavior and close quarters with his family, he kept them to himself, and he does not seem to have begrudged his sisters or cousins their fun when it came to the social opportunities the billeting soldiers brought with them. In fact, on February 1, 1779, Robert addressed a playful letter to his young cousin Bob, in which he commented on one young woman's removal from the town's social life "to keep out of the way of the teasing addresses of the officers," though he supposed her absence was actually due to her concentrating her efforts on winning over just one of them in particular. And it was not only the British soldiers who were enjoying a lively winter. High spirits seem to have prevailed in Oyster Bay that season, even among the locals. "I am told that you are now quite the man of pleasure; that you are acquainted with all the young Ladys in the country," Robert teased his cousin, "and that you have been sporting with the rural dames of the Hollow, and the amorous lasses of the South Woods . . . some of which will, I expect, in the course of a few months, proclaim you the cause of their ruined reputations."[38]

The Townsend girls and their peers were not the only young women enamored with their British guests. Liss was also quite taken with them, spending whatever spare time she could find in their company and chatting with them unabashedly. Years later, in fact, Robert would recall in a letter that Liss was thought to be both more "fond of the British officers" and more "fond of Company" than the family felt prudent.[39] Contact between Simcoe, his men, and the Townsend family slaves would have been unavoidable, of course. Liss would have had the added duties of washing and mending Simcoe's clothing and bedding, not to mention emptying and cleaning his chamber pot, preparing the parlor for daily officers' meetings, straightening the room afterward, tending the fireplace, offering refreshments to Simcoe's officers, and waiting on a steady stream of visitors. Every morning, Simcoe's slackened bed ropes needed tightening, and in the frigid evenings, because his room had no fireplace, Liss carefully filled the heavy bed warmer with hot coals and ran it under his covers, so they were warm when the colonel slipped beneath them. In fact, moving freely in and out of chambers with laundry, meals, and firewood, Liss would have had much more intimate contact with him than any heavily chaperoned young white lady of society would have enjoyed.

As gallant as Simcoe was, however, and whatever effect he had on women to make them set aside their social or political hesitations to take up a flirtation with him, he was nothing compared to his good friend John André—the most celebrated and charming young man of his day.

André had been the toast of the town in Philadelphia the previous spring, enjoying his stay in Benjamin Franklin's commandeered house, while that notorious charmer in his own right was away in Paris and powerless to remove the British from his residence. The *Mischianza*—an unimaginably lavish, elaborate ball with more than four hundred guests, thrown to honor the departure of General William Howe as the British commander in chief—had been the triumph of André's tenure in Howe's service. He coordinated and personally oversaw the most blatant parade of royal extravagance ever displayed on American soil. André's reputation as a universally beloved figure made him a legend; his success at the *Mischianza* made him a celebrity.[40, 41] And now, he was serving as the aide-de-camp of General Sir Henry Clinton, Howe's replacement, who was staying at his "country headquarters" in the Hamptons. With winter giving way to spring, Simcoe and André spilled a great deal of ink trying to arrange a visit. André would have liked nothing better than a vacation from work and, due to a persistent illness that he couldn't seem to shake, felt he deserved some time off. But Clinton refused to grant it, at least as of André's February reply to Simcoe: "The General's kind determination, that I shall be a private Gentleman of his country house . . . seems founded on some view of making a little use of me even as an invalid, I cannot combat. I must therefore relinquish my pleasing scheme of visiting you at present; some future period will I hope be more favorable to my visits with your society."[42]

Finally, in March, André succeeded in begging a few weeks of convalescent leave to venture out to Oyster Bay and quickly learned that Simcoe had not exaggerated the town's charms. Unfortunately, André was not able to fully enjoy all the benefits his personal magnetism naturally attracted. In addition to his health complaints, the abnormally cold and snowy weather kept him largely confined to the Townsend home while in Oyster Bay,[43] where he was under the constant care of the family's slaves, including Liss. On March 20, 1779, he wrote to General Clinton, "I have found myself situated here with some conveniency for attending to my health and shall remain within place until the weather mends."[44]

Following his stay, André gushed about the visit to Simcoe in a letter dated April 6: "I assure you my dear Sir that if I were persuaded my company was half so agreeable to you as the intercourse I had with you was to me I should not hesitate to repair to you again as a convalescent. I cannot express to you how great I found the contrast between the sober and various occupations and conversations of Oyster Bay and the Sysiphean labours of Head Quarters."[45]

As much as he enjoyed visiting his old friend, however, André's mind also seems to have been elsewhere. As the spring progressed and his "treacherous complaint" abated under the household's watchful eye, André remained on the lookout for any news of nineteen-year-old Peggy Shippen, the toast of Philadelphia society and the daughter of a prominent Loyalist. She and André had enjoyed a very public friendship during his stay in her city, and now she had announced her engagement and upcoming marriage to a rather surprising choice of gentleman: Benedict Arnold, a widower literally twice her age with three children—and one of George Washington's top officers in the Continental Army.[46] The unlikely pair married in Philadelphia on April 8, at which point André had already left Oyster Bay to report to his next post,[47] where his correspondence with Peggy now included overtures to her new husband too.

The Arnolds were not the only couple to marry that spring. On March 29, at the end of André's stay, Bob Stoddard—the transplanted cousin whom Robert teased—wedded Sally Coles.[48] Perhaps it was he who had etched her name alongside the two graffiti love notes of the officers. If, instead, Miss Coles was being courted by her own British suitor, Bob was the ultimate victor, and the young bride was spared from joining the Loyalist camp.

But other changes were afoot in the Townsend family as well. In May, the Queen's Rangers received orders to push north of New York City; Simcoe packed his kit, offered a farewell to his hosts, and settled his accounts. For the most part, he had been a well-behaved and respectful guest, but he did leave Oyster Bay with something extra that he quietly spirited away from the home. When his regiment pushed out, a certain young woman from the household traveled with them, but in the ordered chaos of assembling 350 men to embark on a long march and new campaign, no one noticed her absence until they were quite a distance from town.[49]

And by then, Liss had managed to disappear into the sea of soldiers, wagons, horses, and camp followers.

## CHAPTER FOUR

# "No Probability of Your Getting Her Again"

IN THE PREDAWN HOURS OF MAY 18, 1779, LISS FOUND HERSELF PAUSING on the threshold of the large Dutch front door as she made multiple trips from the house to Simcoe's waiting wagon. She looked up at the soft green bull's-eye glass that used to frighten her at dusk when she was a little girl. Now the oval panes at the top of the door seemed to stare back at her, bearing silent witness as she moved through the house where she had been born—the only home she had ever known. In a matter of hours, she would be leaving these familiar walls behind, the wide floorboards and the narrow back stairway, as well as the others she had lived and worked alongside, especially her younger sister, Hannah. After she slunk away under cover of the traveling army, would they ever forgive her for leaving them like this, without even a good-bye? But it was too great a risk to share her intentions with them. A sad look or quivering lip might just be enough to make her lose her nerve. Besides, what if they tried to talk her out of it or reminded her of the punishment they had all witnessed when other slaves in the village had tried to escape: being shackled and whipped in the center of town? She had even heard of a woman from a nearby town who had been branded on the face with her master's last name for running away. And what of her master's daughters—Audrey, Sally, and Phebe—with whom she had grown up? Surely they would be shocked by her sudden disappearance; then again, what loyalty did she owe them—the very people who believed she was something to be owned and ordered about, dedicated solely to their comfort? No matter

46

how the family may have treated her, nothing could change the fact that she was still property to them—valuable property, perhaps, but property all the same. Did she really owe them an explanation, let alone a farewell? No, Liss knew what she needed to do and had steeled her will to do it.

The real departure they should be concerned about was that of poor Susannah, who was laid out in the barn in the final stages of what they all knew was smallpox.[1] The disease had been ravaging the colonies for the past few years, granting a bit of a reprieve during winter but picking up its deadly advance again as temperatures warmed.[2] For those who lived in slavery, recovering from the illness became a cruel badge of honor if their masters decided to sell them away; terms like "pock-fretten" and claims that "all have had the smallpox" were used in advertisements as common selling points, right alongside "excellent washer" and "honest and sober."[3] But those who didn't recover suffered the same fate as free men: their bodies were hastily interred, and their remaining personal belongings were often burned to prevent further infection.

Liss tried not to think about the fate of the woman who had been almost like a second mother to herself and her sister or about Susannah's nine-year-old son Jeffrey, who would soon be an orphan. He would bury his mother in the Townsend family cemetery with only a fieldstone to mark her grave—no name, no dates, no loving inscription to memorialize her life in any way. At most, a "T's" might be carved by an untrained hand to denote that the person buried beneath that particular stone had been the legal property of the Townsend family. Slaves were regarded as property even in death, it seemed.

But enough about death. Even in the darkness, the air was alive with the sounds of horses stamping and whinnying as they were fitted with saddles and bits. Men shouted orders to one another, making only a minimal effort not to wake whatever townspeople were still trying to sleep through the racket of 350 men and dozens of camp followers loading up the last of their gear.

Liss carried the last of Colonel Simcoe's bedding to the wagon to pack into his handsome trunk, perhaps newly fitted with the large hinges lately bought at Townsend's store, when Robert had been visiting from Manhattan. The colonel's final purchases recorded in the Townsend ledger on May 5 included a quantity of nails, as well as the two pairs of H-hinges, which might be used for a large trunk like his or even a trap-door fitted into a large luggage cart—something to secure the covering of a space big enough to contain and conceal a great number of personal effects or a single item of substantial size.[4]

The Queen's Rangers would follow roughly the same route Robert took back to the city when they departed their winter quarters in Oyster Bay: west toward Brooklyn, then across the East River by ferry at one of the safer crossings. From there, they would push on to King's Bridge (modern-day Kingsbridge) for a top-secret campaign revealed only to reg-imental commanders like Simcoe and his superiors; all anyone else knew was that the six months of relative leisure on Long Island were over.[5]

As a pink glow spread from the horizon and melted the night, Sim-coe gave the orders to move out. The regiment's departure from town was almost certainly marked by less pomp and circumstance than its arrival as the bleary-eyed residents of Oyster Bay waved farewell to their erst-while guests before turning to evaluate what kind of wear and damage the departing troops had left behind. The town had felt overstuffed with the additional influx of soldiers, but after half a year, it now felt strangely empty—their absence conspicuous in the quiet streets and empty taverns.

And as for Liss, who slipped away unnoticed that spring morning, the world outside Oyster Bay awaited, promising novelty, adventure, and mystery.

—◆—

The circumstances surrounding Liss's departure with the Queen's Rang-ers remain unclear; the only details preserved by history come to us through a letter Robert wrote to his father eight days later:

*New York, May 26th, 1779*

*Mr. Samuel Townsend,*
*Dear Sir,*
*I have received yours of the 23d Inst. by Joseph Latting, and observe the contents.—*

*I now send you by Zebn. Townsend, 4 L Yds Fustian Dimothy, 1L Yds Persian & 2 Yds of Ribbon, as per enclosed account.—*

*Goods are now very high, but expect they will soon be lower, as large quantitys are daily expected.—You may depend that I shall be able to find them as low as any person.*

*The Queen's Rangers are now beyond King's Bridge. When I see any of the officers will make inquiry for Liss—Tho' I think there is no probability of your getting her again—believe you may reckon her amongst your other dead losses.—I am surprised that Col. Simcoe would permit her to go—he certainly must have known it when they left Oyster Bay.—I am*

*Dear Sir,*
*Your dutiful Son*
*Robt. Townsend*[6]

Beyond this, any attempts to recreate the events are pure conjecture; we know only that Liss left with the Queen's Rangers and traveled with them beyond Manhattan. There are, however, scattered clues that, when reassembled, point toward one of three possible scenarios regarding Liss's mind-set, motives, and movements as she left the Townsend home: either Simcoe alone knew of her plan, Robert was also aware of it, or Simcoe, Robert, and Samuel all knew. Each possibility has supporting evidence, but none seems to tell the complete story.

## Scenario #1: Simcoe's Scheming

An outspoken abolitionist, Colonel John Graves Simcoe had for years been encouraging the British army to reach out to African Americans. Lord Dunmore had done so in Virginia in 1775, and well over three thousand slaves made their way to the British side to fight with the promise of freedom awaiting them upon completion of their enlistment; Simcoe believed that such a policy throughout the colonies could potentially swing the balance irrevocably in favor of the Crown.[7]

Finally, in the early summer of 1779, his years of petitioning paid off. As a trusted officer of Commander in Chief Sir Henry Clinton and close friends with his aide-de-camp, John André, Simcoe very likely had advance knowledge of a significant policy change in the Crown's attitude toward runaway slaves. Perhaps due in no small part to Simcoe's own advocacy of such measures, on June 30, 1779—six weeks to the day since the Queen's Rangers left Oyster Bay—Sir Henry Clinton published a proclamation to be run in every Loyalist newspaper throughout the thirteen colonies that all enslaved people in British North America who escaped their masters and joined the royal cause would be emancipated.[8, 9] Though women did not have the option to enlist, they could nevertheless serve in useful capacities alongside the camp women as laundresses, cooks, or seamstresses. Perhaps Simcoe made Liss a similar assurance of freedom in exchange for faithful service to the army, since he knew the policy was about to become law.

Or perhaps he made no guarantee other than the promise of excitement and novelty in the city, which would have certainly held appeal for a lively young woman who had never ventured beyond the town where she was born. It would have been relatively easy for Liss to slip away from the Townsend house in the bustle of the great departure and just as easy for her to disappear into the city, though the employment options for a young African American woman were predictably limited.

Whatever the case, Robert seems very confident in his assertion that Simcoe must have been aware of Liss's plans, given the close proximity of colonel and slave as she carried out her household duties. The question remains, however, how Liss could have made her escape unnoticed. Certainly the chaos of an army on the move would have helped, but as the slave of one of the town's preeminent families, she ran a high risk of being recognized and caught before she even left the village. It is here that Simcoe's purchase of two pairs of H-hinges and nails hint at a tantalizing clue. Did they have some practical use for a soldier headed out on campaign, or might they have been fitted to a substantial trunk or a trapdoor in the false bottom of a wagon? Either space would have been large enough to conceal a person for long enough to travel safely out of town. Then again, Simcoe may simply have been funding repair of some damage to the Townsend home sustained during his stay. The enigma is intriguing.

With her departure, the Townsend family would be facing a material loss of at least £100 (approximately $9,000) as well as Liss's lifetime of labor and the value of any future children she bore, made even more essential by the impending death of Susannah. The pocketbooks of a family struggling to maintain its business interests in the face of wartime risks and limitations to the shipping industry would have felt her escape keenly. If Simcoe persuaded, or at least assisted, Liss in any way, he was doing so fully aware of the financial impact her loss would have on his hosts. As an ardent abolitionist, however, he probably would have considered the breach of both colonial law and gentlemanly protocol excusable, though certainly not defensible in court.

It seems surprising, however, that as prominent a man as Simcoe would concern himself so intimately with the plans of a young enslaved woman. Given his views on slavery, he certainly may have been willing to assist her, but would he have gone to so great an extent as to concoct an elaborate plan simply to allow one young slave (among a dozen in the Townsend family alone) to escape?

Surprisingly, the answer may be yes. Exactly one year after Liss's escape, Simcoe and André not only helped another young African American get away from his master in South Carolina but also used him as a source of intelligence on local matters.

Following his regiment's participation in the surrender of Charleston in May 1780, Simcoe extended a special invitation to André, his close friend who also served as the British spymaster: "We hunt & barbecú in a grove of laurels tomorrow, I wish business would permit you to partake of what I expect a novel Pleasure."[10] In addition to the pleasantries, Simcoe explained that he was sending André an escaped slave who had valuable local knowledge and for whom, after André's debriefing, he intended to arrange a place within the regiment: "I send you a very intelligent Negro Boy, within the Circle of his knowledge—When you dismiss him I will be obliged to you to pass him to the Quarter House, as I mean to keep him."[11]

The "Quarter House" was a large inn with a racetrack in Charleston used as a resort and for social events in times of peace and as a British officers' barracks during the occupation of the city.[12] This "Negro Boy" may have been one of four escaped slaves who joined Simcoe's regiment as musicians following the Siege of Charleston, recruited to play the drums, horns, and trumpets used to communicate signals during battle. One of these musicians, a sixteen-year-old boy named Barney, served in the Queen's Rangers not only as a trumpet player but also as a "vidette," or sentry. During a 1781 skirmish in Virginia, he showed both intelligence and bravery when he tricked the American forces into following him in the wrong direction, giving his regiment time to assemble and mount a counterattack. Simcoe later recalled the incident in his military journal: "Trumpeter Barney, who had been stationed as a vidette, gave the alarm, and gallopped off so as not to lead the enemy directly to where the cavalry were collecting their forage and watering, and, with great address, got to them unperceived by the enemy, calling out 'draw your swords Rangers, the rebels are coming.'"[13] Later that day, that same young man saved the life of a captain during a hand-to-hand fight and was seriously wounded. Following the surrender at Yorktown, Simcoe allowed Trumpeter Barney, who took the name Bernard E. Griffiths, to travel with him back to England.[14]

This was not the only time Simcoe served alongside escaped American slaves. During a series of skirmishes in New Jersey in late June 1780, Simcoe and a contingent of the Queen's Rangers fought with an unofficial British regiment called "The Black Brigade," led by former slave Colonel Tye, who had a reputation as a fierce fighter. New Jersey newspapers covered the exploits of their combined forces: "Yesterday morning a party of the enemy consisting of Ty[e] with 30 blacks, 36 Queen's Rangers, and 30 refugee tories, landed at Conascung."[15]

Not all of his attempts to help slaves escape were successful. When Simcoe permitted an African American man and woman from Charleston to travel back to New York by boat with his regiment in early June 1780, several of his men took it upon themselves to sell the couple back into slavery when they arrived at Staten Island. Colonel Steven Jarvis later wrote about his involvement, as well as that of Captain John McGill, the same officer who had etched his name into the windowpane of Samuel Townsend's house. Jarvis recorded the incident in detail years later in his account of the war, noting that on the passage from Charleston to New York, he discovered the presence of the African American couple. Two members of the regiment approached Jarvis, informing him that "there was a man who wished to purchase the negroes." Jarvis, playing the role of Pontius Pilate, simply told the men not to do anything without the approval of McGill, who was temporarily in charge since Simcoe himself was traveling separately. This order was followed, McGill's consent was obtained, and the free man and woman traveling under the protection of the Queen's Rangers were sold. "The only hand I had in the matter was to divide the money between them," Jarvis recalled, "and I thought nothing more of the matter for some time."

A few weeks later, the Queen's Rangers returned to Oyster Bay for their third and final visit. As they entered the village, Jarvis received good news: some of the officers had heard he was up for promotion. Not long after, he was called before Colonel Simcoe, who had just settled into his familiar room at the Townsend home, and Jarvis went in to speak with his commander in the highest of spirits, expecting a hearty congratulations. Thanks to Jarvis's careful recreation of the interaction, the soldiers' exact words are preserved.

"Young man, what is this you have been doing? I understand you have been selling negroes," Simcoe demanded, his face filled with anger.

"Sir, I have not," Jarvis insisted, bewildered by the drastic change in tone from what he was anticipating. "Some of the men have, not me, I assure you, Sir."

Simcoe replied simply, "Go to your Troop, Sir"—an order which Jarvis quickly obeyed.

"Imagine what my feelings must have been at this moment, but I had yet a much greater mortification still," Jarvis recalled of the incident. That evening he wrote "a true statement of the facts" to a relative, outlining McGill's approval of the entire incident. Jarvis noted everything to his confidante in detail, "enjoining him to secrecy; that he was not to divulge it until after my death," and asked a fellow officer who was going to Manhattan to mail the letter for him. His conscience clear, he once again imagined the matter was over.

The following morning, however, he discovered that Simcoe was far from satisfied with his explanation of what had occurred. Jarvis recalled, "The next day there was a Court of Enquiry, a Captain and two Subalterns. I was examined; I told my story, as it happened, except how far

Mr. McGill was concerned, but one of the men flatly told the Court that McGill had given them leave to sell the negroes." With this new damning testimony, Jarvis was cross-examined but still refused to give up McGill. At this point, his loyalty to his friend became almost manic: "I was then called again and examined as to that fact. To this I refused to answer. Whatever I have done I must be the sufferer, for I would say nothing that would in the least to injure Mr. McGill."

The matter was dismissed by the Court—but not by Simcoe. Still enraged, the commander meted out his own punishment. Jarvis recounted, "The next morning after the men were assembled for the morning parade, Colonel Simcoe called me to him, and laying his head down on the neck of his horse gave me one of the most serious reprimands I believe man ever received, and told me decidedly 'that I had lost my promotion and his countenance forever. Go Sir and join your Troop.' I returned to my duty more dead than alive."

Jarvis was so upset by Simcoe's disapprobation that he claimed, "I lost my appetite, and my sleep went from me; my frame decayed, and in a few days I was a complete skeleton." But he had still not heard the last from his commander. Somehow, Simcoe obtained the letter of confession Jarvis had penned, and he once again called him and McGill to his quarters:

*One evening after parade was dismissed, both Mr. McGill and myself were desired to attend the Colonel, and after all the officers had retired, he then taxed McGill of giving the men liberty to sell the negroes, which he denied. The Colonel then turned to me and said, "Jarvis, did he not give them leave?" I replied, No Sir. He gave me one of those stern looks, which spoke volumes, taking a letter from his pocket handed it to me saying, "Is not that your handwriting?" I was thunderstruck, and it was some time before I could answer. "Speak Sir, speak, is that your letter?" and "Is what you have stated true?" I then answered, Sir it is my letter, and since I must answer, the contents are true, but Sir you must give me leave to say that if I could have imagined that my friend would betrayed me the confidence that I had placed in him I would have suffered death before I wrote that letter now in my hands. "Go to your Troop," was his reply. What he said to Mr. McGill I forbear mentioning.*[16]

As this drama played out, both within the Townsend home and in the streets of Oyster Bay, it is very likely that Hannah, Lilly, Jane, Gabriel, Jeffery, and the many other enslaved members of the household witnessed the lengths to which Simcoe persisted in sorting out the matter and punishing the men responsible for selling innocent people into slavery. And they no doubt thought of Liss, who had left with him the year before.

In light of Simcoe's repeated pattern of assisting people seeking freedom, it is hard not to consider whether Liss's escape was yet another example. Did he simply want the young woman to be allowed her liberty, or could he also have intended to use her as a source of information? Or was there, perhaps, another factor driving Liss's decision to leave?

## SCENARIO #2: ROBERT'S PLAN

It is curious that, given the substantial financial blow Liss's absence would have had on the family, Robert so quickly encouraged his father to write her off as one of his "dead losses," especially since recovering her was his legal right and he already knew exactly where she was and with whom she was traveling. In fact, Robert's seeming certainty about the troops' movements and a conspicuous absence of entries in his shop's ledger book at the same time suggest that he may have been following the Queen's Rangers at a distance as they marched beyond New York city on their secret orders. King's Bridge, the site of a large British encampment and a toll bridge connecting upper Manhattan to the Bronx, was just over sixteen miles removed from Hanover Square, where Robert maintained his store. From the city, the round-trip journey would take a full day on horseback.

On the surface, it may seem that Robert's reluctance to pursue and reclaim Liss stemmed from a natural disinclination to tangle with the British; however, his assertion that "when I see any of the officers [I] will make an inquiry for Liss" indicates he certainly had free discourse with them. Perhaps he feared retribution from the Queen's Rangers for levying the challenge that Simcoe left in full knowledge that he was carrying off a family slave, but since he does assure his father that he will make inquiries among the officer corps, this seems unlikely.

Why would a young man well within his legal rights, in full knowledge of the runaway slave's location, and apparently on cordial terms with the leaders of the group with which she was traveling not make his petition known? Absolutely nothing about his life or his habits at this point shows any indication that Robert was a budding abolitionist. If he wasn't afraid of the British and wasn't dragging his feet on moral grounds, some other motive must have discouraged him from demanding Liss's return.

## SCENARIO #3: A FAMILY AFFAIR

As unlikely as it may seem on the surface, there remains a third possibility: that Robert and Samuel were both aware of Liss's departure ahead of time. When Robert writes that he is replying to his father's letter "of the 23rd," one is forced to question why Samuel would have waited five days before writing to Robert about Liss's disappearance, given that the Queen's Rangers were very obviously headed toward Manhattan en route to an undisclosed location. Surely, were Samuel genuinely concerned about intercepting his runaway slave, he would have reached out to Robert as soon as Liss's absence was noticed in the hopes that his son could bring her back before the regiment was out of reach.

Even more intriguing is the total absence of any advertisement or public notice regarding Liss's escape. Newspaper notices for escaped slaves were common throughout the colonies. In 1779 alone, well over fifty such ads were placed in the New York papers, promising sums from $1 to $1,000 for the return of runaways, while threatening that anyone who harbored them did so "at their peril" and could "depend upon being prosecuted." The ads, appearing in virtually every edition of every paper, featured details of clothes, hair, and other physical descriptions to provide clues for identification. For example, Isabella, eighteen years old, who ran away in April, had a large scar on her forehead and was dressed in men's clothes when she escaped.[17] Esther, who was "full eyed and talkative," was wearing a calico short gown and looked "rather thin" due to a recent illness.[18] Similar notices were run for, among scores of others, Augustus, who was "slow of speech";[19] Bett, "marked with the small pox";[20] Charles, who had "a large burn on his leg" and played "on the fiddle";[21] and Peg, with a "white straw hat" and a "scar upon her left cheek."[22] But no one placed an advertisement for an Elizabeth or Liss. Samuel Townsend did not run a single notice about her in any extant New York newspaper in the days or months following her escape.

A runaway slave was a serious matter in terms of both the owner's financial loss and the rumors around the neighborhood; the matter was to be dealt with publicly and severely to discourage anyone else contemplating escape. If Samuel was truly troubled by Liss's flight, his actions do not mirror his concern. The inconsistency between his letters with Robert and his lack of pursuit lead one to question whether his correspondence with his son was all for show, should he later be questioned on the matter. But why?

━ ∼ ━

Two seemingly unrelated events occurred as May turned to June in 1779. The first is that Benedict Arnold was court-martialed for thirteen charges of misbehavior, including misuse of army property for personal gain and the sale of surplus goods for profit. Arnold would eventually be cleared on most counts, though he did not escape completely unscathed: he received a written reprimand from General George Washington, and his reputation suffered a serious blow. None of that was resolved until six months later, however; his initial trial was interrupted by the second event, a series of skirmishes that put the Hudson River into play.[23]

The Continental Army held the Hudson Valley, but it was no secret that General Washington had set his sights farther south on New York City. The deep-water ports were invaluable for importing supplies, and access to the city's economic power could not be underestimated—not to mention that, quite simply, British control of one of the largest cities in the colonies was a finger in the eye to the Patriot cause.

In a classic case of wanting what one cannot have, the British were firmly planted in New York City but continually sought ways to advance up the Hudson River, one of the great inland waterways of the northern colonies. Fort West Point was the jewel of the Hudson, and

Sir Henry Clinton wanted nothing more than to seize the defensive garrison and gain control of the river, connecting the British strongholds at New York City northward to Canada, effectively splitting the colonies in two.

Standing in his way was a physical barrier called the Great Chain, the engineering marvel put in place by the Americans; running across the river from bank to bank beneath the cliffs of West Point and Constitution Island, it infuriatingly blocked the British. The ironmaster who forged seventy-five tons of iron into the massive chain was the same Peter Townsend with whom Solomon was now residing in Orange County.[24]

In late May 1779, Clinton assembled a force of eight thousand men near Stony Point, a poorly defended but key American holding on the lower Hudson River. Situated exactly halfway between the sixty miles separating Manhattan from West Point, Stony Point and nearby Verplanck's Point, on the opposite bank, proved the perfect location from which to put the squeeze on the American control of the Hudson. As Simcoe's Queen's Rangers, John André, and many thousands of British soldiers silently gathered, a mere forty colonists were stationed to defend the two positions. On May 31, Clinton led the attack and, after a quick victory with only one British fatality, gave André the honor of accepting the American surrender the next day.

The British relished the victory and moved quickly to continue their press toward West Point, but their celebration was short-lived. Six weeks later, on July 16, the Americans retook the position, inflicting heavy losses and driving the British back toward New York City.[25]

Here, again, questions surrounding Liss's fate begin to emerge. When André returned to headquarters, did he take Liss with him? Had Simcoe already made arrangements for her to labor in the service of another officer garrisoned in Manhattan and tasked André with delivering her? She would still be enslaved, true, but she would not be destitute on the streets. Or, as would shortly happen to the couple on the boat, could a member of the Queen's Rangers have sold her for a quick profit while she waited with the wagons at King's Bridge? Only one thing is known for certain: Liss traveled with the regiment for less than three months; by mid-August, the Queen's Rangers had returned to Oyster Bay without her.[26] And Samuel Townsend does not appear to have questioned Simcoe regarding her absence.

Though the tug-of-war in the vicinity of Stony Point in the summer of 1779 did little in terms of advancing one side or the other, Washington did find that some of his strategies were playing out nicely. He attributed much of his success at Stony Point to his extensive intelligence network in the region, which fed him information essential to formulating a counterattack. A former spy himself during the French and Indian War twenty years prior, Washington understood the vital role espionage could play in uncovering plots, finding weaknesses, and judging the strength of the enemy's position. Washington relied heavily on secret reports from agents throughout the war, but he sought to concentrate the majority of his New York–area intelligence gathering under the leadership of Major Benjamin Tallmadge. The Americans' main strategy was to identify a sympathetic and well-vetted local who could then build up his or her own network of trusted informants and couriers either living openly in their communities or undercover, embedded with the enemy. Either way, what mattered most was that these sources could be counted on to deliver reliable information, in an inconspicuous manner, to the agent in charge, who could then deliver the intelligence quickly and stealthily to Tallmadge's headquarters in Connecticut.

And unbeknownst to nearly everyone, in June Washington began receiving valuable information about troop movements from an informant who promised to be his most valuable agent of all: a shop owner in Hanover Square named Robert Townsend.[27]

CHAPTER FIVE

# Spies and Traitors

"I ONLY REGRET THAT I HAVE BUT ONE LIFE TO GIVE FOR MY COUNTRY."
Those words, purportedly spoken by Nathan Hale, are cherished as the
last utterance of a brave American spy who was captured and hanged by
the British. But although he is widely remembered today, Hale was completely forgotten in the years that followed his death. In fact, the earliest
account of Hale's demise, published in 1799, presented his narrative only
as a counterpoint to that of the ever-popular John André—who in death
had achieved a kind of cult status, even in the United States—and concluded with a harsh criticism of Hale's lack of notoriety: "To the memory
of André, his country have erected the most magnificent monuments[.]
To the memory of Hale, not a stone has been erected, nor an inscription
to preserve his ashes from insult."[1]

A generation later, several American newspapers retold Hale's
story, first in 1816[2] and again in 1820, outraged that "every body has
heard of and pitied Major André, an Englishman who would have
ruined the United States, but who has heard of Captain Nathan Hale,
an American, who would have saved them?"[3] If the public's attention
to André's memory had waned in the first few decades following the
Revolution, perhaps Nathan Hale's story would never have resurfaced
at all. The truth was, not many of his contemporaries had ever heard of
Hale, and by the 1840s few people still living could remember the war
at all. So when historian Henry Onderdonk began research in 1846 for
his new book, *Revolutionary Incidents*, he sought out Ebenezer Seeley
of Oyster Bay, who had lived for decades with several members of the

Revolutionary generation—all family members of his much older wife, Phebe Townsend.[4]

Some years prior, an aging Robert Townsend had told his younger sisters and brother-in-law the story of an unfortunate young man named Nathan Hale who was captured near Huntington in September 1776, after being tricked by a British officer who had been patrolling the local harbors.[5] That officer was Colonel Robert Rogers, the first commander of the Queen's Rangers, whom Colonel Simcoe would replace a few years later.[6] Robert recalled how the would-be spy hailed a vessel he thought was manned by Patriots rowing over from Connecticut but was actually a small boat from the much larger *Halifax* manned by Colonel Rogers, and "thus committed himself, before he was aware of his mistake, into the hands of his enemies." Lieutenant William Quarme, captain of the *Halifax*, admitted to Robert that "when he found out what a fine fellow [Hale] was . . . he was sorry he had fallen into his hands."[7]

In fact, Robert Townsend, who himself would not be identified as one of George Washington's spies for another seventy-five years, served as one of the earliest sources of the legend of Nathan Hale that finally took root in the American mythos, wherein the unfortunate spy's final utterance encapsulated patriotic duty for generations. Robert's account that Hale was captured near Oyster Bay, in Huntington, was widely disputed until 2000, when the unpublished eyewitness narrative of a Tory named Consider Tiffany was discovered in the Library of Congress, putting to rest more than two centuries of dubious claims by various locales.

Ironically, Hale's fame was due to his failure. Had he succeeded in his mission, his cover as a schoolmaster looking for work on Long Island would never have been blown. He would have returned to Connecticut with vital information for the Patriot cause, leaving little trace of his visit.

Hale's ill-fated mission began with Washington's call for volunteers on September 10, 1776, the very day Samuel Townsend was forced to sign an oath of allegiance to King George in Oyster Bay. During the ensuing seven years of British occupation, many spies for both sides would collect intelligence in New York City, on Long Island, and within the streets of Samuel's own village, with varying degrees of success and secrecy.

One such spy was young David Maltby, just eighteen or nineteen years old, with a backstory remarkably similar to Nathan Hale's: he crossed Long Island Sound in the early years of the war and took up residence in Oyster Bay, posing as a schoolteacher in need of work, then began to send letters with his intelligence back to Connecticut. However, unlike Hale, whose entire mission from arrival to hanging lasted only ten days, Maltby managed to maintain his cover for several months, delivering reports disguised as letters to his family through an old man named Seeley (likely related to Ebenezer). The elder Seeley regularly rowed across Long Island Sound from Oyster Bay to Stamford at night with mail from the other side. What Maltby didn't know was that Seeley was a Loyalist refugee, and struck by the inordinate number of letters Maltby was writing, the old man finally opened one. "500 men would easily dislodge the British here," Maltby had scrawled, confirming the old man's suspicions. Seeley immediately reported Maltby to the British authorities, and the young man was captured while trying to escape across the sound.

He was tried as a spy, found guilty, and condemned to death by hanging, but his sentence was not carried out as swiftly as Hale's. Instead Maltby was held in British custody in the guardhouse just a short distance from the Townsends' home. Whether Robert visited Oyster Bay during this time is unknown, but one thing is certain: his father, the former justice of the peace, and all other members of the household—including Liss—were aware of the traveling schoolmaster-turned-spy who was waiting to die just steps from their door.

A little girl named Elizabeth Wooden, a cousin of the Townsends, was allowed to visit the condemned young man to bring him food. Her father had known Maltby before the war and perhaps thought his ten-year-old daughter would be an unsuspected courier of aid. Only a day or two before his execution was scheduled, Maltby and another prisoner somehow broke free, slipped past the guards, and disappeared. In her 1846 account of the incident for Onderdonk, Elizabeth Wooden, now an eighty-year-old woman, relayed that unbeknownst to Maltby, his execution had been stayed just prior to his escape.[8]

Nearly six years after his first capture, Maltby was arrested as a spy for the Americans for a second time, on New Year's Day in 1783, but now he was confined in the Provost, a notorious British prison in lower Manhattan, located on the current site of City Hall Park.[9] His trial date was set for Thursday, February 13, but fortune smiled on Maltby again.[10] Perhaps due to the ensuing end of the war and dismantling of the British court system in New York, his case was never tried. Records show he returned unscathed to Connecticut and married after the war, living out the rest of his days with his family in Fairfield County, eventually remembered only in the childhood recollections of a spinster in Oyster Bay.[11]

Among the most successful intelligence operations in Long Island and New York City was the now famous Culper Ring. The group was formed in early August 1778, when Washington enlisted the services of Lieutenant Caleb Brewster, a skilled whaleboat pilot, and directed him "to use every possible means to obtain intelligence of the Enemys motions" on Long Island, requesting "that you will, by every devise you can think of, have a strict watch kept upon the Enemy's ships of war, and give me the earliest notice of their Sailing."[12]

Later that month Benjamin Tallmadge, who would soon become George Washington's director of intelligence, recruited a farmer from Setauket named Abraham Woodhull, who was also a former Suffolk County militiaman and cousin of the fallen General Nathaniel Woodhull. Tallmadge knew Woodhull personally and conveyed his confidence in the man's loyalty to Washington, who replied back with a certain degree of caution, "You should be perfectly convinced of the integrity of W—previous to his embarking in the business proposed—this being done I shall be happy in employing him." However, Washington warned Tallmadge to keep his new operative from visiting headquarters, "as a knowledge of the circumstances in the enemy might blast the whole design."[13]

Now using the code name "Samuel Culper," Woodhull traveled into New York City and back to Setauket, while Brewster rowed messages across the sound to Fairfield. There, Tallmadge's corps of mounted dragoons would be waiting to receive the letters, which they would swiftly deliver to American headquarters. In October 1778, Woodhull made mention of a trusted new informant, announcing that he had been "particularly successful in engageing a faithfull freind and one of the first Charecters in the City." This source, which seems to have been Robert Townsend, "should make it his business and Keep his Eyes upon every movement and assist me in all respects and meet & Consult weekely in or near the City."[14]

Though Woodhull was a willing and frequent correspondent, by late March 1779, Washington began to experience doubts about both his methods and his ability as an effective spy. Writing to Tallmadge from Middlebrook, New Jersey, where Washington and a force of over eight thousand troops were staying for the winter months, the general made the first of many requests to find a shorter route for the Culper letters. Woodhull's commute on horseback from Setauket to lower Manhattan was over one hundred miles round-trip. Then Brewster's voyage to the opposite shore was another thirteen miles, sometimes with rough waters and heavy winds. Once there, the dragoons still had to make their way to Washington's location, which in this case was a distance of over eighty miles.

In addition to his reservations about the circuitous route, Washington also expressed concern that Woodhull often stated matters of conjecture as hard facts. Besides creating confusion, this led Washington to doubt his reporting, even when it was factual. Then there was the issue of Woodhull's home base in Suffolk County. Washington reasoned that since "the fountain of all intelligence must originate at, & proceed from the head Quarters of the enemy's Army, C[ulper] had better reside at New York—mix with—and put on the airs of a Tory to cover his real character, & avoid suspicion."[15]

However, the suggestion that Woodhull, a struggling farmer without the means, capacity, or desire to do so, would move from Setauket to Manhattan was unrealistic. Washington's instructions to "cover his real character" and "put on the airs of a Tory" were likewise nearly impossible; despite his great loyalty to the Patriot cause, Woodhull lacked the social skills, higher education, and maritime connections for which his commander was looking.

Washington's request to relocate hit Woodhull hard, and his April 10 letter began with a frank confession of self-doubt:

*When ever I Sit down I always feel and know my Inability to write a good Letter. As my calling in life never required it—Nor led to consider, how necessary a qualification it was for a Man—And much less did I think it would ever fall to my lot, to Serve in Such Publick important buisiness as this, And my letters perused by one of the worthiest Men on Earth. But I trust he will overlook any imperfections he may discover in the dress of my words—And rest assured that I indevour to collect and convey the most accurate and explicit intelligence that I possibly can, And hope it may be of Some Service towards Alleviateing the miseries of our disstressed Count[r]y.*[16]

On April 23, Woodhull set off again for Manhattan, and it was very lucky for him that he made the trip. The next day, his father was badly beaten and the family home in Setauket ransacked by Colonel Simcoe, who had traveled from the Townsend home in Oyster Bay with a detachment of soldiers, following up on a tip that a man named Woodhull was gathering intelligence. Outraged by the attack on his father and deeply shaken by the knowledge that he had almost been caught, Abraham was filled more than ever with paralyzing fear.

After another close call in June, in which he "had the good fortune to escape confinement," he reluctantly admitted to Tallmadge that the experience "hath rendered me almost unserviceable to you." He utilized a code to explain he could no longer make visits to the city and "purpose[d] quitting 10 [New York] and residing at 20 [Setauket]. As I am now a suspected person I cannot frequent their camp as heretofore." Explaining that his services would now hardly be worth the expense, he announced, "I shall endeavour to establish a confidential friend to step into my place."[17]

On June 20, Woodhull reported to Tallmadge that he had effectively handed over the reins of the operation—at least within New York City—to his friend, Robert Townsend:

*I have communicated my business to an intimate friend and disclosed every secret and laid before him every instruction that hath been handed to me; it was with great difficulty I gained his complyance, checked by fear. He is a person that hath the interest of our country at heart and of good reputation, character and family as any of my acquaintance. I am under the most solemn obligation never to disclose his name to any but the Post who unavoidably must know it. I have reason to think his advantages for serving you and abilities are far superior to mine.*[18]

As the well-connected son of one of Long Island's most prominent families, Robert was perfectly positioned for the job. He operated a shop in Hanover Square, within the same square in lower Manhattan that also housed James Rivington's Loyalist printing press and coffeehouse, a meeting place very popular with the British brass.[19] Robert quickly began assembling his own network of reliable informants and started passing intelligence letters in June 1779—the same time Liss was traveling beyond King's Bridge with the Queen's Rangers.

The handoff of the ring could not have come at a better time for Woodhull. On July 2, the British attacked Tallmadge's camp in Connecticut. The spymaster escaped with his life, but ten of his men were not so lucky. Additionally, a number of horses were stolen, including Tallmadge's own, which bore letters in its saddlebags from General Washington.[20] A few inquiries and arrests followed, based on names and clues in the captured spy letters, but there was thankfully little to substantiate any charges. Still, the raid reemphasized what Tallmadge and Washington already knew: they needed a better system for protecting their operatives, and they needed it fast.

That summer the ring made two improvements to its methods that gave Robert an even greater edge to avoid detection. The first was Tallmadge's establishment of a "Dictionary Code," wherein certain words were represented by numbers; the list of key words was selected from the 1777 London edition of *Entick's Spelling Dictionary*. To this, Tallmadge added several names and places, as well as a straightforward alphabet-to-number code for adding any words not included. "Rebellion" was 581, "signal" became 600, and "tyranny" turned into 646. Woodhull's code name, "Culper, Sr.," became 722; Robert, aka "Culper, Jr.," was 723; "Washington" was 711; and Tallmadge, code name "John Bolton," became 721. A courier named Austin Roe, who owned a tavern in Setauket, was listed, alongside Caleb Brewster and, curiously, the newspaper printer across the square, Rivington. The places given code numbers included New York, Long Island, Setauket, Hanover [Square], Headquarters, and a long list of colonies and countries.[21] Now members of the ring could refer to one another and well-known persons without running the risk of unmasking informants or plans. Most famous, perhaps, is 355, the code for the word "lady," which appeared tantalizingly just a single time, when Woodhull boasted on August 15, 1779, that "by the assistance of a 355 of my acquaintance, shall be able to outwit them all."[22]

The second new method was the introduction of an entirely new invisible ink formula developed by Sir James Jay, a London doctor and brother of Patriot lawyer John Jay.[23] For quite some time, British spies, especially André, had been making use of two different versions of invisible ink. André would write in one of these solutions in the blank spaces between the lines of a dummy letter, enabling the recipient to, quite literally, "read between the lines" after applying the proper reagent. One ink was revealed by applying heat; the other, by applying something acidic, like lemon juice. To inform the reader which method was needed, André would doodle either the letter "F" or "A" in the margins; as he explained, "In writings to be discover'd by a process, F is fire and A acid."[24] Of course, the Americans could not employ either of these inks with confidence, as the British regularly tested any suspected letters for covert messages. James Jay's new formula was a revelation and a profound secret to be kept in closest confidence.[25]

Washington sent a supply of ink to Townsend and Woodhull both, via Tallmadge, in September 1779. He included detailed instructions on how one might use it, including writing inside innocuous-looking books or listing information between the lines or on the backs of otherwise ordinary letters.[26] Robert, as a purveyor of writing paper, had a better idea—to hide an invisible-ink letter, which came to be called a "blank," in a full stack of fresh paper. A hint in the receipt or accompanying letter might tell the recipient which seemingly blank page contained the message. Armed with this "white ink" or "sympathetic stain," as they called it, Robert could now write nearly undetectable messages on paper that was otherwise indistinguishable from the other new sheets in the ream.

The ink was an especially fortuitous development, as its chemistry was wholly unique and known only to Sir James himself; there was little risk of the British being able to reveal the hidden information even if they did suspect a covert message. But the ink's greatest merit was also its biggest flaw: it could only be produced and disseminated in small batches and therefore had to be used sparingly for only the most sensitive messages.

Even so, the code and the ink together rendered the Culper letters nearly unbreakable and undetectable by the enemy. With those two elements firmly in place, the biggest obstacle the spies continued to face was time. As Robert wrote at the end of July, "I have received your Dictionary, and will be glad to have the stain as soon as possible, when shall endeavor to find some shorter route to forward my Letters."[27] But a shorter route continued to elude them. By the spring of 1780, Washington grew increasingly concerned that information about troop counts and rumored campaigns would become obsolete before it even reached him, and once again he began to urge even greater expediency. Townsend, equally frustrated when his intelligence was rendered useless, began experimenting with different couriers in the hopes of conveying his letters via overland routes or across more direct British lines and cutting the transit time nearly in half.

The first courier Robert tried from outside the ring, his young cousin James, proved an abject failure. The teenaged boy nearly blew his cover trying to impress some young women while pretending to be drunk. Robert's invisible message was hidden between the lines of a bawdy poem mocking the great lengths to which fashionable women went to change the appearance of their body-shape. Though the secret message is no longer readable, the humorous verses remain, copied in Robert's signature lacey script:

> Let her gown be tuck'd up to the hip on each side;
> Shoes too high for to walk or to Jump;
> And to deck the sweet creature compleat for a bride,
> Let the cork-cutter make her a rump.
>
> Thus finish'd in taste, while on Chloe you gaze,
> You may take the dear charmer for life;

> But never undress her—for, out of her stays,
> You'll find you have lost half your wife.[28]

No doubt Robert hoped the reader would be too busy laughing to suspect treachery, yet this communique and the bundle of letters in which it ended up were only successfully delivered after James Townsend was tackled by the young woman's father, landing in American custody briefly on suspicion of being a spy for the British—a debacle that necessitated an emergency bail-out by General Washington.[29]

The second outside courier, Colonel Benjamin Floyd, a member of another well-regarded Long Island family, proved more successful. Floyd had already been of some service to the Culpers, causing Woodhull to ask for special consideration on his behalf when Floyd was captured as a suspected Loyalist and held prisoner in Connecticut in February 1779. Woodhull requested that Washington release him on parole and permit him to remain on his estate unharmed so that Floyd could continue to help the Culpers: "I earnestly wrote you for his discharge—I repeat it again, I anxiously desire you would not forget. I am very likely to Stand in need of his Services."[30]

Though Floyd was not recaptured, in late October Woodhull reported, "Night before last a most horrid robbery was committed on the houses of Coll. Benj. Floyd and Mr. Seton, by three whale boats from your shore," adding that over £3,000 had been looted by the American raiders.[31] These raiders had also been harassing Caleb Brewster's boat as it crossed the sound with their secret correspondence, threatening the entire operation: "I would further observe that the boat that crosses for dispatches from C has been chased quite across the Sound by those plunderers[.] Indeed if some stop cannot be put to such nefarious practices C will not risque, nor 725 go over for dispatches."

The covert assistance of Colonel Floyd was particularly emphasized by Tallmadge, as were his secret efforts for the Americans, in spite of any outward appearances to the contrary. "One of the gentlemen who was plundered was Col. Floyd," Tallmadge confirmed to Washington on November 1, 1779. "From a long and intimate acquaintance with this gentleman I believe him to be of more service to the Whig interest in Setauket than every other man in it, tho from his family connection I believe he has been in favor of Royal Government."[32] Tallmadge later acknowledged Floyd's collaboration with Robert in a July 22, 1780, letter, explaining, "The Letter from C. Junr is directed to Col. Floyd at Brook-Haven because he is a disaffected Person, & should the Bearer of that letter be stopped & searched nothing of importance could be discovered, as the letter appears to be on matters of business."[33]

Colonel Floyd successfully delivered at least three key intelligence letters written in the invisible ink, including one that was sent with Woodhull's accompanying letter conveying some of the Culper's most important intelligence to date: an urgent warning that British warships were en route to attack the French fleet that had just landed in Rhode Island.[34, 35]

Much of Robert's success was owed to his incredible variety of sources. He had access not only to the customers who frequented his store and to the visitors at his boardinghouse, owned by Abraham Woodhull's sister, Mary Underhill, but also to the officers who lounged in Rivington's coffeehouse just steps away. Additionally, Hanover Square was located only a few streets from the deep-water slips in lower Manhattan, where Robert could converse with the many ship captains whom he knew from years in the shipping business, while observing nearly the whole of New York City's naval activity simply by taking a casual walk.

Interestingly, Robert also enjoyed an acquaintance with Hercules Mulligan, a fellow shopkeeper and tailor by trade, as well as a fellow spy for General Washington and Alexander Hamilton. Along with his African American slave Cato, Mulligan also collected information on troop counts and campaign rumors, which the two Americans quietly passed on to the general. In fact, Robert's ledger book notes several instances in which the independent operatives engaged in commerce with each other. In late January 1780, Hercules entered Robert's shop and purchased five gallons of "spirits."[36] As the war drew to a close in February 1783, Robert returned the favor, visiting Mulligan's tailor shop and placing an order for "a new Coat, Pockets and Sleeve-linings, 1 Dozen buttons," lined in silk.[37]

Robert also had the distinct advantage of being well connected with the shipping industry in New York Harbor and on Long Island, which gave him a good excuse to spend time along the docks, counting boxes and making notes of cargo. This information not only offered a broader picture of what the enemy might be up to next but also enabled him to obtain detailed information to confirm or enhance his reports from Manhattan. The Townsend family's long-standing kinship with the Buchanans further bolstered Robert's access to potentially sensitive information. Although outwardly Loyalists, the Buchanans maintained a close relationship with the Townsends through both business and family, using their influence to assist Samuel when his political leanings caused legal headaches, such as his arrest in 1776. Thomas Buchanan's diary from 1780, which functioned as a kind of shipping log, was a document to which Robert might easily have been given access. Each entry began with a blithe comment on the weather, then recorded information gathered on the docks of Manhattan in startling detail. For example, Buchanan's entry for September 13 reads, "Cool and pleasant, with rain in the afternoon. This day Admiral Sir Geo. B. Rodney with 10 sail of the line arrived at Sandy Hook, also a retaken vessel from Charleston who confirms the account of General Gate's defeat of the 16th August last near Camden."[38]

Robert also employed less conventional tactics to obtain intelligence, taking the rather dramatic step of enlisting with a Tory volunteer company organized by his former boss, Oliver Templeton. Often mistaken as an oath of loyalty to the king, a template document to join this company, in Robert's own handwriting, pronounces, "We the Subscribers . . . have formed ourselves into a Volunteer Company, under a command of A___ B___ and faithfully promise to follow such orders as we shall receive from our officers, for the purpose of Co-operating with his Majesties Troops in the protection and defense of the City and Island of New York."[39] A ledger entry of Robert's from 1783, "for work done in 1776," makes payment for what may be the construction of his volunteer company uniform, complete with the British army's signature red coat, listing payment for "dyeing 18 yards of Claret Cloth," for "sewing and pressing," and for a "silk shirt."[40]

As part of the Loyal Volunteers of the City of New York, Robert stood guard, dressed in his full regalia, outside General Guy Carleton's headquarters on Broadway near the Battery at the southern-most tip of Manhattan. This was no insignificant posting on Robert's part, as Carleton had recently taken over from Clinton as commander in chief of the British army in North America. Years later, one of Robert's nephews noted how he and his siblings "often joked" with their Patriot uncle about the red coat packed away in a trunk in the family home.[41]

But for all his daring, one plot ultimately broke Robert, and it began in his very own home, on the first of the Queen's Rangers' three stays.

On March 20, 1779, during his springtime visit to Simcoe in Oyster Bay, John André wrote a letter from the Townsend home to his boss, the British commander in America, Sir Henry Clinton. The letter was precipitated by a visit from another spy, a low-level British operative from Pennsylvania named Christopher Sower III, who had stumbled into Oyster Bay on that chilly spring morning, seeking the Townsend home, where his boss, spymaster John André, was staying.[42]

Sower was the youngest of three generations of printers from Germantown, a settlement just north of downtown Philadelphia; the Sower family ran a book bindery, printed Bibles in German and a yearly almanac, and also published pro-British pamphlets. Christopher Sower II, the current patriarch, was a devoted member of a religious sect called the Brethren, who were opposed to war on moral grounds, so when he refused to sign an oath of allegiance to America, he was accused of being "a foe of liberty." In May 1778, the elder Sower was dragged from bed and marched barefoot in his nightshirt toward Valley Forge. His beard, a sign of his faith, was partially clipped off, red paint was smeared on his face, and he was brought bloody and disheveled before Washington. When he still refused to swear his allegiance to the Continental Army, he was declared a traitor, causing the Sower family to be legally "attainted."[43] This meant that all their assets, including their land, money, home, print shop, paper mill, book bindery, and personal possessions, were confiscated and sold at auction to benefit the American cause.[44] The younger Sower fled with his wife to British-controlled New York, where he joined a ring of Loyalist spies with Pennsylvanian connections. Information about a cache of munitions discovered by this group brought Sower to the Townsend home, carrying a letter intended for Sir Henry Clinton, who was then staying farther east on Long Island in the Hamptons.

Naturally André perused the letter, and what he found shocked him. Unbelievably, the novice spy had not only enumerated the stash of weapons his comrades had found but included the first and last names of every member of his operation. Exasperated, André collected pen, ink, and paper and (by his own account) sat down in the parlor, in full view of the Townsend family and their household slaves, to compose a redacted version, with "fill-in-the-blank" lines where the names had been.

After explaining to Clinton how Sower had nearly "laid bare" his whole operation, André detailed his comfortable stay in Oyster Bay, his continued illness, the poor weather, and lack of haste to leave. Then he coyly mentioned "a certain event" that he and Clinton were both "on the watch" for, which André promised to inform the general of "by immediate express." Barely two weeks later, Benedict Arnold married the beautiful, young, dynamic, and staunchly Loyalist Peggy Shippen, a girl André had likely shared a brief flirtation with the summer before. Within a month of the wedding, the couple was in correspondence with André about how to send covert messages, and on May 23, André sent a letter in his own "Dictionary Code" to Arnold. The great deception had begun.[45]

The following summer, in 1780, Arnold finally received his appointment as commander of West Point, a post for which he had been lusting for nearly a year. André wrote less than four weeks later to propose the surrender of the fort. By August, the plan was set: Arnold had named his price—£20,000 (roughly equivalent to $3 million)—and the British had accepted.[46] Simcoe was visiting Clinton's headquarters in eastern Long Island at the time, and Clinton and André informed him of the scheme. Years later, writing in his military journal, Simcoe detailed learning about Arnold's premeditated treachery and how he planned to go to West Point with his regiment once the plot came to fruition.[47] By the time Simcoe passed back through Oyster Bay for his third stay in the town, the planned betrayal was less than one month away.

While Simcoe stayed at the Townsend home again in August and September 1780, André wrote him at least two letters, on August 29 and September 12, hinting to his friend about the imminent deal. Ten days later, at a secret meeting, Arnold handed over the maps and plans of the fort.[48] There was just one hitch: the British warship *Vulture* that had delivered André to the meeting was fired on by cannons on the cliffs above the Hudson and quickly sailed downstream. André was now stranded and would have to make the thirty-mile journey back to Manhattan on foot through dangerous "neutral ground." Changing from his officer's red coat into civilian clothes and stashing the plans of the fort in his boots, André was supplied with a special pass using an alias, which read, "Permit Mr. John Anderson to pass the grounds to White Plains, or below, if he chooses, he being on Public Business of my Direction," signed by General Benedict Arnold.

The plan seemed flawless until André was intercepted in the early morning hours of September 23 by a small Patriot detachment. This group of militiamen, like many on both sides who patrolled the neutral zone, moonlighted as robbers to supplement their income. When André was unable to produce any cash, the men demanded that he remove his leather officer's boots, which were themselves a fine prize. As he removed them, out fell the plans. In desperation, André produced his pass from the general, but the whole business struck the militiamen as suspicious, and word was sent back to West Point that a shady stranger had been captured trying to pass himself off as a friend of Arnold's. Arnold, tipped off that the plan had gone awry, quickly slipped out the back of the fort, raced down to the river's edge, and caught a rowboat out to the *Vulture*, which had returned to the area. By mere coincidence, early that morning General Washington arrived at West Point with Alexander Hamilton and Benjamin Tallmadge to inspect the fortifications and discovered the horrendous plot that might well have lost the Americans the war. Incensed by Arnold's betrayal, Washington sent urgent word to André's captors to hold him as a spy.

Simcoe had such a clear idea of André's timing for the takeover of West Point that he had departed from Oyster Bay with his regiment just one day before André's capture, heading toward the fort in anticipation of a British victory. When word of André's arrest reached Simcoe en route, however, he immediately sent a detachment to watch the road to

Philadelphia and launch a rescue effort. Benedict Arnold, meanwhile, arrived in New York City, taking refuge in the British-held city. When talks of a prisoner exchange broke down and André was executed by hanging on October 2, the British launched a retaliatory offensive, rounding up nearly forty American spies—including operatives Robert knew personally.[49]

Terrified of being caught, Robert ceased his Culper letters, quietly leaving the city for three months until the fervor died down. In January 1781, he sent word of his return to Washington via Woodhull[50] and then promptly ended his lease at the boardinghouse on Water Street where he had been living; he also dissolved the partnership under which he had been operating his store in Hanover Square. It was as if he wanted to cut all former ties with anyone who might have reason to suspect him. Now, he signed a new lease for an apartment[51] he called "Bachelor's Hall" with his younger brother William and cousin John, situated above a new shop they opened together in Peck Slip.[52] No longer paying for meals with his lodgings, as he had done for years in boardinghouses, Robert took on most of the domestic duties, including cooking and managing the affairs of the household. But most notably, he reverted to being merely an informant, passing intelligence on to Woodhull in person but not putting pen to paper himself for almost two years. In fact, no Culper letters were sent by any member of the ring between August 1781 and May 1782.

Of all Robert's relationships, most of them severed, one was newly rekindled—or perhaps simply maintained. On August 7, 1781, Robert made an unusual note in his ledger of a personal purchase of "hourhound tea for Elizabeth." Horehound was a common medicinal tea to treat respiratory issues. What it is striking is his use of the singular name "Elizabeth." Throughout the ledger books from his store and his household accounts, Robert reserved the sole use of Christian names for members of the Townsend family and household; everyone else he recorded more formally with both a first and last name. The only Elizabeth with any close connection to Robert was his father's slave, who ran away in 1779. The assumption is, of course, tenuous at best, as Elizabeth was one of the most common names for women in the American colonies; far more concrete, however, is the entry in the same household account book on May 3, 1782, where Robert records the purchase of a "thimble and thread for Lis [*sic*]."[53]

Liss had unquestionably reentered Robert's life at some point by the spring of 1782, though under what circumstances it is impossible to know. She was, at that point, owned by a British officer, having left the Queen's Rangers some time prior to August 1779. But if she had not maintained some connection with Robert, how did she know how to find him in the whole of New York City after three years—especially since he had recently moved? And why does he record his purchases for her so casually in his ledger? Could they have been in contact throughout that period? Could Liss, in fact, be the mysterious 355—or at least one member of Robert's extended espionage network, passing intelligence from the household of a British officer?

Interestingly, the same month that Liss reappears unambiguously in Robert's ledger, the Culper letters resume, composed by Woodhull with information transmitted verbally by Robert. Something or someone triggered Robert to begin sharing intelligence again, and he continued to do so throughout the summer of 1782, as the inevitable end of the war became clear and Loyalists in New York started making plans to evacuate to British-held Canada.

Then, three months later, Robert did something radical. On August 14, he paid his father "£70 for a Negro Wench."[54] As he would explain in a future letter, referring to himself in the third person, as was common in such writings, "The person she was first sold to being about to leave this state on the evacuation by the British, and she not willing to go with him, apply'd to our R.T. to repurchase her, which he did."[55]

If Samuel had previously been unaware of Liss's escape plans, this must certainly have come as a shock to him. As it is, there is no record of whether Samuel was surprised in any way by his son's actions. He records his receipt of the money in his own ledger on August 28, confirming the transaction was indeed for Elizabeth, noting "£70 received for Liss" from "Robert Townsend's own account."[56]

Liss, meanwhile, had taken up residence at Bachelor's Hall, owing not only to Robert's purchase of her but also to the fragility of her condition. She was now three months pregnant.

# Part II

# In the Course of Human Events

## CHAPTER SIX

# "A Child with Her Then Master"

No one passing the simple storefront on Peck Slip on August 14, 1782, would have given a second thought to the young woman standing outside, clutching a bundle and looking distressed.

Located on Manhattan's East Side near Pearl Street, the Townsends' store did steady but unremarkable business with all manner of people. Not much about a sundries shop run by two brothers and a teenaged cousin was likely to attract attention, which was precisely the reason Robert had moved it from bustling Hanover Square at the height of his spying activities two years earlier. No one would have suspected any cloak-and-dagger goings-on in ordinary Robert Townsend's ordinary little store. Especially not now, in the roiling tumult of New York in the midst of an evacuation.

The site of people carrying all their worldly possessions had become strikingly commonplace as the British and the staunchest Loyalists prepared to move out of the city. Some were headed to the Caribbean, happy to leave behind the bone-chilling winds of New York winters for His Majesty's dominions in the West Indies; Jamaica was said to be positively lovely in January. A few were headed east, back across the Atlantic to the motherland itself. Life in the colonies was fine for some, but New York simply wasn't London. Most of the evacuees, however, were headed north to Canada. It was a relatively short journey—just a few days by ship to Nova Scotia, where Halifax stood ready to welcome King George's loyal subjects to a portion of British North America that was not choked by rebellion.

The city was certainly in transition but, so far, the process had been orderly. There were many who were determined to ride out the war, still believing the American bid for independence was simply too farfetched a notion to ever actually succeed. A recent copy of the *Weekly Mercury* newspaper had urged the public to continue life and business as usual, despite the proposal of independence for the "Thirteen Provinces" at the ongoing negotiations in Paris. Its first article cautioned, "Until a general peace can be ratified, we cannot know what is to be the eventual condition of the country."[1] Nevertheless, those who had read the embargoed tea leaves correctly predicted that it would be better to sell out now before the panic set in and the market was glutted. Advertisements began filling newspapers, hocking "the effects of Officers going to England," offering for sale everything from "a compleat camp bed" and "men's wearing apparel" to a fine "fowling piece."[2]

A number of British senior officers were among those headed northward, moving on orders to withdraw from the rebellious thirteen lower colonies to what remained securely within the boundaries of King George's domain. Life in New York had been comfortable and lucrative. Many high-ranking soldiers had built small households for themselves that now proved far too difficult to transport to Canada and were selling furniture and slaves unable or unwilling to go,[3] as masters sometimes preferred simply to start over with local slaves in their new duty station. There was a relatively sizable black population in Nova Scotia, due to several factors, including Dunmore's Proclamation, which had welcomed fugitive slaves from the colony of Virginia as far back as 1775. By the 1780s, several thousand free people of color were living in Halifax, but slavery still existed on the island, and a move to Canada for New York slaves did not necessarily mean emancipation, just enslavement somewhere else. Some protested, not wanting to leave behind family in the city or familiar surroundings.

Newspapers bear witness to the objections many slaves had toward emigrating with their masters. "Valuable Negro Wench . . . the property of a gentleman going to the West-Indies," one typical 1782 advertisement read, "and sold for no other reason than her being averse to be carried there: she is a good plain Cook, and an excellent Washerwoman and

Ironer, her title is undisputable."⁴ The clear title mentioned was invaluable. It meant the woman in question could be legally purchased by another buyer; that there was correct documentation meant that she had been paid for in full, so there was no question of a lien against her or of her being a runaway. A number of slaves had used the chaos of the war as cover to either slip away to live as freemen (albeit, without manumission papers) in large cities; other runaways enlisted in the British army, lured by promises of freedom at the end of their service. Those slaves who had such an indeterminate status posed a problem for their current masters, who could not provide the proper provenance and, therefore, could not sell them as easily. In most cases, these individuals were eager to leave the United States in the hopes that they might have a better chance at eventually gaining their freedom elsewhere. But in other cases, they objected, fearing that their runaway status might be revealed in the transition due to a lack of ownership papers or because they did not want to miss reuniting with family members on the chance that they, too, escaped or were emancipated.⁵

The mass exodus of the British from New York was a complicated process, but it was not the only reason that Elizabeth now stood at Robert's front door, and it was not the reason she was scared about the future.

On September 19, 1782, Robert handed his last Culper letter to Benjamin Tallmadge, having left Manhattan five days prior in order to ride to Westchester, New York, to deliver it in person. "The last packet, so far from bringing better news to the loyalists, has indeed brought the clearest and unequivocal Proofs that the independence of America is unconditionally to be acknowledged, nor will there be any conditions insisted on for those who have joined the King's Standard," Robert wrote. "Indeed, I never saw such general distress and dissatisfaction in my life as is painted in the countenance of every Tory at N.Y. . . . I am myself uncertain when the Troops will leave N.Y. but I must confess I rather believe if the King's Magazines can be removed, that they will leave us this fall."⁶

The report was Robert's first intelligence in almost two years. It was also his last report of the war.⁷

Why he chose that moment to reengage the Culper Ring for one final mission is unclear. Perhaps his motive was tied to his undercover work with the City Volunteers, who had been reactivated in mid-September after a lengthy hiatus. As *Bauermeister's Journal* recorded just a few weeks later, "The inhabitants of New York and vicinity were again called upon to do the greater part of the garrison duty of the city."[8] Robert had once again donned the red wool uniform he secretly despised and stood sentry outside British headquarters for at least one night.[9] What he saw or heard may have prompted him to reach out once more to Tallmadge.

It is also possible, however, that something in the information he obtained within a month of Elizabeth's arrival at his door struck him as significant enough to take one final risk in smuggling covert information out of the city. If she had, indeed, been acting as an informant for Robert for the past two years, her appearance at his doorstep now, in the final days of New York's British rule, may have been an act of both tremendous bravery and self-preservation if she was afraid of being unmasked as an American agent. After ensuring the message was safely in Tallmadge's possession, Robert quickly returned to Manhattan and the unusual household there of which he was the de facto head.

The apartment upstairs from the store had the distinct air of bachelors' quarters; the young men hadn't even bothered to hire a housekeeper, rendering the place utterly devoid of a woman's touch. Robert, now twenty-nine years old, William, aged twenty-five, and John, just eighteen, lived as comfortably but simply as three single men from respectable families might.

William and John were still young enough that their marital status was not questioned, but Robert's lack of a wife was beginning to elicit gossip. To Robert, it seemed he was completely surrounded by married couples, which made his own singleness stand in stark contrast. True, he was not yet thirty, but as a successful young man from a prominent family who had no need to postpone marriage until he could support a household, he was expected to find a wife and settle down soon. He couldn't even use the instability of the war or his precarious career as a spy as an excuse to himself anymore; his covert compatriot Abraham Woodhull had married Mary Smith the previous year. Ever since his oldest brother Solomon had married their cousin Anne in February, Robert had been warding off questions from nosy relatives who wanted to know when he, too, would take a wife.

Samuel's wedding gift to his oldest son and daughter-in-law had been a married pair of slaves from the Townsend household. This last point sat especially uneasily with Robert. Let the family gossip about his personal life as they saw fit—they had done so anyway regarding his service in the Loyalist City Volunteer Company—but he was beginning to develop scruples regarding the giving and receiving of human beings as presents to be passed around. Solomon and Anne were staying with her family in Chester to avoid crossing into British-held territory, and the enslaved couple, Gabriel and Jane, were to be "given" to the Townsend newlyweds "upon their marriage,"[10] but no one had yet made the trip to deliver the slaves. Robert, as a merchant, could easily obtain passes out of the city, as evidenced by his frequent jaunts outside Manhattan, but he seems to have declined to transport human chattel.

Robert's refusal to conform to expectation had long been a source of amusement in the family, but it was beginning to become a source of tension. Among the four surviving Townsend brothers, Robert was certainly the quietest and the farthest in temperament from their genial and outgoing father, Samuel. But as he grew older, Robert's quirks seemed only to grow stronger, and his noncompliance with the general Townsend approach to life and respectability began to seem troublesome. As Solomon would write a few years later, "His manner of living is rather indolent and by no means commendable in a person of his time of life. . . . [Robert should] make himself a more useful member of society."[11]

The more Robert looked around him, the less he was concerned with accepted norms or keeping up appearances. The time for that had passed when he agreed to keep operating his shop in New York and associate openly with the British officer corps—even donning the despised red coat of King George's finest—for the sake of smuggling intelligence to General George Washington. It was a good thing Robert cared so little about what others thought about him or whispered behind his back, because the Townsends' comfortable bachelors' quarters were about to be shaken in a way wholly unimaginable to the three men who resided there.

Robert's decision to welcome Elizabeth into his home could not have been an easy one: an unmarried, pregnant woman living alone with three men would have raised many an eyebrow and set more than a few tongues wagging.[12] Complicating the issue even further was Elizabeth's liminal status as both a runaway slave and a seemingly repentant supplicant. Keeping her in his home, when she was legally considered stolen property belonging to his father, gnawed at Robert's conscience. Yet he did not want to return her to Oyster Bay, where she would likely be made to work despite her condition. And he certainly did not want to be a slave owner himself, though to any outside observer he would certainly have looked like one.

The day after he paid his father for Liss, he made purchases for his new houseguest, including "thread for towels, a tumbler glass" and "an earthenware plate."[13] Robert further seems to have reconciled his conscience to the matter by hiring a white Irish housekeeper, named Polly Banvard, to assume all domestic duties instead of using Elizabeth for such tasks. The arrangement was not ideal—Robert still had no idea what he would do once the baby arrived—but for now Elizabeth was safe.

For her part, Liss was likely stunned by the sudden shift in her circumstances once again; suddenly living as a guest rather than as a slave, she remained under Robert's protection for the remainder of her pregnancy. Two things remain unclear, however: the name of the father and the circumstances under which Elizabeth became pregnant.

To the first point, her British master lurks in the background as an anonymous but powerful presence who is never identified by name. This ongoing lack of specificity in reference to him is curious, as Robert certainly would have been aware of his identity through Liss. The fact that Robert's letters go out of their way not to give the man a name necessarily raises the question of whether he was a high-ranking officer whose unwitting connection to Robert would have attracted unwanted attention to and questions about Robert's connections and wartime activities.

To the second point, consensual sexual relationships between soldiers and camp women were very common, and Elizabeth was described as being "too fond of the British officers" and "too fond of Company."[14] Unfortunately, rape was also common between slave and master, and Liss appears in Robert's shop ledger on May 3, 1782, at nearly the same time she would have been impregnated. Might she have been assaulted by her British master and sought out Robert for safety?

Or is it possible that Robert himself was the father of Elizabeth's child? In two separate letters he notes that she was "brought up in our Father's family," but he never states whether he viewed her with filial affection or took a less chaste interest.[15] In calling upon Robert for protection, perhaps she was appealing not simply to his benevolence but to his sense of duty.

Whatever the case, Elizabeth's fortunes seem to have improved when she turned to Robert for help: she now had a comfortable home, at least temporarily, and female companionship in Polly Banvard. The young Irish woman became a permanent fixture in the Townsend household, a live-in housekeeper and on-call midwife. Handsome, dashing William took to teasing Polly, and a flirtation quickly grew up between the two, even as Elizabeth grew larger through the autumn and winter, and Robert grew more concerned about the future after her baby arrived.

On November 30, 1782, the United States and Britain signed a preliminary peace agreement, though the war would not officially end until a full treaty had been ratified by both parties. Still, the evacuees streamed out of New York. Those last holdouts for a Loyalist victory set forth for friendlier climes or else accepted their new reality and prepared for life in an independent nation. With many of King George's troops now fixed in Canada, Liss could at least let go of any lingering fears that her former master would lay claim to her and demand her emigration at his side. For the moment, at least, she could rest comfortably knowing the Townsend apartment was home.

William and John's reaction to Liss's sudden presence in their home has been lost to history, but it is safe to assume that they vacated the premises as soon as her labor pains began on February 19, 1783, and stayed away until her screams were no longer cutting through the plaster walls of their apartment. Where they spent their time on that chilly morning is uncertain, but the home they returned to would not have been much quieter than the one they left: Elizabeth had given birth to a baby boy Robert described as "mulatto," whom she named Harry.[16] Robert was now as involved as any father could be, whether the child was his or not, as long as the boy and his mother lived under his roof.

As soon as it became clear that the pair were healthy, Robert faced the question that had been pressing on him since Elizabeth first turned up at his doorstep: What next? But in this, as in all things, he refused to be ruffled.

———

Richard Sharwin's sudden death on July 25, 1783, proved as conveniently timed as such unfortunate events can be.[17] The London-born saddler had emigrated to Boston, where he had taken an active role in at least one street brawl in 1775 (where he was arrested alongside eight British officers), before settling in New York to do brisk business during the peak of the war years. Ultimately proving himself neither a Patriot nor a Loyalist but a capitalist, he had provided finely worked saddles to whoever had ready money and a willingness to part with it. He had operated a shop in Hanover Square for several years, then moved with his wife, Ann, a few blocks north to a finer house on Wall Street. But with the British largely gone from the city, combat greatly reduced, and most skirmishes shifting to the south, demand for his products was about to drop sharply, so the Sharwins returned to their old neighborhood in June. Now that his services were no longer in such high demand, his heart obligingly gave out in his forty-sixth year, and Ann suddenly found herself a moderately wealthy woman.

The move uptown to Wall Street had been exciting, but there was something comforting about being back in the old shop on Hanover Square, in the midst of former neighbors and familiar buildings—especially as a new widow. Still, Ann was lonely. The Sharwins had never had children, and the new home had barely been unpacked since the move in June. Now, the house that had once held such happy memories felt empty—and a little exciting. Her newfound freedom lay before her, offering boundless possibilities. She found herself an able businesswoman, liquidating a large amount of inventory from the saddle shop and collecting on the outstanding debts still owed to her late husband—especially from British officers now evacuating to Canada. "His Widow requests that all those who have demands on her late Husband's estate," declared an ad Ann submitted to the *Royal Gazette*, "will please to deliver in their accounts to be settled and paid; and humbly hopes those indebted to said estate will immediately pay the same, especially the Gentlemen who are leaving this City."[18] She was not yet old, she was not destitute, and she had both the means and desire to live comfortably, but she did not want to live alone. The solution, for now, it seemed, was to get herself a lady's maid.

As Ann cast her eye about her, looking for a suitable companion, she became aware of an attractive young slave woman residing with the Townsend bachelors in nearby Peck Slip. It was an unusual situation, to be sure, and a few discreet inquiries filled in whatever holes gossip had left. The infant Harry was six months old by the end of the summer, and Robert seemed eager to find a more suitable situation for mother and child. Ann knew Robert from their mutual time in Hanover Square and respected him as an honest businessman; she now had the opportunity to get to know Liss and her abilities as well. It seemed a natural solution: Liss and Harry would join Ann Sharwin's household.

There was only one catch: Liss was still legally a slave, and due to a technicality in New York state law, Robert was unable to free her with a simple stroke of the pen.

The manumission process in 1780s New York was a complicated affair. Prior to 1785, slaves were granted freedom by their masters, but these manumissions were not often recorded in town records. When a master legally freed his slave, he had to post a bond, usually £200, intended to support the slave should he or she become indigent.

The law changed twice more between 1785 and 1788, before a "gradual abolition" law was enacted for the state in 1799. But in 1783, manumissions were still subject to the old standard, and £200 (equivalent to approximately $18,000 today) was an exceedingly large sum to post in cash during wartime—especially since Robert had already just paid his father £70 on behalf of Elizabeth.[19] Further complicating the matter is the fact that it is unclear whether Robert was issued a bill of sale for Elizabeth on making payment to his father. Since she was born into the Townsend household, she never had a title for Samuel to possess in the first place.

As a result, the deal that Robert struck with Ann Sharwin was not a straightforward transfer of ownership. Sharwin was to pay Robert £70—the same price he paid his father for Elizabeth, despite the fact that she now had a child who promised to be a strong and capable boy in a few years. Apparently Robert was not willing to profit from the sale of human beings. Sharwin could not, however, simply elect to sell Elizabeth if she ever decided she was finished with her services. Instead, she was required to come to Robert first and allow him to purchase the pair back for the same price at which he initially sold them. He wrote, "Mrs. Sharwin . . . knowing the Wench, applyd to purchase her, and she being willing to live with her, he sold her with the child and particularly stipulated that whenever Mrs. Sharwin should incline to sell her, he would, rather than she should be sold to a place she should not like or sent out of the State, take her again and return the amount of what he sold her for."[20]

Liss, for her part, seems to have been pleased with the arrangement. Though she was still enslaved, she was in a comfortable situation, close to her family in Oyster Bay, and guaranteed to remain in New York with her child. Given her time and place, she could hardly hope for better circumstances.

Liss and Harry were settled into the Sharwin home in the late summer of 1783. An entry on August 1 in Robert's household ledger for "cartage of household furniture and portage" may refer to her move.[21] She began work eagerly and performed her duties well. "From this time," Robert wrote, "[I] never understood but the mistress and wench were perfectly satisfied with each other." Elizabeth was treated kindly, and Harry continued to grow, starting to talk and taking his first steps under Ann's roof. The Townsend apartment became a bachelor pad once again, with only Polly staying on in her role as housekeeper.

Then, in the spring of 1784, two things happened that would change everything.

One was the reestablishment of Alexander Robertson's dry goods store in Manhattan.[22] Corpulent, beak-nosed, underhanded but charming, and apparently silver-tongued, Alexander Robertson was the perfect melodrama villain. The Scottish-born merchant built a small fortune for himself in the years leading up to the war selling in his two Manhattan shops certain British imports banned in the colony of New York. By smuggling them in from Philadelphia, where they were still legal, he assumed both the risk and the reward. In 1769, however, he was brought up on charges before the New York Committee of Merchants and his reputation publicly decried. "Alexander Robertson," the *New-York Journal* charged,

> *not having Love of his Country at Heart, but being instigated by the sordid views of a little paltry Gain, hath most notoriously and willfully committed a high Crime and Misdemeanor against the Liberties of the People of this City in particular, and the American Colonies in general . . . and it is not doubted but that all Ranks and Degrees amongst us, both Men and Women, will unite in all legal means to shew their just Abhorrence and Detestation of such scandalous Practices, that they will avoid any Connections and all Intercourse with him, treat him on all Occasions with the Contempt he deserves, regard him in the odious Light of an Enemy to his Country.*[23]

Nevertheless, Robertson continued to operate both stores for at least five more years before leaving the city for the span of the war. But his wife, Mary, was in the final stages of a "languishing illness,"[24] and Alexander Robertson was a man of big appetites—for luxury, for profits, and for women. New York was the only city that could satisfy them, and an empty storefront in Hanover Square, not far from the home of a financially secure widow and her attractive lady's maid, seemed just the place to stage his return to Manhattan.

The other thing that happened in the spring of 1784 seemed like a bit of déjà vu. Liss and Harry had been gone not quite a year when the Townsend bachelor quarters was again filled with the sounds of a crying infant. Polly Banvard give birth to a baby boy—whom she named Robert Townsend Jr.[25]

CHAPTER SEVEN

# "Ensnared into Bondage"

WILLIAM TOWNSEND WAS THE VERY MODEL OF A REGENCY-NOVEL RAKE. Charismatic, angelically handsome, and always up for fun, the fourth Townsend son enjoyed the nickname "flower of the family." But along with those good looks and "agreeable manners" with the ladies came a recklessness and a cavalier attitude that strained relationships with his siblings and cousins, and eventually landed him back under the watchful eye of his once doting parents. For not quite two years, William enjoyed life in Manhattan, playing the charming foil to his somber older brother Robert and watching his young cousin John emerge as a promising flour merchant, but the temptations and allurements of the city proved over-powering for William, and those relationships quickly soured.

By early 1784, at the age of twenty-six, William had returned, "a dis-sipated young man," to his parents' house in Oyster Bay, due in no small part to his casual relationship with money, including more than £1,000 owed to him by his cousin and housemate John, but also influenced by the open secret that William had sired Polly Banvard's child.[1] Samuel, for his part, had naturally fostered hopes of a good match for his attractive and popular son—a daughter of a wealthy family well connected with business interests—but rumors of illegitimate children could hardly help William's cause with the most respectable families.

Years later, after a tragic accident claimed William's life at age forty-seven, Solomon eschewed eulogizing his younger brother, noting instead that "he was for several years a very unhappy man, and has at times been the occasion of much distress to the family" and that "he had his faults, and some to excess." The scrawled entry in Solomon's pocket diary recalled that their interactions were always filled with "bickerings, disputes and disagreements," but William "is now no more in this world."[2]

What caused "much distress" to the rest of the family seems to have hardly fazed Robert. On February 1, 1784, just a few weeks after William departed the city and almost exactly one year since Harry was born, Robert likely once again found himself fetching a midwife to aid a woman in labor at Bachelor's Hall. Though he failed to record his reaction to the birth of this second baby boy, Polly's choice of name, Robert Townsend Jr., speaks loudly to his character. William's refusal to take responsibility for impregnating a housemaid was hardly unheard of, but to Robert it was intolerable. In William's absence, as her pregnancy came to term, her son's name must have been an immeasurable comfort to Polly, whose own father had died when she was only eleven years old. To buck social convention and take a stand for a person with limited resources was a Townsend tradition, though in the case of both Liss and Polly, Robert showed no inclination to receive praise for his assistance.

Though the public assumed that Robert was the father, even the boy himself knew better, and years later he privately hinted that William was more likely the "uncle" who had caught his mother's eye. When Solomon's youngest son cornered an aging Robert on the matter, he came to the same conclusion and wrote in his scrapbook, "I believe my Uncle Robert thought that he might as well have owed his paternity to his Brother Wm.," but added, "The subject was *never again* renewed between us."

By lending his name, Robert helped to ensure broader acceptance for the young man than that given to a fatherless child who bore his mother's surname. In fact, even after Polly married a widower named Marmaduke Buskirk two years later, Robert Jr. retained the Townsend moniker. As he grew, his family struggled financially, with Polly working throughout her adult life as a washerwoman. With Robert's financial assistance, however, Robert Jr. attended school and even learned French.[3]

The elder Robert, it seems, had long ago given up any concern for upper-middle-class eighteenth-century social norms. A few months after Polly gave birth, in the summer of 1784, he forged a business partnership with Solomon at the same time that Solomon and Anne welcomed their first surviving child, a girl they named Hannah. Solomon was, by all accounts, following the script for how a Townsend man's life should look, but Robert was a different story. He was now thirty-one, had never been involved in a courtship, was willing to shelter unwed mothers in his home, and had little interest in the social climbing and snobbish aspirations of many of his peers. Since his identity as a Patriot spy was unknown but his service in a local Loyalist brigade was not, he was even believed by some of his family to have cast his initial allegiance with the wrong side of the conflict. But none of this seems to have bothered Robert—not his tarnished reputation or his failing social standing or even his family's opinions about his life. And now, a son of one of Oyster Bay's largest slaveholders was beginning to dabble in the abolitionist movement.

Men who have successfully slayed one giant will rarely stop there. Almost from the moment that the Treaty of Paris was signed to officially end hostilities in the American Revolution, many of New York's most ardent Patriots shifted their focus to stopping the trade in human beings and ending the practice of slavery. Efforts had been made for decades previously, mostly without success, but now that the British tyrant had been defeated, more people in positions of power shifted their focus to the next great evil.

In 1777, despite the fact that he himself owned slaves, John Jay had hoped to use the momentum for American independence to promote the cause of abolition by drafting a bill in the New York legislature to end slavery throughout the state, but it failed to gain support. By 1785, however, many of the leading figures in the state had decided to pool their considerable social and political equity to form the New York Manumission Society (NYMS). The eleven original members, including John Jay and Alexander Hamilton, laid the groundwork for an organization that grew rapidly to include the likes of attorney Robert Troup, Hamilton's college roommate; tailor-turned-spy Hercules Mulligan; merchant and secretary of the New York Chamber of Commerce Adam Gilchrist; William Backhouse, one of the wealthiest merchants in the city; and Robert

Townsend, who officially joined the NYMS at its second gathering, on February 4, 1785, just ten days after its inaugural meeting.

The earliest members represented a wide array of religious and civil doctrines. Jay and Hamilton were ardent Federalists, while another charter member, Melancton Smith, was an outspoken anti-Federalist and likely the anonymous author of several popular political tracts in that vein. Many were Quakers, like Robert Bowne and William Shotwell, while the religious affiliations of other members ranged from Presbyterian to Anglican to Baptist to none at all. Some were among the wealthiest lawyers and landholders in New York; others were middle-class professionals and tradesmen. Many joined the society while still owning slaves themselves. The NYMS even boasted as honorary members the English abolitionist Granville Sharpe and the Marquis de Lafayette.[4] In short, it was a relatively diverse group for a collection of white men, but all had united for the sake of abolishing within their state's borders the buying, selling, and owning of human beings.

The exact path by which Robert became involved with the society in its earliest days is unclear; perhaps he had the future of Liss and young Harry in mind or else was influenced by the impassioned work of John Jay, whose invaluable contribution to the safety and success of the Culper Ring via his brother's invisible ink was known intimately by Robert. Jay was, after all, the most vocal of all the NYMS members. Not only did he spearhead the failed 1777 vote on abolition, but he also allied with Aaron Burr to champion later efforts for the same cause.[5] The NYMS wasted little time in getting to work. Just a few months after the founding, members campaigned ardently for the passage of several measures to end the importation of slaves into New York and to streamline and simplify the process by which a master could free a slave. Simultaneously discouraged and emboldened by these small victories that promised a slow but eventual path to total abolition, the NYMS appealed directly to the public for support of their cause in 1786 by widely publishing the story of George Morris.[6]

Although the first Fugitive Slave Act was not passed by the United States Congress until 1793, it had long been common practice for local law enforcement to capture runaway slaves, return them to their masters, and levy fines against those people who had assisted in their escape. There was money to be made in functioning as a kind of bounty hunter, but certain unsavory elements of society soon recognized even more potential in selling unprovenanced African Americans at the full going rate for a slave on the auction block. Abductions were so common, and some perpetrators were so notorious for their involvement in such trafficking, that many newspapers began to run ads warning people of color that those particular individuals were in the area and to be alert for their own protection.

On March 15, 1786, "A Hint" appeared in the New York papers cautioning, "Now riding in this harbor, the sloop Maria, Captain Tinker, and will probably sail for Charleston in a day or two. She has on board a considerable number of negroes; some of these distressed objects were seen ringing their hands, and praying to their relentless proprietors that they might be permitted to remain in New-York, but by these hardened people their petitions were treated with disdain. It would be well for free negroes to be upon their guard, lest they should meet with some kidnappers, and share the fate many have heretofore done." The message was signed simply "Benevelous"—one of the pennames employed by Benjamin Franklin.[7]

But this was hardly the first time, or the last, that Captain James Tinker would ply his trade between New York and Charleston. In late February 1786, three weeks *before* Benevelous's ominous caution appeared in two New York papers, a local merchant and member of the South Carolina Legislature named Richard Lushington found himself enjoying a brisk morning walk when he wandered into Charleston's infamous slave market, one of the largest clearinghouses for human trafficking in the country. The colony was more than 50 percent African American at the time, and the specter of slavery cast its shadow on everything in the city. From the bulky sacks of rice, to huge bundles of indigo leaves, to immense bales of cotton, to barrels of rum to the huge ships that carried them all over the world—many of which now had empty hulls from hauling human cargo from Africa—the evidence of slavery as the economic engine of the region was unmistakable.

Richard Lushington, a devoted Quaker with ties to Philadelphia, was a man of many contradictions. While most Quakers adhered strictly to the "Peace Testimony," requiring Friends to actively oppose participation in war, during the Revolution he not only served as a captain in the Charleston Militia but also commanded a regiment of local volunteers, including at least thirty-four shopkeepers of the Jewish faith. On February 3, 1779, Lushington's "Jew Company," as it was known, distinguished itself in the low country of South Carolina at the Battle of Beaufort, courageously fighting and inflicting heavy casualties on the enemy.[8]

After the war, he continued to lead a busy and varied life, commanding the local militia, importing and selling goods through his Philadelphia Quaker connections, winning election to the legislature, supporting various philanthropic causes, and operating a large rum distillery. And as the owner of 750 acres of land, despite the teachings of his faith and his work as an abolitionist, he owned as many as eleven slaves himself.[9]

As Lushington observed the goings-on at the Charleston slave auction that February day, he was possibly musing on lines from J. Hector St. John's *Letters from an American Farmer*, published just four years earlier. A French immigrant from minor nobility, St. John had moved to Orange County, New York, in 1759 and become a naturalized citizen. He traveled the country extensively before compiling a series of letters ostensibly authored by the eponymous American farmer, which describe the wonders and curiosities of the young nation to British readers across the Atlantic. In Letter IX, one of the most famous passages, the narrator visits Charleston, South Carolina, and balks at the wretched state of the slaves he sees for sale there. He muses (rather naively), "We have slaves likewise in our northern provinces; I hope the time draws near when they will be all emancipated: but how different their lot, how different their situation, in every possible respect!" He then goes on to describe the lives of southern slaves:

> *The day in which they arrive and are sold, is the first of their labours; labours, which from that hour admit of no respite. . . . They are neither soothed by the hopes that their slavery will ever terminate but with their lives. . . . Cheered by no one single motive that can impel the will, or excite their efforts; nothing but terrors and punishments*

*are presented to them; death is denounced if they run away; horrid*
*dilaceration if they speak with their native freedom; perpetually awed*
*by the terrible cracks of whips, or by the fear of capital punishments,*
*while even those punishments often fail of their purpose.*[10]

The letter closes with a lament on the deterioration and wicked-
ness of humanity and a description of an instance of sadistic torture
the author had witnessed firsthand on a plantation. Though it enjoyed
more success in Europe than it did in the United States, *Letters from an*
*American Farmer* was nevertheless much read and discussed among an
educated American readership. While terribly shortsighted in terms of
northern slavery, the divergent regional approaches to the practice were
nevertheless a significant mark of cultural distinction between the North
and South in the 1780s, and Charleston's reputation as a hub for human
suffering was already well established.

By chance, as he observed the proceedings of the auction, Lushington happened to notice one athletic-looking young man, who was
especially distressed as he awaited his place on the block, and struck up a
conversation with him. In this way did Lushington meet George Morris,
who had been kidnapped and transported roughly one week earlier from
New York City by two men: one was named Abrahams, and the other
was the infamous Captain Tinker.[11]

Morris was born free in Philadelphia in the late 1760s, apparently to
a relatively well-to-do and cultured African American family, enjoying
the liberty afforded him by life in a colony that had abolished slavery in
1780. In 1785 he became the avid student of an itinerant dance master
named John Griffith, who made stops through Connecticut and Massachusetts before arriving in Philadelphia. Griffith offered classes in a
variety of dances ranging from the classic minuet to more loosely choreo-
graphed jigs and reels. He introduced his students to the latest cotillions
straight from Paris and taught them a few of his original dances, like
one he called "Griffith's Whim."[12] When he announced he was headed
to New York City to open a studio at the Grand Assembly on Broadway, Morris ignored the warnings of his friends and relatives, packed his
things, and followed Griffith to Manhattan.

Young George wasn't completely unaware of the risk he faced by moving to a state where slavery was still legal. Understanding the vital importance of protecting his freedom papers and entrusting them to the care of a respected community figure, Morris filed his certificate with James Shuter, clerk to William Backhouse, a prominent merchant and well-known NYMS society member. Backhouse was currently involved in plans for the new African Free School, an academy for free black children, which would open later that year, so he seemed a natural choice as a safe repository for such an essential document.

On February 20, 1786, Mr. Griffith and his dance academy scholars put on their finest clothes and gathered in the assembly room at 6 p.m. for a grand ball, after weeks of planning and rehearsal. Their public announcement made clear to all attendees that "no person will be admitted whose appearance may give umbrage to the company."[13] But as the music began, one dancer failed to show. George Morris surely wished he could have been dressed in his grandest finery, performing the minuet at the ball. Instead he was stripped to the waist as he waited his turn to step up onto the auction block, 750 miles to the south.

Richard Lushington's sober Quaker dress and manners were surely familiar to Morris as a Philadelphia native. When Lushington addressed him with the formal use of "thee" and "thou," a relieved Morris recognized him as a sympathetic figure and spilled his harrowing tale, from his days as a dance student to his journey south as a captive of Captain Tinker, and revealed the exact location of his certificate of freedom.

Moved by his plight, Lushington wrote to fellow politician John Jay, whose abolitionist efforts in New York were well known and appreciated by the Society of Friends. "I take the liberty of addressing thee; understanding that thou art a friend to the distress'd of whatever colour, that have been ensnared into bondage," he began, informing Jay of the case and beseeching him to investigate Morris's claims. "I am persuaded that many are kidnapped, brought from New York, and sold here, and I could wish some mode might be adopted to prevent and deter people from pursuing so villainous a practice." Hoping his urgency would prompt Jay to pledge his assistance in freeing Morris, he added, "These poor unhappy people have but few friends here, and many who wish to be friendly are much afraid to appear and vindicate their cause publicly."[14]

Jay did one better. Not only did he track down the freedom papers in question and verify Morris's story, but he aggressively pursued criminal charges against certain known kidnappers. He also published portions of Lushington's letters in newspapers in New York, Philadelphia, and Boston, along with commentary informing readers that he "made complaint thereof to authority, who, on sufficient proof, confined one of the transgressors and admitted another to bail. There is no doubt but such miscreants, as have been accessary to this violation of the laws of God and man, will shortly meet with their just deserts [sic]."

Jay pleaded with the public to recognize that Morris's case was, tragically, not unique and that the abduction of free people of color to sell into slavery was a frightfully common practice. The story, he hoped, would "command the attention of every good citizen, and shew the necessity of a spirited exertion, in [sic] behalf of those unfortunate people that may become the victims of unprincipled, cruel, avaricious men." To this end, Jay also shared Lushington's letter with the rest of the NYMS. "They are taking proper measures on the occasion," he wrote back, "and I flatter myself that our Legislature will interpose to prevent such enormities in the future. It is much to be wished that slavery may be abolished. The honour of the States, as well as justice and humanity, in my opinion, loudly call upon them to emancipate these unhappy people. To contend for our own liberty, and to deny that blessing to others, involves an inconsistency not to be excused."[15]

Almost immediately, the public's knowledge of the Morris case had a real and tangible effect. Passengers aboard Captain Tinker's vessel witnessed his attempt to trick another free African American young man onto his ship and ultimately intervened.

Tinker had devised an elaborate scheme whereby an accessory named John Passmore offered the target a generous sum of money to go on a journey with him aboard Tinker's vessel. Sent ahead to safeguard a trunk he was told contained $100, the victim boarded the ship and "faithfully guarded this supposed treasure until the vessel was hoisting sail." As the ship left harbor and headed for the open seas, Tinker informed the man that his supposed travel companion was not coming and produced a key to the trunk, which, when opened, contained only a pile of old shoes. "To pacify the poor Black," the account read, "Tinker offered him the same wages he allowed to the other hands on board." The ship, however, was headed to Charleston, which all but sealed the young man's fate. Luckily, the journey was cut short when a storm turned the boat back to New York. Because they had recently read about the Morris case in the papers, passengers immediately informed the NYMS, and the "ensnared African was released from that complicated scene of painful existence."

The newspaper account of this incident, signed only by "A Friend to Mankind," concluded with a call to action from the NYMS: "How long will Americans view these violations of that which should be the distinguishing characteristics of a free and enlightened people, with an eye of so much indifference? Is it not time that our laws should discountenance such reproachful and inhuman practices?"[16]

Robert's abolitionist views were also intensifying, bolstered at least in part by the highly publicized Morris case. Robert and Solomon knew Richard Lushington as a business associate, having sold him a number of goods, including several shipments of iron anchors from Solomon's ironworks.[17] They were also acquainted with Lushington's business partner, a Quaker named John Kirk Jr., who had grown up near Oyster Bay in Jericho, Long Island, and whose father had been arrested in 1776 alongside Samuel Townsend. Robert knew Lushington to be an honest, if unconventional, Quaker (he did go against his faith's pacifist views by taking up arms during the war, after all), driven by a genuine desire to do right by all people and by his own conscience. The lengths to which he went to resolve Morris's case were evidence of that. Robert felt relieved that Liss and Harry had been settled so conveniently and with a contractual guarantee that they would return to his family's household if Ann grew dissatisfied, rather than potentially being shipped south. It had been quite some time since he had visited them, but they had seemed content, and Ann had given no indication that she was anything other than pleased with the arrangement as well.

Robert did not know that his relief was nearly two years out of date.

When Mary Robertson died in July 1784,[18] her husband, fifty-two-year-old Alexander, wasted little time. Almost immediately after attaining widowerhood, he sought an avenue out of it—and his Hanover Square neighbor Ann Sharwin was just the sort of woman he wanted. She was wealthy and respected, with no children of her own—and, in her mid-forties, she was likely past the point of bearing any. Alexander could only have viewed this as an asset, as he already had an enormous brood of eleven with his late wife, so his home could hardly contain any more. Ann, for her part, had been living with Liss and Harry for nearly a year, and by all accounts the arrangement suited them all quite well. Ann probably counted herself lucky; healthy, rich widowers were in high demand in a society still recovering from the effects of war, and Alexander's children promised to fill her life with boisterous laughter and vitality as the family she never had. The pair were married on Christmas Eve, just five months after Mary Robertson breathed her last.[19]

Almost immediately, however, discord erupted between the newly-weds over Liss, who had caught Alexander's eye first for her attractiveness and then, when Ann apparently objected to his salacious behavior, for her potential to make him a quick profit. Less than three weeks after the Robertsons married, Liss caused a "derangement in his family" and "his separation from Mrs. Robertson." For Alexander, there was a silver lining to the whole debacle; he could "turn her into money."[20] Liss was sold out of state, without her child, without warning, and without regard to the contract with Robert. She was quickly and quietly loaded on a ship, the *Lucretia*, bound for Charleston. The captain? None other than James Tinker.

The same day the *Lucretia* arrived in Charleston, the New York Manumission Society held its first meeting mere blocks from the dock where she had departed. Harry, who was not quite three, was left behind in the shattered household of Alexander Robertson, bewildered and inconsolable, without his mother or anyone who cared what had happened to her.

And for almost two years, no one said a word about Liss.

## Chapter Eight

# "A Townsman with a Cudgel"

THERE ARE SOME PEOPLE WHO FIND THEMSELVES PERPETUALLY AT odds with life. They are reckless with opportunities and trample on second chances; they survive by finding loopholes and slipping through the cracks; they see discord as entertainment and mercy as weakness. And then, finally, with prospects disappointed and hopes dashed, they rage that they never had a fair shot in the first place and that life was a deck stacked against them. Such a man was Richard Palmes.

Born around 1740 in New London, Connecticut, to Edward Palmes and his wife Lucretia, Richard grew up hearing stories of the greatness of his lineage and how the immense inheritance that should have been his was long ago unjustly stripped away by the courts.

In 1660, his grandfather, Major Edward Palmes, married Lucy, the daughter of Connecticut's first governor, John Winthrop Jr., whose own father, John Winthrop, had been the founding governor of the Massachusetts Bay Colony.[1] The Winthrop family landholdings were vast, and their wealth and influence in the colonies of both Connecticut and Massachusetts were immeasurable. But all the promise of such a fortunate marriage was lost when young Lucy died childless in 1667, just a few months after the death of her powerful father.[2] Described as a "disappointed and ambitious man," Major Palmes remarried but continued for decades to petition for his deceased first wife's share in the enormous Winthrop estate, even taking the case to the high courts of England, only to lose any inheritance rights in 1707 at the hands of his powerful brother-in-law, Fitz John Winthrop, then governor of Connecticut.

In the midst of this bitter entanglement, Major Palmes joined a group of "malcontents" and "enemies of Connecticut" who attempted "to take away her charter," arguing to the Crown that the colony had "unjustly deprived the Mohegans of their land." Their efforts sparked the so-called Mohegan Controversy of 1704, a drawn-out court battle that continued until 1823 and is considered the first legal case to rule on indigenous land rights. Early histories of Connecticut utterly rejected the notion of indigenous rights and instead describe Major Palmes as one of a cast of villainous schemers. As one such account from 1704 recounts,

> *Major Palmes, who had married the daughter of John Winthrop, Esq. the first governor of Connecticut, under the charter, had imagined himself injured by the administrators of the governor's estate, and had brought an action against them. Losing his case before the courts in this colony, he had appealed to England. He was particularly irritated against the colony, and against his brother-in-law, Fitz John Winthrop, Esq. then governor of the colony. These malcontents all united their influence, by the grossest misrepresentations, and all other means in their power, to injure the colony in its most essential interests.[3]*

By the time of Richard Palmes's birth, these distant stories of injustice had turned to legend, and his father, instead of enjoying vast properties, made his living by operating a humble New London inn.[4] This establishment became an official meeting place for debt collectors to confer with creditors; in many of these meetings, individuals would come to the inn to receive their share of a settlement after the debtor's estate had been liquidated by the courts.[5] Unfortunately, instead of gleaning important lessons about the pitfalls of insolvency, young Palmes seems to have picked up tips on how to better hide his own debts and evade collections—a habit that he practiced for most of his life.

In 1763, now in his early twenties, Palmes opened a mercantile and apothecary shop in his hometown, offering customers an assortment of pharmaceuticals, spices, and groceries, ranging from "Turlington's Balsam of Life" and "Hooper's Female Pills" to figs, mustard, chocolate, and "all kinds of surgical instruments."[6]

By May 1765 he had moved to Marlborough Street in Boston and opened a shop "Next Door to the Sign of the Fan." He married a woman named Mehitable, a member of the prestigious Lillie family, and now focused his business interests primarily on food, spices, "English Stone Delph and Glass Ware," and "a few drugs and medicines very cheap."[7] Mehitable and her brother Samuel, born only one year apart, had lost their father when they were just ten and eleven years old, followed by the death of their mother two years later. The orphans' inheritances were held in trust by legal guardians for over a decade, but in September 1765, the siblings had finally come of age and were set to receive their long-awaited shares of the Lillie estate.[8] Perhaps the old tales of the lost Winthrop fortune caused Richard Palmes to go on a spending spree, or maybe he had wildly over-spent in anticipation of Mehitable's windfall—but by the end of October, his bills had become seriously overdue, and his wife's newfound money was either gone or kept out of his hands. A local paper ran a notice that Robert Palmes had "absconded or [is] concealing himself" from paying his outstanding debts. In November, a published list of Boston "bankrupts" included his name. On December 6, 1765, while still in hiding, Palmes wrote a letter to Chief Justice Thomas Hutchinson that he was willing to surrender all his property,[9] and six months later, on June 12, 1766, an auc-tion of all of his personal effects was conducted to settle his debts, with the majority purchased by his wife's brother, Samuel. An auction advertisement indicates his tastes were far above the means of a young merchant, and the items sold may well have included his wife's family heirlooms, including "a handsome Eight Day Clock, a handsome Marble Slabb, Mahogany Tables, Black-walnut Chairs, large Looking Glasses, Cases of Draw[er]s, Cham-ber Tables, Bureau Tables, japann'd Tea-Tables, [and] Feather Beds, . . . a variety of China," brassware, pewter, and "all sorts of Kitchen furniture."[10]

A second auction was held in 1768, after which Mehitable no longer appears in any records bearing Palmes's name, indicating that they may have separated at some point. But Palmes barely had time to feel the sting of his first material loss before the city was thrown into crisis: British troops began to occupy Boston in October 1766, and hostilities and civil unrest grew.

The following August, Palmes's name shows up on the rolls of a boisterous group of political radicals known as the Sons of Liberty. The listing from the 1769 gathering of those who "dined at the Liberty Tree" in Dorchester also included Samuel Adams, John Adams, Paul Revere, and John Hancock.[11] Though history has come to view the "Sons" fondly, it is impossible to deny that their methods were sometimes violent by modern standards. They burned public figures in effigy and in at least one case tarred and feathered a British customs official. Boston's particularly active chapter of the Sons of Liberty torched the offices of Andrew Oliver, the administrator charged with enforcing the Stamp Act, destroyed and robbed the home of governor Thomas Hutchinson, and famously incited the so-called Boston Tea Party a few years later.

Palmes's most particular role as a revolutionary, however, was as the "townsman with a cudgel" at the Boston Massacre. Despite usually being portrayed in modern reenactments as an old, scraggly drunk, Palmes was actually in his late twenties, broad chested, and quite physically imposing; he doubtlessly swung his club-like stick with tremendous force. Several famous paintings of the massacre depict Palmes front and center with his weapon raised high.[12] One widely published version of the event gave a blow-by-blow account of the brute force of his assault on the British soldiers: "On this the Captain commanded his men to fire; and more snowballs coming, he again said, 'D[am]n you, fire, be the consequence what it will'—One soldier then fired; and a townsman, with a cudgel, struck him over the hands with such force, that he drop[ped] his firelock; and rushing forward, aimed a blow at the Captain's head; which grazed his hat, and fell pretty heavy upon his arm."[13] A 1771 editorial pointed out the severity of the captain's injury, noting that "the violent blow to Preston . . . wounded him so that he was under the doctor's hands for weeks."[14]

Although this account maintained that Palmes only wielded his club *after* the first shot was fired, another eyewitness account, given by an enslaved African American named Andrew, told a different story—one contending that Palmes, whom he called "a stout man," was the cause of the eruption of gunfire:

> *A stout man forced his way through [and] came up between me and the Grenadier. He had a stick in his hand. I saw him strike at the Officer. Persons were talking with him. I saw him [the Officer] dodge*

*and try to fend off the blow with his arm. He [Palmes] then began to strike on the Grenadiers Gun who stood about a yard and a half from the Officer on the right. I saw the Grenadier attempt to stick him with his Bayonet. He put it aside with his left hand, step'd in and gave a lick upon the Grenadiers neck or Shoulder with his Club. It was a cord Wood stick not very long. As he struck I turn'd about, looked at the Officer. There was a bustle. The stout man had still hold of the Bayonet. . . . While I was looking at the Captain the People crowded me on between the Soldiers, upon the Man's having the advantage of the Grenadier, crying "kill 'em, kill 'em, knock 'em over." . . . They rush'd back very quick making a great noise or screeching huzzaing and bid the Soldiers "fire damn you, you dare not fire." I jump'd back and heard a voise [sic] cry "fire" and immediately the first Gun fired.*[15]

Ironically, given his political associations, Palmes proved one of the key witnesses in acquitting the British soldiers. To conduct the defense, the Crown hired prominent Boston attorney and ardent Patriot John Adams, who questioned dozens of witnesses and participants. Palmes, who was acquainted with Adams through the Sons of Liberty, admitted to throwing the first blow in the hand-to-hand melee that erupted and confirmed the soldiers' story: the assembled mob had thrown snowballs, ice, and other objects at the armed men, taunting them to shoot, before someone—possibly an American member of the crowd and not the British officer in charge of the troops—had shouted, "Fire!"[16]

Following the Boston Massacre in March 1770, Palmes was involved in a series of court actions, the first in 1771 when he accused the sheriff of Suffolk County, Massachusetts, of unlawful imprisonment, claiming that the previous August, Sheriff Steven Greenleaf "without any lawfull Cause did assault, arrest, and imprison the said Richard, and without any lawfull Cause or Warrant did there hold and keep the said Richard in Prison and in his Custody." In the first trial, Palmes's attorney was Boston's celebrated lawyer and pamphleteer James Otis, famous for having first stated "Taxation without representation is tyranny." When this case was lost, Palmes took it to superior court, and this time his counsel was none other than John Adams, who wrote in his "Pleadings Book" that the arrest arose as a backlash against Palmes's status as a witness in the Boston Massacre trials. With the assistance of attorney Josiah Quincy, Adams convinced a jury of Palmes's innocence.[17]

Palmes's propensity for unchecked violence got the better of him again two years later, when he issued a public apology on March 15, 1773, to another deputy sheriff of Boston, named Joseph Otis Jr., brother of his original attorney. Though the circumstances of Palmes's attack on Sheriff Otis are unclear, his apology admits that he beat the deputy and acknowledges that he committed the act in a state of uncontrollable rage:

> *Whereas I the Subscriber, being in a Passion, did oppose, beat, and otherways ill-treat Mr. Joseph Otis, jun, of Boston, Deputy-Sheriff, when in the Executive of his Office (which I am sensible was a great violation of the Laws of this Province, which Laws I ever desire to be governed by,) and am sorry for so doing; and ask his Forgiveness in this public Manner.*
> *R. Palmes*[18]

Palmes's third brush with the law in 1771 arose not from his temper but from his other bad habit: refusing to pay his bills. A local doctor and fellow member of the Sons of Liberty named Joseph Warren had rented a small house in an area called New Boston to Palmes, who had failed to pay his rent for eighteen months. The doctor sued him for the back rent and legal costs, winning the case in February 1773.[19] Just two years later, while serving as president of the Massachusetts Provincial Congress, Warren dispatched Paul Revere and William Dawes on their midnight ride to warn that "the British are coming," and on June 17, 1775, having attained the rank of Major General, he died heroically at the Battle of Bunker Hill.

As the war began, Palmes made use of his reputation as a strongman, as well as his long acquaintance with John Adams and a recommendation from John Hancock, to obtain a commission from the Continental Congress as a captain of the Marines on July 23, 1776, at which point he began his rather colorful military career.

The Continental Marines, a corps formed in 1775, served as security forces on naval vessels with a primary duty of guarding the ships' officers. Palmes's first post was aboard the frigate *Boston*, commanded by Captain Hector McNeill, but almost immediately Palmes's temper landed him in trouble.[20] Following the capture of two enemy vessels and the blockading of the *Boston* by the British in 1777, he ran afoul of the captain, who claimed an impudent Palmes had repeatedly disobeyed orders and even destroyed his own naval commission by "casting it into the fire."[20] On August 10, McNeill sent a formal letter of complaint to Palmes, announcing, "Your unofficer like behavior and repeated breach of my orders obliges me to confine you to your birth [*sic*]."[21]

With that he placed Palmes under arrest on charges eventually defined as "misapplication of the Ship Stores, Neglect of duty, disobedience of orders, and attempts to Excite Murmuring and Mutiny among the Ships Company."[22] Given that another primary role of the marines aboard any naval vessel was to subdue a mutiny, these charges were especially egregious. It did not help Palmes's case that McNeill apparently fostered a deep personal disdain for him, noting, "You may thank your own folly and impertinence for what has now befallen you. I despise your insinuations of Cruelty, as indeed I do Everything Else you can say of me consistent with truth. You may go to the house of the Office as often as Nature calls, provided you return immediately to your berth and keep your Tongue Still as you pass and repass." McNeill also recommended Palmes, whom he called a "frothy Fool and Knave," for court-martial.[23]

In November, Palmes found himself in front of two members of the Eastern Naval Board and, after presenting his own version of events, rather fortuitously found the charges against him dropped. Commander McNeill protested that the decision would destroy the chain of command, arguing, "If precedents of this kind be permitted once to take place, farewell discipline and good Order, farewell Honor, and honesty. The Service will then become a receptacle for unclean birds."[24]

However, McNeill was notoriously unpopular and currently faced charges on his own of withholding from his officers their portions of the financial prizes the *Boston* had earned in its maritime capture of several

British vessels. Palmes was reassigned to a different ship for a time, while McNeill was relieved of duty.

In early 1778, Palmes rejoined the crew of the *Boston* under its new commander, naval captain Samuel Tucker, and soon found himself reunited with an old friend who singled him out for a special assignment. On February 13, John Adams and his eleven-year-old son, John Quincy Adams, boarded the vessel that was to take them to France, where the elder Adams was to assume diplomatic duties alongside Benjamin Franklin, with Richard Palmes assigned as their bodyguard. Just four days after the *Boston* pushed into the open Atlantic, they encountered a fierce nor'easter, a three-day blow that battered the ship severely. Three weeks later, on March 11, the *Boston* saw more action when it engaged in a firefight with the fourteen-gun British ship *Martha*, bound for New York. Under strict orders to protect his distinguished passengers by any means necessary, Captain Tucker was dismayed when John Adams suddenly appeared on deck in the middle of the battle, wielding a gun hastily entrusted to him by Palmes, who would have had responsibility for all the firearms aboard the ship. Nevertheless, the battle ended quickly, the *Martha* was subdued, and Adams had a story of bravery in combat that he would trot out nearly two decades later when he was running for president.

The *Boston* dropped anchor at Bordeaux on April 1, and Palmes joined Adams and his son as they traveled to Paris and acclimated there. It was during this time that Solomon Townsend also arrived in Paris and made his petition for a certification of loyalty to Franklin.

While ashore, Palmes recruited a number of French marines to help fill out the *Boston*'s severely understaffed rolls, but there was such a clash of personalities that all twenty-four French marines and twenty-three French sailors who had signed on left the vessel just a few weeks later. As Captain Tucker prepared to depart, Benjamin Franklin and John Adams trusted Palmes to deliver their important correspondence, writing, "We have dispatched Captain Palmes [with] your orders for your future government," urging Captain Tucker to "take particular care that these orders may not, in case of misfortune,—which God forbid,—fall into the hands of the enemy."

When the *Boston* finally set out for America, it did so with a depleted crew, but sailing in convoy with Solomon's ship, the *Providence*, the small fleet arrived safely back on American shores in late October.[25]

Palmes then moved to another ship, the *Warren*, in early 1779, but despite Adams's mentorship of the young man, his impetuous habits seem to have resurfaced. Naval records indicate that later that spring Palmes went absent without leave and was charged with having "left his duty at a critical time without the leave and against the judgment" of a superior. He was again recommended for court-martial and again seems to have escaped it on a technicality. In November, he was back aboard the *Boston*, headed south to the Carolinas, but the ship was captured the following spring during the Siege of Charleston, and Palmes was held as a prisoner of war for two months before being freed in a prisoner exchange. He continued to serve aboard various American vessels through the end of the war, apparently finding his calling more among the rough-and-ready Continental Marines than in the staid, sedentary life of an apothecary.[26]

Whether he grew accustomed to South Carolina's warmer climate during his imprisonment, or viewed the colony as a place to start over fresh, where no one knew his reputation as a borderline scofflaw and bankrupt thug, or just became one of thousands of northerners who settled in the South after the war due to the near economic meltdown of the financial system, Palmes remained in Charleston. By 1785, he had settled on an estate on the outskirts of the city and proceeded almost immediately to once again land himself in significant debt, outfitting his home lavishly.[27]

But mahogany chairs and billiard tables were not the only luxuries with which Palmes sought to adorn his home. As he pressed his petition with the United States Navy to pay him a greater share of the war prizes from foreign vessels captured during the war,[28] Palmes also splurged on at least one indulgence that lay just a bit out of his financial reach.

~◆~

The firm of Parker, Hopkins, and McLane was just one of many in New York that functioned as a kind of clearinghouse for imported goods. Much like the auction house of Templeton & Stewart, Robert

Townsend's former employer, the firm of Parker, Hopkins, and McLane, sold an ever-changing array of home goods, delicacies, and other sundries imported from other colonies and far-flung countries. A newly established mercantile, they advertised heavily in the city's papers: "They are now ready to receive and sell on commission, all kinds of goods, wares, merchandise, and effects whatever, either by private sale or public venue. They will negotiate all sorts of public securities, and perform everything appertaining to the business of Auctioneers and Brokers, with dispatch and punctuality, and on the lowest terms. Their auction room is completely fitted for the business and is known to be one of the best stands in the city."[29]

Interested sellers were instructed to bring their wares at least one day in advance for the sake of determining the quantity and quality of the items being offered. Business seems to have taken off quickly for the firm; not even three weeks after its initial posting, it was conducting wholesale auctions on site, such as the one to be held at 12:30 p.m. on April 24, 1784, which included "a large quantity of best English Cheese; Forty-eight bottles best Ketchup; forty-eight ditto best anchovies, forty-eight ditto best Sallad [*sic*] Oil; one chest Bohea Tea; a few crates Earthen Ware; and a large quantity of excellent pickled Tripe."[30]

Within a year, however, the partnership dissolved, with Hopkins and McLane joining the stream of businesses shifting southward, while Parker remained situated in New York.[31] In fact, in January 1785, Mr. Hopkins himself sailed for Charleston on the brig *Lucretia*, captained by the notorious James Tinker, alongside a large shipment of household goods he intended to take to market as he and McLane reestablished themselves in their new city. Among the barrels of cherry rum, ship's bread, Burlington hams, hyson tea, and "double refined loaf sugar" was Liss.[32]

Hopkins and McLane, while not direct importers of slaves from the coast of Africa, had no qualms as to the goods that passed through their warehouse, so they (like so many other businesses at the time) didn't bat an eye when approached by a man named Alexander Shirras to help facilitate the sale and transfer of a young "negro wench" to South Carolina. A prolific merchant who also dabbled not only in trading African and African American people but also in bounty hunting for runaways, Shirras cut a no-nonsense figure in the world of Charleston's merchant class. A June 24, 1785, advertisement Shirras ran for a runaway slave woman named Sally described her as "a short wench, from the Gulla country, about 24 years of age, speaks tolerably good English, pronouncing it rather slow; had on when she went away a wrap[p]er and petticoat of lincey—brown, white and orange stripe." He included a somewhat ominous postscript: "A further reward of Five Guineas will be paid to any person who will bring proof of her being harboured by a white person, mulatto, or free negro, and Three Guineas if by a slave."[33]

It was through Alexander Shirras that Alexander Robertson arranged for the swift sale of Liss, with Hopkins and McLane escorting her 750 miles to her new master, Richard Palmes.[34] The curious point, however, is why Palmes would have gone through the immense trouble of importing a slave from New York when he could have had his pick of any of the dozens of housekeepers who came up for sale in the massive Charleston slave market each day. No records indicate that he knew Robertson to make a personal arrangement for the easy sale of a slave from one friend to another. No extant advertisements describe the sale of Liss or what price any of the managing parties attached to her. The only certain facts are that (1) Liss was quickly and quietly put up for sale by Alexander Robertson within a month of his marriage, in breech of Ann's contract with Robert Townsend; (2) Richard Palmes was attempting to create for himself a rich man's estate appointed with the finest furnishings available; and (3) Liss's asking price was more than Palmes could afford to pay outright. He applied for and was granted a £50 mortgage, which was held in Manhattan by Shirras, to complete his purchase. Whatever it was about Liss that made Palmes go through all the extra effort and expense of securing a loan and shipping her to Charleston, he clearly wanted to purchase her badly.

Absent personal journals or detailed records, there is no way to know for certain why Liss held such a strong attraction for Palmes, especially since he had likely never laid eyes on her before she arrived in Charleston. Given that she was approximately twenty-two or twenty-three years old, however, and is not noted elsewhere as having an extraordinary skill in cooking or sewing, it is not unreasonable to suppose that she may have been an especially beautiful young woman, and Palmes was certainly seeking out lovely accessories at this same time to help outfit his home. It was quite common for people in search of slaves with a specific skillset to reach out to a trader they knew to be on the lookout for an enslaved person who might meet that need, and Palmes may have contacted an agent directly—be it Hopkins or McLane, Shirras, or even Captain Tinker—to secure for him a young, attractive house slave.

Further evidence to support this view is the fact that Liss was sold without Harry. As common as the barbaric practice of separating families was, such enforced divisions were actually not the norm for mothers of children under the age of four. It was certainly not unheard of, but young children—even those intended to work the fields someday—required basic care. Selling a mother separate from her baby or toddler necessitated finding some other custody arrangement for the child, so, more often than not, mothers with children were sold as a unit if the child was too young to learn a useful domestic, trade, or agricultural skill. The purchaser would then have the benefit of an able adult worker, plus the promise of another one learning alongside the parent. That child would then become a much more valuable asset either as a worker or as a trained commodity to be sold separately when older. The fact that Alexander Robertson kept Harry and only sold Liss indicates that she was marketed as more than just a typical servant whose sole job would be to focus on running a household.

As for Liss, the journey was doubtlessly terrifying. She had already fought to stay in New York once rather than evacuating to Canada with her British master, so to be forcibly removed three and a half years later, after believing herself safe, may have led to feelings of tremendous fear and great betrayal by Robert Townsend.

The *Lucretia* docked in Charleston on January 25, 1785, after a voyage of approximately four days.[35] But Liss was not immediately handed off to Palmes; instead, she was held for an additional eight days, perhaps because Palmes was unavailable to claim her or maybe for quarantine on Sullivan's Island, though those "pest houses" were more commonly used for ships arriving from international destinations like Ireland, the Caribbean, and West Africa. There is no indication that the white passengers aboard the *Lucretia* were detained upon arrival, so there was no concern about smallpox or yellow fever aboard; instead, Liss was possibly treated simply as another piece of cargo that needed to be registered, inventoried, and stored until arrangements could be made for her retrieval. Unlike George Morris, who had been kidnapped by Tinker and begged a sympathetic Richard Lushington to help retrieve his freedom papers while he awaited sale at auction, Liss had no recourse. She had been legally sold, purchased, and transported to a new state. Where she slept and what she ate during this eight-day holding period are not recorded; we know for certain only that on February 2, 1785, she was handed over to the custody of Captain Richard Palmes and became his legal property, in the eyes of South Carolina and the United States, to dispose of as he saw fit.

Undated photograph (with damage) of a 1772 portrait painting of Captain Solomon Townsend. The painting was commissioned in Lisbon, Portugal, when Solomon was twenty-six years old and is now held in a private collection. COLLECTION OF THE FRIENDS OF RAYNHAM HALL MUSEUM

Portrait of Solomon Townsend, 1808, by Ezra Ames (American, 1768–1836), oil on canvas COLLECTION OF THE FRIENDS OF RAYNHAM HALL MUSEUM

The *Holy Bible Containing the Old and New Testaments* (Edinburgh, Scotland: Alexander Kincaid, 1771). Originally owned by the family of Samuel Townsend, the Bible was passed down to Howard Townsend, MD, of Albany, his great-grandson, and acquired by the Friends of Raynham Hall Museum in 2004. The Bible was used to record the births and deaths of some of the enslaved persons owned by the family from 1769 to 1795 and includes the names of seventeen individuals.
COLLECTION OF THE FRIENDS OF RAYNHAM HALL MUSEUM

Sketch of the Townsend homestead, now known as Raynham Hall, c. 1840, by Benson J. Lossing, for his *Pictorial Field Book of the Revolution*, published in 1850 COLLECTION OF THE FRIENDS OF RAYNHAM HALL MUSEUM

Miniature of Adam Gilchrist, c. 1785, attributed to John
Ramage (Irish-American, 1748–1802), watercolor on
ivory IMAGE COURTESY OF THE GIBBES MUSEUM OF ART/CARO-
LINA ART ASSOCIATION

the officers not much anxious for it &c &c — I
think there is no probability of your
attention again — believe you may return
and amongst your other dear ones — I am
happy that Coll: James would himself
for to go — he certainly must have known
it when they left Boston Bay — I am

Dear Sir,
Your affectionate

Robt: Jenkins

Letter, Robert Townsend to Samuel Townsend, May 26, 1779. This letter from Robert Townsend to his father, Samuel, reveals a startling fact: a young enslaved woman named Liss had escaped with Lieutenant Colonel John Graves Simcoe and his British regiment, the Queen's Rangers, as they departed Oyster Bay. COLLECTION OF THE FRIENDS OF RAYNHAM HALL MUSEUM

The only known likeness of Robert Townsend was sketched by his nephew Dr. Peter Townsend in 1813, when Robert was sixty years old, and is pasted into Peter's sketchbook. COLLECTION OF THE FRIENDS OF RAYNHAM HALL MUSEUM

## CHAPTER NINE

# "Derangement and Separation"

ROBERT TOWNSEND SIGNED HIS NAME WITH A FLOURISH, NOT OUT OF any artistic impulse but from the surge of emotions that he had not fully expended in the bitter words of his letter. The fact was, the family was owed money—a lot of money—and while the war may have signaled a new beginning for many things, it certainly did not mean that every debtor started over with a clean slate. This letter—just the latest in a series of missives to individuals and businesses whose accounts were in arrears—would be sent by the next ship to North Carolina.

With Solomon too focused on his growing iron empire, it had fallen to Robert to shoulder the responsibility to revive overdue accounts and pursue old debts that had built up during the tumultuous years of the Revolution. Looking back, Robert admittedly had lost sight of his own best interests during the war, spending countless hours gathering intelligence, composing coded letters, and traveling miles from the city on horseback to hand off his secret correspondence, all the while putting his faith in a business partner who he realized too late was an outright thief. It was not uncommon for unscrupulous people to take advantage of wartime chaos to broker shady deals, skim profits, or dodge debts, and Robert had the unfortunate luck to have been briefly aligned with one such figure. He had only begun the partnership in 1779 with Henry Oakman because of his new commitment to lead the New York City intelligence operation as "Culper, Jr." He needed someone to run the store's day-to-day operations and cover his many unexplained absences, and Oakman came with a strong recommendation from Robert's old boss, Oliver

Templeton, who claimed he was "a very good man." However, over the next year and a half, as Robert stood guard in his red coat, dodged British sentries, and waited in the dark for midnight meetings with Woodhull, his partner managed to steal profits left and right. The most egregious example involved using Robert's money to buy a vessel while he was on Long Island, only to sell the boat for a large profit and pocket the proceeds. As Robert's misgivings about Oakman grew, he asked around only to find he was not the first partner to be cheated by him. He noted afterward, "I then was fully convinced of what I just before began to have some suspicions of, that he meant to take advantage of me, and I likewise had warning from a person who had heard of some of his transactions with another person. I inquired of this person and found that he had taken an ungenerous advantage of him. I now conceived it high time to endeavor to sever myself."[1]

Thus, Robert's fortunes, which were already negatively impacted by the war, along with just about everyone else's, suffered a double blow. Even the long partnership of Templeton & Stewart, where Robert had first apprenticed, was torn apart by the end the war. Thomas Stewart, like so many others, had relocated to Charleston, and in a 1784 letter, Robert reported to him on Templeton's struggles: "Mr. Templeton left this [New York] for Nova Scotia; I have received letters from him dated in August in which he informs me he has no prospect of recovering any money from those who owe him, and that he shall return to this place in a short time."[2] Like those of Oliver Templeton and so many others, the Townsend family fortunes had taken a sharp turn for the worse, and Robert did not want his to be the generation that saw the family fall into ruin.

Beyond the challenge of unscrupulous individuals, however, merchants like Robert faced an uphill climb to rebuild their livelihoods. Business was down for a dozen different reasons. First, there was the flood of refugees who had come to the city from the ravaged countryside, followed by the mass evacuations of British troops and Loyalist families from New York. While it may seem at first blush that the one crisis could balance out the other, this was hardly the case. People fleeing for their lives rarely had extra capital to spend on the kinds of modest but nonessential goods Robert generally stocked, and the number of people liquidating their furnishings and household contents before they followed the Crown to friendlier territories glutted the market anyway. There was also the additional insult that trade with the British-held territories of Canada and the Caribbean, the closest international trading partners, had been shut off to the Americans following the war in a retaliatory act. And, of course, the fact that inflation was rampant and much of the rest of the world considered American currency barely better than printed scraps presented additional challenges for merchants and financiers alike.

The truth was, the years immediately following the Revolution were a time of tremendous instability for nearly everyone in the fledgling nation. Both in civic and commercial sectors, chaos bubbled just below the surface as each state tried to cobble together its own version of a republic while also healing from the deep physical and economic wounds of war. And Robert, like countless other business owners, was exhausting himself trying to recoup his losses as best he could, even if it meant going after debts that were a dozen years old. It was not work he particularly relished, but he regarded it as highly necessary. To him, the matter was as much moral as it was financial; honorable people reconciled their debts. That was simply the way the world ought to work, social niceties be damned.

For this reason Robert had recently taken to poring over the family's old financial records in an effort to identify those who still owed money on past deals, including one rather significant account established way back in 1773, when his brother, Samuel Jr., was still alive and working for the family in Wilmington, North Carolina. When Robert took over the operations for Samuel Jr., he managed the relationship with Ancrum, Forster, and Brice, which sold a small fortune's worth of flaxseed, tobacco, tar, and rum for the Townsends.[3]

As the war began just a few years later, many who had kept their political feelings separate from their professional concerns found that they could no longer continue "business as usual." This was especially true for Ancrum, Forster, and Brice, as the partners were split politically; John Ancrum was an ardent Patriot serving on his local Committee of Safety, and John Forster was also described as "a warm friend to American liberty," while Francis Brice broke in the opposite direction and followed the Loyalist cause.

In an April 10, 1776, letter to Robert, the firm explained, "We knew not when we should be under a necessity of quitting town, which we have been obliged to do about eight weeks ago." Prior to fleeing the city, they had liquidated most the Townsend's goods on credit "as the times would not admit a circulation of cash," and the rest had been packed up and "stored in the Country, so that we have not had the opportunity of disposing of a single article."[4] In July 1777, John Forster was killed while serving as an American commissary, and in September 1779 John Ancrum also died at the hands of the British, after the sacking and destruction of his plantation. Francis Brice, the lone British sympathizer of the trio, survived the conflict.[5]

In 1784, when Robert wrote Thomas Stewart about Templeton's financial troubles, he also enlisted his old friend to put him in contact with a Charleston lawyer named Henry Toomer, who served on a Wilmington commission handling disputes between merchants and debtors. Thus began a chain of increasingly scathing letters spanning the next fifteen years, as Toomer chased after the outstanding debts of Ancrum, Forster, and Brice. Insisting first on full repayment plus interest, Robert pursued the case with an almost manic sense of outrage.[6] Francis Brice, no matter his genuine desire to pay back whatever he could, was in a difficult position. The firm had long since dissolved, the credits given for goods a decade ago had been hopelessly lost in the tumult of war, and any stores of hidden goods in the countryside of North Carolina had long since been pillaged. Brice faced a further challenge in the fact that he had sided with the Loyalists during the conflict, now making him persona non grata in local business. As to the subject of being charged interest, Brice argued that he could not "think of allowing Townsend interest during the war, as it was impossible that remittances could be made to Townsend within the British lines."

Robert retorted, "If my being within the British lines is the only reason for not allowing interest, and if Mr. Brice, or any others concerned in the estate of Ancrum, Forster & Brice, should offer that as the only reason for not allowing interest, I shall not think it sufficient."[7]

Robert eventually relented on the interest, pursuing instead repayment of the capital and, finally, whatever he could recover. On May 5,

1785, he recorded in his ledger receipt of a bond for just over £285, which Brice promised to pay within one year's time.[8] This small victory was short-lived, as Toomer soon sent word that Francis Brice had skipped town and fled to Montego Bay, Jamaica, and that "his affairs are much confused in this place."

Robert felt himself ill-used by both Brice and Toomer as well as a handful of other debtors and legal experts. The complaints against lawyers that fill Robert's personal notes from this time reveal his increasing frustration with the solicitors on whom he relied to work as his proxy in most collection issues. He seems to have held a special fondness for the anonymous essayist "Junius," who frequently contributed letters to New York newspapers as early as 1769. Robert copied out several of Junius's scathing remarks regarding lawyers and sometimes even entire articles. "Subtlety is soon mistaken for wisdom, and impunity for virtue," one piece insisted as it artfully attacked the character of the legal profession. Robert seems to have fully embraced such a view, carefully replicating it in his own writing and storing it alongside the various replies from lawyers as to why one client or another's payment was forestalled again.[9]

Discord was also brewing within the family itself. As the financial struggles continued to plague everyone, a business dispute arose among the Townsend relatives regarding the sale of certain certificates or bonds. Robert's cousin John, the flour merchant with whom he used to share a house, had racked up an enormous debt, now owing several thousand dollars to the family. Robert wrote a scathing letter to his failed cousin for recovery of the loss.

John was unapologetic for his financial reverses and insinuated that his old housemate had treated him quite unfairly. "I received your [letter] of the 5th: inst., and observe with surprise, its contents," John opened. "Whatever your reasons for writing such a Letter may be, the suspicions hinted in it have hurt my feelings most sensibly, and though I should be justified in taking no notice of it, I will still answer it to the best of my recollection." After laying out the conditions of the sale of the certificates or bonds, he closed the message by remarking, "What circumstance . . . has justified you (as you say) in writing me such a Letter, I should be glad to know."[10]

Though his indignation may have been righteous, there was no denying that across Robert's letter-writing campaign and debt-recovery efforts, his personality seems to have undergone a rather dramatic shift. Never as concerned with the rules of proper society as Solomon nor as jovial as William, Robert had grown even more reticent. He became withdrawn and appears to have struggled with bouts of deep depression to such a degree that they strained quite a few personal relationships. As he withdrew from his business partnership with his older brother, Solomon hardly noticed as he was now more interested in growing his fledgling iron business. Having worked for the Sterling Forge for the last five years of the war, in 1783 Solomon built his own forge nearby, called Augusta, and purchased large tracts of the surrounding forest, eventually owning over thirteen thousand acres. Solomon then opened an "iron-mongery shop" on Queen's Street in New York and focused his energy on the enormous responsibility of running Augusta's industrial complex, which included a blast furnace, forge, smithy, anchor shop, gristmill, saw-mill, and carpenter's shop.

As Solomon became less and less attentive in their shared ventures, Robert had more on his mind than just troubling business prospects and collecting on old accounts; he found himself pondering the challenges brought on by intimate connections that weigh on a man's soul when he feels too much on behalf of others. An essay he took pains to carefully copy out, titled "On the Advantages and Inconveniences of a Retired Life," reflects, "In proportion to the alliances which he forms with a great number of persons who thereby become dear to him, as their vexations give him concern, their pains torment him, and their sorrows oppress him." The essay muses that as long as people are involved in any kind of engagement with other people, they "are always obliged to participate in what affects them, and their affections rebound partly upon ourselves."[11]

It was while he brooded in this state of mind that Robert first heard the rumors that Alexander Robertson had moved his family back to the neighborhood.

The marriage of Alexander Robertson and Ann Sharwin leaves little evidence that it was a happy one or that it lasted long at all. Her name appears next to his in no records besides their marriage announcement,[12] and later writings by family neglect to mention her altogether except to note that Robertson, apparently an eventual powerhouse in the linen trade, took a "third wife" named Janet upon a trip to his native Scotland some years later—an indirect acknowledgment that there had also been a second wife at some point. It may be that Ann suffered a fate similar to that of the noted third wife, as a grandson recalled, "After they had been home a little while, he found that the bride had pinched . . . his youngest and favorite daughter, so he rose in his wrath and shipped her back to Scotland, and she was heard of no more!"[13] If Robertson was not above casting off a wife who displeased him for upsetting a favorite child, it would certainly not be out of character for him to behave similarly with a wife with whom he had experienced "derangement" and "separation" less than a month after their wedding. In fact, the only remnant of his marriage to Ann appears in a July 1785 advertisement for Alexander Robertson & Co. After listing scores of fancy fabrics, such as "Marcelles quilting with borders" and "ribbons and sewing silks," he offered "a large and choice selection of Saddlery, which will be disposed of much under prime cost."[14] Clearly, he was trying to unload the last of the inventory his new wife still possessed from her late husband's saddlery business.

A year later, Robertson resettled his substantial household at 52 Smith Street, quite near to Robert's home in Peck Slip,[15] and Robert soon roused himself from his melancholy to make inquiries about Liss and Harry, whom he had not seen in nearly two years. What he learned snapped him out of whatever gloom had settled upon him in the intervening months and sent him into a fiery rage.

The confrontation between Robert and Robertson was anything but cordial. Robert demanded an explanation as to Liss's absence, and Robertson lamely replied simply that his wife "did not like her." But Robert refused to accept this explanation, insisting that Ann had never expressed any displeasure with Liss when their household consisted only of the two women and Harry. The linen merchant explained the sale in simple terms: Liss was the source of tension in the Robertson household, and the shrewd businessman saw an opportunity to make a handsome profit. "It was principally owing to some derangement in his family occasioned by his separation from Mrs. Robertson," Robert wrote, "and to turn her into money at a great price." With Ann not present for this altercation—she may already have been permanently estranged—Robert had no one to verify the terms of Liss's original sale. (That did not excuse Ann from culpability, however; as a widow, she legally had the rights of a "dower," meaning that any property she brought into a subsequent marriage remained her own rather than automatically transferring to her new husband. Had she wished to stop Robertson's sale of Liss, she would have been well within her legal rights to do so.) Robertson further insisted that he had no knowledge of any preexisting contract between his wife and Townsend regarding Robert's right to purchase Liss back should Ann ever seek to sell her, and it was too late anyway. Liss was no longer in New York, and no amount of railing about breached contracts could bring her back.

Robert grilled Robertson for every available detail regarding the circumstances of the deal, carefully recording names, dates, and places so that he could immediately set about the apparent fool's errand of trying to track down a single woman of color shipped to Charleston two years prior. The sale itself, finalized on February 2, 1785, was to one Captain Richard Palmes, living in the vicinity of Charleston. The man who held the bond in New York was named Alexander Shirras, and a pair of merchants named Hopkins and McLane had executed the transaction and been responsible for physically transporting Liss. Had he known that the notorious Captain Tinker, whose horrific crimes he had followed through the efforts of the New York Manumission Society (NYMS), had captained the vessel Liss was transported in, Robert might have lost all composure.

He did take one other step, a dramatic gesture that the linen merchant could have sued him for, had he wished to press charges. Robert immediately—and without apology or payment—removed Harry from the Robertson home. Exactly how he would care for a four-year-old does not seem to have occurred to Robert in the moment. He simply seized the motherless child and departed before Robertson could do the boy any more harm.[16]

"In what manner soever we adhere to those we are related," Robert had copied out, "our tranquility depends partly on theirs." So, it seems, did Robert Townsend feel the great burden of all the pain to which he had unwittingly been a party—both by his active involvement in selling Liss and Harry in the first place and by his subsequent absence from their lives. He had spent the last two years attending meetings in hopes of bringing an end to slavery, but he had failed to watch over the very people he sought to help—the people who depended on him the most.

The Townsends of Oyster Bay, who were celebrating Samuel's election to yet another term in the New York State Senate in January 1787,[17] were probably not adequately prepared for Robert's surprise visit to the family homestead, bringing with him a "mulatto" child from the city. Any whispers about William's ignominious return a few years earlier were certainly eclipsed by whatever the local wagging tongues made of serious, sober-minded Robert's sudden appearance with a biracial child he treated with special concern and care.

Harry, for his part, must have been traumatized not only by the separation from his mother two years prior but by now being plucked abruptly from the only home he could remember and being carried by a strange white man to a small village far removed from the noise and busy streets of Manhattan. Nevertheless, this was to be his home now, and the boy was folded into the Townsend household, most likely under the care of Liss's sister, Hannah, who was herself six months pregnant.

If Robert had kept the goings-on at Bachelor's Hall with Liss and the birth of Harry a secret from his parents, everything was now laid bare. Their son was not just failing in business and stubbornly refusing to marry; he had given his good name to his brother William's illegitimate son and was now bringing home a light-skinned slave boy, raving that the mother—gone from their house for seven years—must be brought back to New York immediately.

After ensuring Harry's adjustment to his new life and returning to the city, Robert focused on the extraordinary task of tracking down Liss and bringing her home to Oyster Bay, but he would need to enlist the help of his brother Solomon, whose iron business had established many accounts in the Charleston area. No matter how disapproving his older brother would be, he had to explain the whole ugly and complicated affair and convince him to help find and rescue Liss posthaste.

The first order of business was identifying a contact in Charleston whom they trusted well enough to carry out the rather delicate business. Given the possible challenge of seeking out a slave sold under questionable circumstances, as well as Robert's current opinion of lawyers, it makes sense that the brothers chose, among their numerous business connections, a Charleston firm Solomon had engaged to sell his anchors and that included Richard Lushington, well known to Robert through the NYMS. In fact, Lushington may have been an automatic choice, given his role in freeing George Morris and returning him to New York the previous year. There was another point in favor of employing Lushington for this purpose as well. His business partner, John Kirk Jr., was from a well-respected Long Island family and was also an acquaintance of the Townsends. In fact, John's father was one of the men arrested alongside Samuel Townsend in September 1776.

With this trusted pair enlisted for the task, Robert felt confident that the matter would be carried out with the utmost care for Liss's well-being. He was understandably wary of third-party brokers at this point, given Alexander Robertson's shady dealings, but two men who held staunch abolitionist views and who were known personally to his family seemed the ideal proxies in a far-from-ideal situation.

The second matter Solomon and Robert needed to resolve was not quite so straight-forward as selecting the agents, however: namely, they needed to find the means by which to make the substantial purchase and to cover the transportation of Liss back north. It was here that their past business dealings with the firm of Lushington & Kirk became essential. The Townsends owned a schooner named the *Sally* (a different ship from their larger brig of the same name), and in 1785, while being captained by James Farley, the schooner had suffered severe damage in a hurricane off the coast of Barbados.[18] Limping home, the boat had been made seaworthy, but the family had decided to put the vessel up for sale.

No buyer having been found in the New York market, in 1786 she was sailed to Charleston with a load of lumber, captained by a man named Ebenezer Gilbert.[19, 20] Lushington and Kirk offered the schooner for sale on behalf of the Townsends. Gilbert, along with two other men named Wentworth and Elderkin, who had also served at one time as captains of the *Sally*,[21] signed a bond promising to purchase the vessel as a group.[22] However, an entire year had passed with no money forthcoming. The rebuilt vessel, "burthen about twenty Tons, built with good materials, eighteen months old," was currently moored at Cochran's Wharf in Charleston.[23]

The Townsends quickly composed a letter to Lushington and Kirk on January 17, 1787, requesting that the promised money for the *Sally* be used to repurchase Elizabeth from Richard Palmes. They evidently anticipated that the transaction would be carried out quickly—that Palmes would be easy to locate, that he would be willing to let Liss go, and that the long-awaited money for the ship would be obtained from the three captains. Robert was so confident of the matter's being resolved before spring that he included a touching request for new clothing items for Liss to make her comfortable as she traveled north and sought to assure Lushington and Kirk that this transaction was rooted in the most unobjectionable of intentions, with no eye toward making a profit or mistreating Liss. In the final line of the letter, Solomon and Robert took pains to stress that this was to be treated not as a mere business transaction but as "an act of justice."

*New York, Jany.17th:1787*

*Messrs Lushington & Kirk,*
*Gentlemen,*
*We are now to request the favor of you to purchase a Wench, named Elizabeth, sent from this place by Alex. Robertson, and sold by Hopkins & M'Clane, the 2d of Feb'y 1785 to Capt'n Rich'd Palms [sic] of your place state, and send her to us yr first good opportunity. If you are not acquainted with Capt'n Palms [sic] you can be informed of him*

*by applying to Alex. Shirras & Co. of your place, who have a bond for the amount of what the Wench sold for. This Wench was brought up in our father's family and sold for no material fault but that of being too fond of the British officers. The person she was first sold to being about to leave this state on the evacuation by the British, and she not willing to go with him, apply'd to our R. T. to repurchase her, which he did with a child which she had while with her then master.*

*Mrs. Sharwin, since Mrs. Robertson, knowing the Wench, apply'd to purchase her, and she being willing to live with her, he sold her with the child and particularly stipulated that whenever Mrs. Sharwin should incline to sell her, he would, rather than she should be sold to a place she should not like or sent out of the State, take her again and return the amount of what he sold her for. From this time he never understood but the mistress and wench were perfectly satisfied with each other, nor did he know that she was sent to Carolina till sometime after she was sent. He has inquired of Mr. Robertson the reason of her being sent, and he could give none but that Mrs. Robertson did not like her; he then asked him why he did not inform him of his intention before he sent her, he answer'd that Mrs. Robertson had not acquainted him with the circumstance above mentioned. We believe it was principally owing to some derangement in his family occasioned by his separation from Mrs. Robertson, and to turn her into money at a great price: The child was left behind, and is now here. We suppose Capt.n Palms [sic] will not ask more for her than will purchase another equally as valuable to him, but if he should ask more, four or five pounds more, we request you will give it, and pay for her, out with the money you may receive for E. Gilbert & Wentworth & Elderkins note, and what you may give more, out of the proceeds of anchors shipped by Sol. Townsend. She was sold the first time for seventy pounds this currency: We hope this sum will purchase her again from Capt'n Palms [sic]. If you should purchase and send her before the weather becomes moderate, we request you will furnish her with such cloathes as may be necessary to keep her comfortable on the passage, and pay for them as before directed. We are sorry to give you*

*this trouble, but as we intend it as an act of justice, we are convinced*
*you will cheerfully undertake it.*

> *We are,*
> *Gent.n*
> *Yours etc etc*
> *Sol & Rob't Townsend*

To guarantee delivery, two copies of letter were sent south, one by Captain Elliot and a second with Captain Flyer. Robert carefully wrote out his own copy, so that every detail could be tracked and recorded—and then he waited.[24]

## Chapter Ten

# "Principled against Selling Slaves"

After waiting a full month with no reply, and in order to appease Robert's unrelenting demand to take immediate action, Solomon finally agreed to bring up the subject of their unusual request with Richard Lushington and John Kirk Jr., but this time he would do things his way and with none of his brother's high-minded verbiage. Though Solomon had agreed to include his name on the signature line, the phrasing of the request (complete with the unseemly details of babies born under Robert's roof and the affections of the family's "negro wench" for British officers) had been entirely composed by Robert, who quietly glossed over the fact that Liss had been a one-time runaway who returned to the family. The whole situation was highly irregular, not to mention that Solomon had his reputation as a professional merchant to consider. If he were to broach the subject again with his own pen, then matters of invoices, orders, and accounts were his preferred lexicon. His scrawled copy of the February 26, 1787, letter to Charleston set a much more businesslike tone:

*Gentlemen,*
*Your favor of the 10th November received in course, since which have not heard from you. Wrote you in January with my Brother Robt. concerning a Black Woman which we wanted to have purchased and sent to N. York. Shall be glad to know how you are likely to succeed. We want much to know how you have settled the matter with the Schooner. Shall be glad to be informed and what sales you have made of the anchors.*

The letter went on to detail the troubles of shipping on the North River in the middle of a particularly severe winter. Ever the anchor salesman, Solomon guaranteed the pair that he would keep them "supplied with such sizes as you think most saleable." New opportunities were opening up in the East Indies, he bragged, creating "a new channel of trade" expected to result in large sales of iron goods in the coming months. He closed the letter with no more mention of Liss, but rather with impressive statistics on the output of his ironworks: "This year the works turn out about 100 tons of anchors—the next season they expect to increase one half more."

In the next letter in his copybook, dated March 1, he wrote to another Charleston merchant, who was more of an old family friend than strictly a business contact, named Adam Gilchrist. What Robert didn't seem to understand in his haste to arrange for Elizabeth's repurchase was that much of the money he was counting on—including sales from his anchors and even the old schooner debt—was already spoken for. Now Solomon had to embarrass himself yet again and tell his old friend Gilchrist that he might have to wait for his payment. If Lushington and Kirk somehow managed to find and pay for Liss, Gilchrist would be the one left hanging until Solomon could raise more funds in the next few months. However, if they didn't succeed in buying her back, then Gilchrist could be paid after all. He was fairly confident his friend wouldn't mind this runaround, though another retelling of the affair was painful and confusing, at the very least:

> Shipped some anchors some time ago to Mssrs. Lushington & Kirk— expect they are sold by this [time] and intend paying you out of the net proceeds of them and some other moneys which they have in their hands . . . but wrote them some time ago to purchase a black Woman which if they do they will not have sufficient [money] in their hands; if they do not will direct them to pay you if it is agreeable for you to receive it there and the exchange can be fixed on, but if you had rather have the money paid here to you brother Mr. J. will have it paid by May and cannot conveniently sooner.

Referencing the unpaid money for the *Sally*, he added, "It would have been settled long before this but some unforeseen disappointments has prevented."[1]

For Robert, the wait to hear back from Lushington and Kirk was interminable, with recent actions by the New York Manumission Society (NYMS) only serving to feed his fears of the horrors he might uncover once Liss was found. The society had once again sought to put an end to Captain James Tinker's business in human kidnapping, placing another warning in the New York papers on February 20, 1787: "A CAUTION: THE FREE NEGROES in this city are desired to be very careful lest they should be kidnapped, and carried on board [by] Captain Tinker, who intends shortly to sail for Carolina, and is supposed, is ready to take with him, all such blacks as may become the victims of cruel, unprincipled and avaricious men." The notice went on to accuse Tinker, claiming he had "several times been guilty of taking Free Negroes," and specifically mentioned that the NYMS would be "particularly attentive" and "endeavor to detect any attempts that may be made on the liberties of that helpless class of citizens," signing the warning "A Friend to Mankind."[2]

Perhaps their actions had begun to have an adverse effect on the legal side of Tinker's shipping business, since just three days later the captain took the audacious step of printing a response in his own defense, titled "To the Impartial Public," calling out prominent members of the NYMS: "The dark and infamous attack made upon the character of the Subscriber by a despicable scribbler—a certain Mr. Shotwell who lives with Lawrence Embree—a few days ago in this paper, renders it in some degree necessary for him to appeal to the public." Tinker went on to declare that he was "willing to stand the test of an impartial jury" to clear his name, calling their accusations "groundless aspersions thrown out by a base assassin against the reputation of the public's most obedient servant." At the conclusion of his declaration of innocence, he also noted, "On Wednesday the 28th, the *Mercury* Packet will positively sail for Charleston."[3]

The court case mentioned by Tinker arose from another recent abduction, brought to light at the February 15 meeting of the New York Manumission Society. The meeting minutes outlined a shocking account of an African American man who was forcibly taken from his home in

Norwich, Connecticut, in the presence of his wife and children. From there, he was transported to New York City and detained in the city jail until Tinker's vessel was ready to sail for Charleston. How the NYMS came to learn of this unnamed man is unclear, but once alerted to his plight, they sprang into action to block his removal to South Carolina. Defying every negative stereotype of lawyers that Robert Townsend had recently begun to believe, the legal experts within the NYMS obtained a writ of habeas corpus and brought the unfortunate man before the chief justice, demanding that he either be charged with a crime or else released. Since there was no evidence that the man had committed any offense, and he was clearly being held in the jail only for the sake of Tinker's convenience, the court was forced to set him free. The NYMS collected from its members the necessary funds to send the man home to his family in Connecticut, and further tragedy and injustice were avoided. But this was just one success. In its notes on the case, the NYMS committee observed that its members knew of "several other cases" of Tinker's criminality.[4]

Similar warnings from "Benevelous" and "Humanus" continued to dot the newspapers in New York throughout the 1780s.[5, 6] And despite any legal actions brought against him, Tinker kept up a healthy side business in exporting free blacks that cemented his place as a villain of the first order in the eyes of northern abolitionists.

Evidence of other kidnappings by Tinker exists outside those cases brought to light by the NYMS. Runaway slave ads in Charleston show just how active his operation was and reveal stories of other victims who found themselves sold into slavery, hundreds of miles from home, with no choice but to attempt the treacherous voyage home on their own to save themselves.

In 1785, just months after Liss's arrival in Charleston, a South Carolina plantation owner named Maurice Simons had purchased a man named Frank from Captain Tinker as he docked his brig on the Charleston wharf. Simons, a civic-minded Patriot much like Samuel Townsend, had been a justice of the peace, had served in South Carolina's Second Continental Congress, and by 1784 had been elected to the House of Representatives, alongside Richard Lushington.

One morning in mid-September, his plantation overseers must have noticed Frank was missing, as Simons wasted no time in advertising the runaway, explaining, "The above Negro was lately brought from New York in the brig *Lucretia*, Captain Tinker, from whom I bought him." The ad describes Frank as "about forty-five years old, 5 feet 8 inches high," wearing "a brown woolen jacket and oznaburg trowsers." Billed as a runaway who "speaks good English" and would "endeavor to pass as a freeman," Frank was also noted as "an artful sensible fellow."[7] In other words, he was no ordinary field hand, and given Tinker's reputation, it is not at all unlikely that Frank was, indeed, a freeman who had been captured in New York and sold into bondage. Interestingly, however, Frank seems to have succeeded in his escape, as the ads seeking him ran for several months with apparently no resolution and then abruptly ceased with his master's sudden death; no further effort was made to recover Frank. Simons, the owner, was famously killed in a duel on November 12 stemming from a slander trial for accusing a man of disloyal behavior during the British occupation of Charleston back in 1780.[8, 9] Because Simons was so well-liked and such a prominent politician, a campaign to end the bloody practice of dueling resulted in a flurry of editorials as far north as Boston.[10, 11] As the public focused on the loss of a man known as a civic leader, owner of a large plantation, and loyal countryman, Frank slipped silently away.

There was also a runaway notice about a man named Will, who in June 1786 "absented himself" from the *Lucretia* while it was being unloaded at the docks in Charleston. In this case, Tinker himself ran the ad seeking Will's recapture, offering $10 reward "if taken ten miles from town" and $5 if taken within the city limits. Described as a "Negro fellow" who was "born in New England," Will was wearing clothes very similar to those worn by Frank, including "an oznabrig shirt and trowsers, a brown jacket, and a large flopped hat." Listing him as six feet tall, the ad detailed that Will had a "smooth face" and spoke "good English," indicating he too may have been an educated freeman. Tinker ran the ad for five days in a row, then ceased, perhaps due to Will's recapture or else Tinker's next regularly scheduled departure for New York.[12]

Though she had not been kidnapped, per se, Liss was certainly in Robert's constant thoughts as stories about Tinker appeared in local newspapers and were discussed during society meetings. The threat of Tinker, the specter of slavery, and the image of Liss languishing in the hands of a man with as violent a reputation as Richard Palmes surely weighed on Robert's mind as he waited anxiously for word from Lushington and Kirk.

At least the work of the NYMS seemed to be having an effect in the town of Oyster Bay. Though in the eyes of many, the group's first attempt to end slavery in 1785 was a failure, the society was instrumental in advocating for a state law passed on March 14, 1785, which prohibited the sale of slaves imported into the state. This law also made it less expensive and easier for slaveholders to manumit slaves by ending the necessity of posting a £200 bond to the town, establishing instead a process by which "Overseers of the Poor" could certify the freeing of a slave, provided the owner could prove the individual was over twenty-one, under fifty, healthy, and able to earn an independent living.[13] In the hundred years since Tom Gall had been freed in 1685, only three individuals had been legally manumitted in Oyster Bay: Tom, his son-in-law Obed (whom he himself set free), and a third man named Dick. However, in 1785, thanks in no small part to Robert and the other members of the NYMS, a flood of manumissions began. The Oyster Bay town records reveal twenty-three in the first year alone, followed by twenty-five more over the next three years.[14] Though neighboring towns like Huntington and Hempstead appear not to have experienced the same flurry of manumissions, at least in his own hometown, Robert could see that he was making a difference.

Finally in March 1787, two months after their initial inquiry, Solomon and Robert received a reply from Lushington and Kirk, but it was hardly the response for which they were hoping. Despite feeling sympathetic to the plight of the enslaved woman, there was an objection to the firm's involvement in the case: John Kirk Jr. flatly refused to participate in any transaction that involved the purchasing of humans on the basis of his strict stance that he was "principled against selling slaves." He would not use others' money to buy her back, as that would leave the stain on his Quaker conscience of having participated in the slave trade.

What was more, when the Townsend brothers had written confidently that Liss would never "be sold out of the family again," it indicated that she would still be regarded as property upon her return to New York. Therefore, Kirk determined, his firm could not be involved in the case in any manner.[15]

Kirk's objections may indeed have sprung from a very deep and complicated battle of conscience, and Lushington's shared Quaker faith may have also led him not to oppose his partner's immovable stance. Since the Townsends had not guaranteed Liss's freedom following her rescue from her current enslavement, the proxies were technically implicating themselves in the very practice they so deeply despised.

However, it is also hard not to evaluate Kirk's seemingly shortsighted reasoning in light of his family's history with the Townsends. Samuel Townsend had walked free just hours after his arrest in 1776, thanks to his family's wealth and connections. But the details of John Kirk Sr.'s arrest and the tragedy that followed no doubt left an indelible mark on his son's life. John Jr. had been twenty-six years old when his father was arrested just days after the Battle of Long Island and might even have been at home on the day when the 17th Light Infantry came for him. Historian Henry Onderdonk later recorded the events in grim detail: "Kirk was in his corn-field stouting top-stalks. When warned of the approach of the enemy and advised to flee, he refused, saying he was ready for his fate now, for should he escape this time, he could have no peace till they seized him. He also had faint hopes from the proclamation of [British commander in chief General William] Howe, promising pardon to all who would quietly remain at home. They conducted the two committee-men on horseback to the house of Samuel Townsend, member of the Provincial Congress."

When John Kirk Sr. finally returned home after nine weeks in the hellish hold of the prison ship half dead from smallpox, he passed the disease on to his wife and young daughter, who both died of it.[16] A weakened John Kirk, along with John Jr. and three surviving daughters, buried his wife and youngest child in the week before Christmas of 1776. Meanwhile, the Townsends emerged from the war almost entirely unscathed. If he carried any kind of grudge, now would certainly have been an opportune time for John Kirk Jr. to relish the shift of power between himself and Solomon and Robert.

Whatever impulses prompted Lushington and Kirk to decline the request to locate Liss and secure her release and safe passage back to New York, their letter left no room for negotiation. They would not carry out a commission they regarded as simply one more act of human trafficking, no matter the intention behind it.

The unexpected response sent Robert into even deeper emotional turmoil. He was so close to securing Liss: he knew where she was; he had a plan for raising the funds; his brother, somewhat begrudgingly, supported the plan; and he was making thoughtful preparations for her arrival. But until they could find another agent to undertake the work of actually securing Liss's freedom, she was stranded at Palmes's estate, not sure if anyone from her old life knew where she was or whether she was even dead or alive.

After consulting with Solomon, they identified Adam Gilchrist as their best hope. Because of his brother's recent correspondence, Gilchrist was already somewhat aware of Liss's predicament and the unusual complications in obtaining the money to repurchase her. No matter how unwilling the Quakers seemed, the Townsends still needed their cooperation to make the plan work. On March 22, 1787, Robert composed a carefully worded response to Lushington and Kirk, emphasizing the importance of securing money from the schooner *Sally* and revealing the startling fact that Liss's pregnant sister, Hannah, had refused an offer to become a free person:

> *Messrs Lushington & Kirk,*
> *Gentn,*
> *We are now to acknowledge the receipt of yours of the 17th Ult'o and are sorry that your Mr. J. K. could not, consistent with his principles, purchase the Wench as requested; we think it might have been done in our names without violating those principles, but as Mr. J. K. could not think so, we would not by any means urge it. It was a principle similar to Mr. J. K.'s which urged our R. T. to request that she might be purchased and sent back, that he might return her to her original*

*master: whether he would give her free immediately we cannot say, but this we can say, that he has offered the sister of this Wench her freedom, which she has declined taking. However, this we can venture to say with certainty, that she will never, in case of her return, be sold out of the family again with their consent. We shall write Mr. Adam Gilchrist on the subject by this conveyance, and send him any order on you for the amount of what you may receive for Ebenezer Gilbert & Wentworth & Elderkins note, which we beg you will pay. We beg you will accept our thanks for your exertions on securing this debt. We are,*

*Gentn,*

*Yours etc,*

*Sol. Townsend*

*Rob't Townsend*[17]

## Chapter Eleven

# "Obtain the Wench from Him"

"I'm going to wash myself," Timbo casually mentioned to the men he was working alongside, asking them to let the master know if he came looking. Then, in his "old homespun shirt and trowsers," he shuffled his way out the door. Heavy-set and "very bandy leg'd, his knees laps [*sic*] over one another," Timbo may have been suffering from rickets due to a vitamin D deficiency, and his appearance was certainly conspicuous; in short, he was hardly considered a flight risk. But on July 17, 1772, with just a brief word to his comrades, Timbo slipped out of the tailor shop of one Adam Gilchrist Sr. and disappeared into the bustle and crowds of Manhattan.[1]

Adam Gilchrist Jr., who was twelve at the time, watched his father run ads for the next three months seeking the runaway. With such malformed legs, running or walking long distances was nearly impossible for Timbo, but New York's busy harbor offered many avenues of escape by boat, prompting the elder Gilchrist to add, "This therefore is to forewarn all masters of vessels to harbor him at their peril."

Whether Timbo was ever caught is not recorded. The advertisements seeking him appeared in the newspapers six times between July and September before he was either recaptured or Gilchrist gave up, but the incident probably made a lifelong impression on young Adam, who eventually grew up to become a member of the New York Manumission Society (NYMS)—though not before first leading a storied military career in the Revolution.

As New York City braced itself for its fall to the British late in the summer of 1776, Adam Gilchrist Sr. moved with his wife and three teenaged sons farther inland to a small hamlet in Orange County, New York, near the Pennsylvania border and only a few miles from where Peter Townsend ran his main ironworks.[2] Almost as soon as the Gilchrist family settled in Smith's Clove, Adam Jr., the oldest son at age sixteen, enlisted in the Continental Army as an assistant general commissary of forage with a Pennsylvanian regiment and within a few months was back where his family had just evacuated—and right at the center of the conflict, stationed at the last American stronghold on the upper tip of Manhattan.[3] On November 16, 1776, Gilchrist was captured, along with 2,836 others, at the disastrous Battle of Fort Washington near modern-day Washington Heights.[4] Following the American surrender, the prisoners were marched south into Harlem and, the day after that, down into the city of New York, where they were loaded onto British prison ships and held for ten weeks before being transferred to Long Island on January 20, 1777. By then, nearly two-thirds of the men with whom Gilchrist had been captured were already dead due to disease, torture, exposure, starvation, and general neglect.[5] For the next year, Gilchrist was held in spartan conditions in a grim camp until finally, on December 7, 1777, he was freed as part of a prisoner exchange. Undeterred by his harrowing experience as a prisoner of war, on May 28, 1777, Gilchrist took an oath of allegiance to America and reenlisted, now with the rank of captain in the Ulster County Militia.[6, 7]

After the Americans retook Manhattan on November 22, 1783—three days before Robert Townsend's thirtieth birthday—the Gilchrist family packed up their home in Orange County and returned to the city. Gilchrist Sr. established himself as the senior member in the firm of Adam Gilchrist & Co, using his background as a tailor to sell fabrics and other goods at 2 Queen Street in lower Manhattan.[8] Young Adam, who was twenty-three and had already spent seven years in military service, joined his family in New York, but his zeal for the Patriot cause was hardly dampened by the end of hostilities.

In 1784, a newly married Adam Gilchrist Jr. began his term serving on a committee dedicated to obtaining compensation from Loyalists for occupation and damage done to private residences by British troops during the war. In direct protest of the Quartering Acts, whereby private citizens were required to put up British troops in their homes without any financial reimbursement from the Crown, this commission sought to defy the old British laws by gathering back rent due to people who were forced to house soldiers or who were driven from their homes and businesses by occupying troops during the war. "Under an impression of the importance of the object of their appointment, and in compliance with the request of their fellow citizens," a public notice announced, the nine members of the commission gravely took their appointment as a means of providing fair restitution and a way to help heal the community from the scars of war. "They . . . feel themselves at full liberty to take such measures (consistent with the laws and constitution thereof)," the notice continued, "as upon mature deliberation may to them appear prudent."[9] Gilchrist's work in this role, alongside prominent New York political voices and NYMS members, such as Melancton Smith, understandably won him considerable support, and from 1785 to 1786, he served as the secretary of the New York City Chamber of Commerce, alongside fellow merchant Alexander Robertson.

In 1786, Gilchrist also signed his name as one of 136 members of the NYMS addressing a letter to the New York Legislature calling for a ban on "the practice of exporting them [slaves] like cattle" and highlighting the inhumanity of "husbands being torn from their wives . . . children from their parents" and the kidnapping of free men and women of color who were then "carried to market in distant parts."[10] Especially significant about Gilchrist's joining the society in 1786 was that he moved his young family to Charleston a few months later,[11] though it appears that when he left New York, he had not firmly decided where his best business prospects might be, in the end choosing to live in a city at the heart of the southern slave trade. Solomon later admitted to Gilchrist, "[I] am sorry you had not determined on settling in Charleston when you left this [New York]. If so, [I] should not have looked to any other than yourself to transact what business I have at Charleston."

Though Gilchrist may have struggled with his choice of money over morality when he moved to Charleston, his timing proved fortunate for the Townsends. With John Kirk's righteous objections still ringing in their ears, Solomon and Robert desperately needed another agent they could trust to carry out the negotiations for Liss. Solomon already enjoyed a strong business relationship with Gilchrist, as evidenced by his letter on March 1, 1787, when he made casual mention of "a Black Woman" he and his brother were hoping to purchase and return to New York.[12]

Just a few weeks later, however, Robert's urgency in resolving Liss's predicament swiftly became apparent. As soon as he put down his pen in composing a letter to Lushington and Kirk on March 22, he picked it back up and began a second letter, this time to the bright, respected family friend and business associate of Solomon's:

*New York, March 22d:1787*
*Mr. Adam Gilchrist,*

*Sir,*
*We wrote Mess.rs Lushington & Kirk in Jany last, requesting them to purchase a Wench, named Elizabeth, shipped by Alex. Robertson and sold by Alex. Shirras, & Co to Captain Rich'd Palms [sic] of your place, which they inform us they cannot consistent with the principles of Mr. J. Kirk. We are now therefore to request that you will purchase and send her to us yr. first good opportunity. We suppose Captain Palms [sic] will not ask more for her than will purchase another, but if he should ask five or six pounds, this currency, more, we are willing that you should give it. We enclose an order on Mssr Lushington & Kirk for the purpose of paying for her—whatever you may give more for her than what you may receive for this order, take from the proceeds of Anchors shipped by our S. Townsend. This wench was brought up in our father's family, and sold to Miss'rs Sharwin, since Mrs. Robertson, for no particular fault but that of being too fond of Company. Our R.T. sold her, and as he is principled against selling slaves, is anxious that she should be repurchased and sent back, that he may return her to her original master, who we have reason to believe will give her free if she chooses to be so. If you should have*

*any scruples about purchasing her in your own name, we request you*
*will do it in our names.*
    *Sol. Townsend*
    *Rob't Townsend*[13]

Lessons from Kirk's refusal echo loudly in this appeal to Gilchrist. The Townsends raise the likelihood of Liss's eventual freedom as well as make clear that Gilchrist is welcome to purchase and ship her home using the Townsend name if he has concerns about using his own in such a transaction.

The day this letter was penned, Solomon wrote an additional business letter to Gilchrist about anchor sales, with no mention of the request to rescue Liss. This letter (and most likely the other two as well) was transported to Charleston aboard the Townsend's sloop *Betsy* along with the latest shipment of iron. While Robert's request appealed to Gilchrist's sense of morality, Solomon's correspondence offered him a potential edge in his anchor sales, encouraging Gilchrist to feel free to undercut Lushington and Kirk by offering his product at a much lower price. Solomon even extended Gilchrist special terms, offering that the inventory need not be paid for until it was sold, but added, "Shall be glad you would not mention this being a consignment" to his Charleston competition.[14] Whether such offers were influential in Gilchrist's decision is unclear, but Gilchrist replied to Robert that he was "happy to serve you in this affair" just a few weeks later. However, his return letter makes clear that what happened next was far from straightforward:

*Mr. Robert Townsend*
*Charleston, 12th April, 1787*

*D[ear] Sir,*
*Your esteemed favor 22nd Ulto I duly received and called on M[r]*
*Lushington who informed me "Palms" was resolved no price should*
*obtain the Wench from him—(this person lives out of town is the rea-*
*son have not called on him). M[r] Shirras says the bond for which the*
*wench was sold is in New York and the payment of the same secured*

*by a mortgage on the wench; it amounts to upwards of £50 Stg. . . .*
*[A]s the payment of this sum [paper mutilated] our late law is by*
*installments of thrice annual payments he is secure in the property of*
*the wench, the original proprietor kept out of his money and no sale*
*till the mortgage is released would be safe—*

*I should be happy to serve you in this affair & the first time I see*
*Capt. Palmes will attend to it.*

*With esteem I am*
*D[ear] Robert*
*Yours sincerely,*
*Adam Gilchrist*[15]

<hr />

Richard Lushington's journey was not a particularly comfortable one.
Even in early spring the tangled woods outside Charleston felt more
like a tropical jungle than a respectable oak forest. The strange, sharp
fronds of the saw palmettos that grew wild here could leave red lacera-
tions on bare skin, and the insects were already active, picking up their
infestation and irritation right where they had left off every year prior,
since hard freezes rarely came to kill them off. Even if one stuck to the
main roads, the southern vegetation had a way of creeping back into the
path, reclaiming almost overnight every hard-fought inch of wilderness
that had been tamed. Palmes's home did not lay deep in some remote,
trackless swamp, but it was not without at least a little concern for his
own safety that Lushington ventured outside the security of Charleston's
gates in an effort to track down Richard Palmes.

Charleston, South Carolina, was often remarked upon by visitors
and residents alike as one of America's most European cities. It wasn't
just that the town was arguably wealthier and more cosmopolitan than
any town south of Philadelphia; nor was it due entirely to the ships that
poured into the harbor from international destinations carrying people
and goods from all over the world. Charleston felt distinctly Old World
in another significant way too: it was a walled city—America's only
urban settlement to be surrounded by such a medieval-style fortification,
including gates to restrict the flow of traffic in and out. As Charleston

grew, it quickly began to expand beyond its original walled boundaries, and in the years following the Revolution, the wall began to be dismantled to accommodate the swelling population. The area outside the city, however, was still viewed with some trepidation by city dwellers.[16] Much like Manhattan, Charleston was situated at the tip of a peninsula. To the north and west, sparse settlements dotted the hills before one met again with the relative sophistication of the "upcountry" in the mountains, which had recently been settled by immigrants from the neighboring colonies of Virginia and North Carolina. Across the river to the south, rice, indigo, and cotton plantations occasionally punctuated the otherwise untamable "low country" replete with alligator- and mosquito-filled marshes and swampy islands.[17]

It was into this markedly less urbane region, where the structure and development of Charleston began to fade away, that Lushington was now trekking in defiance of both good sense and the objections of his business partner, John Kirk, who wanted nothing to do with the whole affair. But Lushington apparently viewed the Townsends' commission as a moral imperative, more than a time for legalistic stances or even old grudges, so it was he who ventured out for the first meeting with Palmes—an encounter that was likely dramatic in any number of ways.

Palmes's estate was not a sprawling plantation, nor did it lie much beyond the boundaries of Charleston. However, Palmes seems to have been seeking a change from country life. In January 1787, just before Solomon and Robert sent the first letter seeking to repurchase Elizabeth, Palmes ran a notice in the local newspaper advertising "TO BE LET, An airy and commodious HOUSE, Without the City, With a large yard garden, and every outbuilding necessary; its stand is suitable for trade, or a tavern" and directing interested parties to locate the property "near the Gates."[18] Thus, it seems, the home was hardly isolated but was still certainly beyond the more tightly packed streets within the city walls.

As Palmes lived outside town, an unexpected visitor would have been a novelty, and as a household servant, Liss herself was likely the person to answer Lushington's surprising knock and to escort the stiffly dressed Quaker inside the well-furnished home. Palmes was retrieved, and following introductions, Lushington explained his business and offered to make payment for Liss. Here Palmes's obstinate and fiery character proved itself unchanged. "Palms [*sic*] was resolved no price should obtain the Wench from him," Gilchrist wrote to the Townsends on April 12, after meeting with Lushington to obtain details of his efforts thus far.

Whether Palmes made that declaration in a passionate rage or a cold, calculated bid to drive up the price is unclear, but he now knew that someone wanted to purchase Liss, and he was determined to play his hand to full advantage. For Palmes, Lushington's visit meant that he might have a way to make a profit. For Liss, it meant that she knew for the first time since she had set foot on Tinker's ship that someone from home knew where she was and, what was more, was looking for her. For the first time in more than two years, she had a glimmer of hope.

Gilchrist, meanwhile, sought out Alexander Shirras, a Charleston merchant who did a brisk business in fabrics, such as "needle-worked lawn aprons," "fashionable silks,"[19] and groceries like "tea, hams, candles and soap,"[20] and also dabbled in real estate (once selling off an "excellent swamp in St. James Parish")[21] as well as slaves.[22] Shirras, besides dealing in fabrics, was also a native of Scotland, and these commonalities with Alexander Robertson may have been a factor in his selection as mortgage broker—a mortgage that happened now to be in arrears.[23] Hoping he could use this as leverage to negotiate a quick settlement, Gilchrist was quickly disappointed when what he learned was hardly more promising than the results of Lushington's encounter. Shirras would not agree to release the bond until it was paid in full—more than £50 was still owed—and a new state law, enacted March 28, just six days after the Townsends wrote their letter to Gilchrist, regulated both the payments of debts and the importation of slaves. Not only did the so-called late law enact a three-year ban on the importation of enslaved people from both overseas and other states—an act that would have served Liss well two years prior—but there was now a three-year extension on all overdue debts. "WHEREAS, many inhabitants of this country before the revolution owed considerable sums of money," South Carolina Act No. 1371 reads, "and of which the embarrassment of the war prevented the payment"—as did the subsequent glutting of the markets thanks to the lifting of British tariffs and restrictions, not to mention several poor harvests following the peace—the law declared that anyone with an unpaid debt was given three years from the passage of the bill to settle it without legal recourse.[24]

In other words, Palmes now had until 1790 to pay off the note on Liss and was under no legal obligation to settle it sooner. The law could keep the owner of the bond, Alexander Shirras, "out of his money," Gilchrist explained, for up to three years. And since Palmes insisted that "no price should obtain the wench from him," it seemed that things were once more at a dead end.

Lushington and Kirk, meanwhile, replied back to Solomon on March 26 (the letter once again sent via Captain Tinker), probably in response to Robert's second appeal for help. Solomon was apologetic when he wrote back on April 23, explaining that "respecting the Black Woman . . . soon after writing was sorry that we had requested the favor when on reflection it occurred to me that it could not be complied with on those principles which you mentioned." Mentioning the new law, instead of voicing concern about Liss, he remarked that he hoped those who had contracted to purchase the schooner *Sally* would not take advantage of the three-year clause. He then went on to detail anchor sales before closing the letter by reiterating that the Quakers might be pulled into the matter of Liss one way or another: "Having sent a few anchors to Gilchrist . . . I have also wrote him about the black Woman which if he executes shall have occasion to draw on you for some money. . . . Must beg you will push the matter of the schooner debt as much as possible and have a final settlement of it."[25] In other words, if Gilchrist could find some way around the debtors' law to manage the purchase, he would still need the money from the sale of the ship in order to pay for Liss. The only problem was that the ship hadn't sold.

On May 5, Lushington and Kirk placed an ad for the *Sally* in the local papers, with the caveat that if no buyer was found within the next five days, the sale would henceforth "be exposed at public, by David Denoon."[26] The schooner had been languishing on the dock at Cochran's Wharf for over a year while they waited for the absconding buyers, who now, clearly, were not going to show. Denoon's auction house specialized in the sale of sloops and schooners, and he surely had a better chance of finding a new purchaser.[27]

When Lushington and Kirk wrote back to Solomon on May 16, they may have informed him of their new push to auction the *Sally*, but it would seem they made no mention of Liss. Solomon failed to reply to them for three months, due to the unexpected death of his father-in-law, the "Great Chain" maker Peter Townsend, which caused him to spend the summer in Chester, settling Peter's affairs and composing scores of letters to associates as close to home as Boston and as far afield as North Carolina, Bermuda, and England. After writing to Gilchrist on August 24, explaining that he "should have answered yours long before this but have been much in the country of late occasioned by the loss of my Father in law," Solomon then sent a letter to Lushington and Kirk a few days later, mentioning his receipt of their letter from May, informing them of the death of his father-in-law, and repeating his desire for money from the sale of the unsellable schooner. In neither of these August business letters did Solomon make any mention of Liss, "the Black Woman" who had filled his letters the previous spring.[28]

With Gilchrist's April 12 promise to "attend" to her sale and no reference to any further complications in the purchase of Liss in his reply to the May 16 letter from Lushington and Kirk, the timing of her voyage back to New York likely falls between those dates. The question, however, is how it was carried out.

Was Shirras paid his remaining debt, and was Palmes somehow enticed to part with Liss? Gilchrist could not draw the money from Lushington and Kirk since the schooner remained unsold. Is it possible that Gilchrist paid the money upfront, amounting to nearly $24,000 in modern currency? If so, this demonstrates a remarkable degree of trust in the Townsends to stand by their word of financial responsibility and honest dealings. It also speaks volumes of Gilchrist's character that he was willing to risk taking on such a debt in order to get Liss home.

However it was that Gilchrist secured enough money to sufficiently satisfy both Palmes and Shirras, a second mystery remains—namely, how Liss reached New York again, in light of the 1785 law spearheaded by the New York Manumission Society, which forbade the importation of enslaved people into the state. According to Shirras, there was an actual bill of sale for Liss, which was held in New York, where the deal was originally struck, so Gilchrist did not have a simple route to manumit her in South Carolina. Complicating matters even further, such a bill of sale could not even be applied for because it would immediately render her ineligible to enter the state of New York and return to the Townsend family, since she was purchased elsewhere. Under New York law, the Townsends could not legally purchase her in South Carolina and have her shipped to them. Gilchrist, likewise, could not purchase her in his name and then legally resell her to the Townsends upon arriving in New York. The only option was to smuggle her in, which, ironically, may have been the simplest aspect of this entire plan.

Several vessels may have carried her home. Gilchrist owned a merchant ship called the *Julia*, which made frequent trips between Charleston and New York, including a voyage that left Charleston in mid-April.[29] Since Liss was traveling without the proper documentation, sailing aboard Gilchrist's own ship would have been ideal; however, if she were to sail on the *Julia*'s impending voyage, Gilchrist would have needed to secure the deal remarkably quickly since the ship was slated to leave just one day after he wrote his letter to the Townsends informing them that Palmes was unwilling to sell Liss. It is probable that only his letter sailed aboard the *Julia* the next day. A more likely transport was the Townsends' own vessel, the sloop *Betsy*, which entered the harbor in Charleston on April 10.[30] Voyages of the *Betsy* appear regularly in Solomon's business letters, making deliveries of iron to Adam Gilchrist and others, returning up the eastern seaboard to New York, Boston, Newport, and Philadelphia. Though there is no official record of the *Betsy* arriving in New York in late April, by May 9 she had come into port in Boston.[31] Did the vessel make an unscheduled stop in Oyster Bay Harbor? If Liss was secreted out of Charleston and delivered to the dock in her own hometown in late April or early May, her arrival was not noted in any record.

There is certainly evidence to support Palmes's willingness to come to a very swift agreement after his initial obstinance, however. In the summer of 1787, he was, predictably, in such severe financial straits that not even South Carolina's "late law" could help him, and he may have viewed this sudden windfall in selling Liss as a convenient way to try to dig himself out of at least some of that debt. But it was too little too late for Richard Palmes. Just a few months later, in September, after absenting his house for a few days on business, he returned home to find his entire dwelling stripped bare. A notice was left from a man named Robert Smither that all of Palmes's possessions had been taken in partial payment of an overdue debt. Palmes filed a grievance with the court against Smither, perhaps seeking to evoke the three-year payment loophole, but on the day of his court hearing, Palmes was a no-show. The angered justices ruled that since Palmes "though solemnly called does not come," he automatically forfeited his case. Furthermore, not only would "the said Richard take nothing," but he was also responsible for paying Smither's court costs, which amounted to "the Sum of three pounds fourteen shillings and three pence." The list of extravagant articles taken from Palmes's "commodious house" was impressive, including, "one Mahogany Table, one Deal Table, four Windsor chairs, six Leather bottomed chairs, two Glass Shades, one Case of Knives and Forks, one Lot of China and Glass Ware, one large looking Glass, one Tea Table, four Waiters, four Mahogany chairs, one Mahogany Table, one Windsor chair, one pair of Fire Dogs, and Bellows, one other large looking Glass, one Bedstand, Bed and Bedding, one coverbed, one Billiard Table, one other Bedstead, Bed and two Pillows."[32]

Had Liss still been under Palmes's ownership in September, she, too, would have been seized by Smithers and her ownership transferred to him. By then, however, Liss was resettled in Oyster Bay, reunited with her son, and no longer the property of the "townsman with a cudgel." But, still, she was not free.

# Part III

# For Ourselves and Our Posterity

## Chapter Twelve

# "Elizabeth, a Black Woman"

Quite a lot had changed in the eight years since the teenaged Liss had run away in the spring of 1779. There were more people and new buildings in town now. Several old families, staunchly devoted to the Crown, had packed up and left; tight clans united by blood and name had scattered in every direction on the compass. In their place others who were strangers to Elizabeth had taken up residence. The community of free African Americans, once composed of just a few households in Pine Hollow primarily named Gall, now included dozens of newly emancipated families. A war had been won—or lost, depending on your loyalties. A child had been born. A nation had been born too. Elizabeth had been sold eight hundred miles away, likely suffered violence at the hands of a brute, and been smuggled back to her birthplace, where the institution that enslaved her was very slowly being phased out. The world was not the same, and neither was the twenty-five-year-old woman who now looked around Oyster Bay with older and more experienced eyes.

For one thing, it appears she went by "Elizabeth" now, having dropped her childhood nickname. She reassimilated as best she could, living in her old home at the Townsends' but hardly stepping back into the same life she had left behind. How could she simply pick up her old routine now that everything had changed?

Then there was Harry. Elizabeth had been sold to Palmes just before her son's second birthday; he may even still have been nursing at the time. Now, he was an independent four-year-old who had little memory of the woman who wanted to talk to him, hold his hand, and pick him up. Just five months earlier, he had been plucked by Robert from the only home he had known and carried to a new home with a new set of people who were in charge of raising him. What did he make of this strange woman who suddenly stepped back into his life and wanted to call herself "Mother"?

Elizabeth's sister, Hannah, was now a mother too, to a baby girl named Violet,[1] and apparently contented enough with her lot that she had turned down an offer of emancipation, as Robert had mentioned in one of his letters to Lushington. Or perhaps Hannah had declined in order to be sure she could stay close to Oyster Bay should Elizabeth ever come home. Even more likely, with a newborn baby to care for, she may have wondered if she could find enough work as a free person to provide for the two of them on her own. After all, Elizabeth had sought her freedom, and now she was right back where she started. Whatever the case, Hannah had rejected the very freedom that had driven her sister from home in the first place. How did the sisters reconcile their respective lots? Did they ever regret their decisions or accuse one another of taking the wrong path?

Even "home" itself, whatever that concept looked like to Elizabeth, was different. While she had been "returned to her original master," his home was no longer filled with the bustle of a British headquarters. At the war's end, Audrey Townsend had married the Scottish sea captain James Farley[2] and now lived on a farm on the edge of town. Sally and Phebe, aged twenty-seven and twenty-four, had spent their teenaged years at war and now were approaching matron status, still living at home with their aging parents. Did Elizabeth slide back into her former role as their ladies' maid, or was that place filled by another of the Townsends' slaves? Had Robert told his family of her harrowing journey—and had the tantalizing gossip of the household inevitably spilled out into the streets?

Those stories, or others dreamed up in a vacuum of information, created a world of uncertainty for Elizabeth. After all, the clandestine means by which she was brought back to New York in the spring of 1787 were quite illegal. How could she explain turning back up at her old master's house after so long and her desire to mother the biracial child Robert had carried into the family home almost half a year prior? And how was she to answer the inevitable questions as to her whereabouts in the intervening years—especially her activities during the war if she had, in fact, done covert work for Robert and the Culper spies? Was she regarded as a traitor by those who knew she had escaped with John Simcoe in the days when she was "too fond of the British officers"? Perhaps it was better if she said nothing, ignored the whispers and sideways glances, tried to forget her old self, and simply became Elizabeth, a black woman belonging to the Townsend household.

Except, *did* she actually belong to the household? Her status would have been ambiguous at best. Elizabeth had no papers to prove she was the property of either Robert Townsend (who had paid for her twice) or his father, and proof of ownership was required by the Overseers of the Poor to be legally freed. To qualify for manumission, the Townsends had to prove she belonged to them, but they could not do so without incriminating themselves for breaking several laws: the 1787 law prohibiting the exportation of slaves from South Carolina, as well as the 1785 and 1788 laws against the importation of slaves into New York—laws passed through the lobbying efforts of the NYMS, of which Robert was a longstanding member. It was the perfect legal quandary. So draconian were the restrictions on importing slaves, in fact, that the 1788 Act Concerning Slaves included a provision reading, "If any person shall knowingly employ, harbor, conceal or entertain, any negro or other slave they shall forfeit to the owner the sum of five pounds for every 24 hours they do so."[3] Had Elizabeth's liminal status been made public, the Townsends would have owed an astronomical sum to her last owner on record, Richard Palmes; she would have been returned to him in Charleston, and all the effort and expense of the past five months would have been for naught.

The new act also provided for the voluntary manumission of slaves in wills, regardless of age, health, or proof of work skills. In these cases, however, the law imposed a steep fee, reverting to the past practice of requiring payment of a £200 bond to the town to ensure the newly free person did not pose a burden to the public. The result of this policy was the same as in the first hundred years, back in the days of Tom Gall and his son-in-law Obed. Oyster Bay manumissions ground to a complete halt after the law was passed in 1788. For the next six years, until they began again in 1794, not a single enslaved person in Oyster Bay was registered as being freed. It is possible that the town-appointed overseers were no longer offering low-cost manumissions in an effort to encourage the more lucrative bond payments. If so, their strategy was a total failure; there is not a single record of the town receiving any £200 fees for slaves freed in wills during the six-year gap. Masters who informally granted freedom to their slaves without paying the bond left the newly emancipated individuals in a perilous situation not unlike that Elizabeth faced: no freedom papers meant no legal status, rendering them especially vulnerable to false accusations of being runaways. Any children born to such individuals might have their freedom questioned. After the death of their former masters, heirs to the estate might lay claim to them and attempt to return them to bondage. Worst of all, they were more vulnerable to being kidnapped and sold south at the hands of men like Captain Tinker, as they had even less legal recourse than victims with freedom papers.

Harry's status, too, was highly questionable. Robert had not provided any proof of his provenance when he brought the child to Oyster Bay, but Harry had to be accounted for somehow if he were ever to be freed as an adult. As he was the only Townsend slave described as "mulatto" and his paternity was never explicitly stated, it is hard not to wonder how he might be treated if a family resemblance began to appear. Would he be treated differently by the Townsends or by the other enslaved members of the household? Would he grow up hearing tales of his strange and sudden appearance in Oyster Bay and understand his inherent difference from the rest of his family?

Complicating matters further was the fact that Samuel Townsend's health had begun to decline, which raised questions as to the future of his estate. Though he was still serving as the New York state senator for Queens County, he was over seventy now, and the man who had once seemed impervious to time, discouragement, and circumstance was slowing down. By the spring of 1789, Robert had closed up shop in Manhattan and come home to Oyster Bay for good to manage the affairs of his ailing father and aging mother.[4] Of the five Townsend sons, the lot fell to Robert almost by default. Solomon, age forty-one, with homes in both Chester and New York City, was stretched quite to the limit after purchasing a second ironworks in Riverhead, on the eastern end of Long Island, adding to his existing Augusta Forge and Manhattan anchor shop. William, twenty-nine, was still living in Oyster Bay and regarded as much too flippant and careless to be granted any real responsibility. David, the youngest son, after surviving seven years of war in the prime of his youth and still unmarried, had died of tuberculosis two years earlier, at age twenty-five, and by now Samuel Jr. had been buried in North Carolina for almost fourteen years.[5] Thus, at age thirty-five, Robert quietly assumed the mantle of oldest son, becoming the man of the house in anticipation of the patriarch's impending demise. Leaving behind the city that had been his place of business for a decade and a half, he returned to Long Island to help with the bookkeeping and daily operations of the family estate.

As much as the world had changed for Elizabeth, the world had certainly changed for Robert too. Besides David's death, he suffered the severing of another fraternal bond when he and Solomon finally dissolved their dwindling partnership in 1788. Solomon had spread himself perilously thin financially, even taking personal loans from his father, from Robert, and from other family members, and Robert was not amenable to his older brother's directives as to his conduct. Solomon, for his part, wrote to their father upon the dissolution to complain about his younger brother's moodiness, personal choices, and unconventional lifestyle, which Solomon deemed unseemly: "It's true there is money due to him from me and in a little time hope it will be convenient to pay him. But had he conducted himself with more temperance and moderation when we were concerned together matters might have been accommodated better than what they were." Possibly referring to Robert's efforts to save Elizabeth, Solomon claimed that Robert was "very unsteady," adding "we differed in opinion too much." Now that his younger brother had retired from the merchant business, Solomon bitterly remarked that he must take up a new profession, insisting, "He should fix on something and make himself a more useful member of society." Particularly galling to Solomon was the fact that Robert declined to take over running a shop and farm the family owned in Marlboro, New York, nearly eighty miles up the Hudson River from Manhattan. Marveling at Robert's apparent desire to stay closer to home rather than accept the Marlboro offer, Solomon voiced frustrations that his brother should choose such a nonproductive and cloistered life, complaining, "His manner of living at present is rather indolent and by no means commendable in a person in his time of life." If Solomon suspected that Robert wanted to stay in Oyster Bay to be near Elizabeth and Harry, he never explicitly said so, but he did go so far as to accuse Robert of performing his melancholy as a kind of act, noting, "Let him pretend what he will, he is not averse to Society."[6]

Robert continued to resist his family's expectations as he resettled himself in Oyster Bay, declining to take a wife or even to join a church. Elizabeth, on the other hand, did accompany Samuel, Sarah, and Sally to worship at the Baptist church located just a few blocks from their house. Elizabeth's name was listed directly adjacent to Samuel Townsend's in the church registry in 1789, with the notation "a Black woman" following it. Though several others, such as "Yano a Black man" and "Hagar a Black woman," appear as well, the other twelve slaves owned by Samuel Townsend at the time are not on the list, which seems to indicate that Elizabeth was somehow different.[7] She may have been regarded by the family as informally freed by that time, even without a legal manumission. Thus, her ambiguous status continued as she lived with and served her old master, perhaps receiving some degree of agency over her decisions and associations.

As Samuel Townsend's long career in state and local politics came to a close, his legacy on Long Island was unmistakable. One of his final efforts in the New York State Senate was passage of the Floyd-Jones Act,[8] an impossibly complicated legal tangle that hearkened back to an incident that had occurred during the Revolution, in the days when Colonel Simcoe was using Samuel's house as both home and headquarters.[9]

On May 1, 1779, Simcoe ordered a small contingent of soldiers to travel under cover of darkness by boat across the sound to Fairfield on a stealth mission to capture an American brigadier general named Gold Selleck Silliman. Bursting into his house after midnight, the men succeeded in capturing both General Silliman and his son and brought them back to Simcoe in Oyster Bay.[10] The entire Townsend household no doubt knew of the midnight kidnapping and likely saw the prized captives as they were paraded out of town to be held prisoner by the British for the next six months.

The Americans, unable to produce an officer of enough importance to exchange for Silliman, mounted an equally audacious night-time mission to capture one of the most highly regarded and ardent Loyalists on Long Island, the Honorable Thomas Jones, a justice of the Supreme Court of New York and son of the former Speaker of the New York State Assembly, who had publicly chastised and jailed Samuel back in 1758. Jones lived in a palatial estate in South Oyster Bay (in what is now Massapequa and Jones Beach), which he had dubbed Tryon Hall, situated on the same six thousand acres that had once belonged to the Townsends. On the evening of November 6, while Judge Jones was hosting an elaborate ball, a band of Americans from Connecticut approached the three-story mansion. While the dancing and music continued in a large ballroom on the lower level, Jones, who was in the upper hall, was caught by surprise as the men burst through the door and carried him off without the knowledge of the revelers below.[11]

The exchange for Silliman, which was negotiated by Major John André, occurred the following April, in 1780, when the two prized captives were exchanged simultaneously on boats in Long Island Sound.[12] Judge Jones left for England in 1781, and after the war his mansion and six-thousand-acre estate could only be claimed by one of his kin, and only under a very strange set of circumstances. Because Judge Jones was childless, the fortunate heir was twenty-five-year-old David Richard Floyd, the only son of Jones's sister and nephew to Colonel Benjamin Floyd, the invaluable courier who had assisted Abraham Woodhull and Robert Townsend as they passed their Culper letters in invisible ink across enemy lines. Due to various complications and loopholes, David could only secure this fortune if his last name was changed from Floyd to Floyd-Jones, which required a special act of the legislature. Samuel Townsend, as representative of Queens County, in which the soon-to-be-inherited estate lay, helped pass the law in February 1790 that made young Floyd-Jones the legal owner, securing for the Floyd clan an even greater position of power and influence among the old, wealthy families of eastern New York.

This act was particularly satisfying to Samuel, as the sting of his punishment for speaking up on behalf of the French Acadians more than thirty years prior had never left his memory. In 1838, Peter Townsend noted that Judge David Jones (1699–1776) was "first Judge of the County & Speaker of the Assembly & during which last office he attempted to persecute his relative, my Grandfather Samuel Townsend, then Magistrate of the Assembly."[13] But Samuel got the last laugh. In one of his final acts of public life, Samuel helped spearhead the law that transferred the land away from his old Loyalist enemy's son and into the hands of the Floyds, whose clan included William Floyd, a signer of the Declaration of Independence, and Benjamin Floyd, who had secretly aided his son. The scars of the Revolution were still shaping the landscape and laws of Long Island.

Just two months after the inheritance was finally settled, President George Washington made a tour of Long Island, visiting war-ravaged areas and famously calling upon a number of his most valuable New York spies. After stopping in Setauket, home of Abraham Woodhull and birthplace of Caleb Brewster, he visited the tavern of the Culper's trusted courier, Austin Roe. The following day, Washington arrived in Oyster Bay, staying in the "private and very neat and decent" home of the Youngs family, which was situated at the water's edge outside the village. The diary Washington kept while on his tour is short on details as to how he spent his time and with whom he met, commenting mostly on the condition of the roadways and the kinds of vegetation he observed from his carriage.[13] According to local lore, Robert Townsend never met with Washington to acknowledge his role as Culper Jr., and neither Samuel nor the Townsend family ever received an official reward for their sacrifices during the war.

Given the gloomy and introverted turn his character had taken, the idea that Robert did not meet with President Washington is perhaps credible. If Elizabeth had indeed been the agent "355" or otherwise aided the Culpers, she may have strained to catch a glimpse of Washington's carriage as it traveled through the village, but she almost certainly did not have an opportunity to meet the president. One can only speculate as to what Samuel Townsend, who carried some of Washington's vital letters himself, knew about his son's intelligence work during the war, but it seems that if he were aware, he could not have resisted meeting with Washington behind closed doors during the president's stay.

It is a quite fitting end to Samuel's story, in fact, that President Washington himself visited the town where Samuel had returned in the fog, after personally delivering to General Nathaniel Woodhull the fateful news that Washington would abandon Long Island in 1776. The once impossible dream of an independent, American New York had become reality, and Samuel had been a part of the process, every large and small step along the way. Barely six months after Washington's visit, and just one day before Robert turned thirty-seven, Samuel Townsend passed away at home in Oyster Bay at "an advanced age, after a long and painful illness."[15] One of the most outspoken and fervent Patriots on all of Long Island lived long enough to see the dream of liberty realized and a duly-elected, beloved president—not a king—set foot in his village to recognize and celebrate the sacrifices they had endured.

But still, thousands of people lived enslaved, without any liberty or justice. And as determined as Robert was to follow in his father's footsteps and dismantle the next institution of human oppression, the fight was bigger than he was and the way forward not nearly as clear.

CHAPTER THIRTEEN

# Uncle Robert and "Free Elizabeth"

Elizabeth marveled at her change of fortune. The thirty-room Fort Neck House, now owned by the newly christened David Richard Floyd-Jones, was grander than anything she had encountered before, its sprawling lawns and palatial rooms far larger than the Townsends' homestead or anything she would have known in New York City. It was exponentially larger even than Palmes's estate outside Charleston. But even if her new home had been a hovel, it would not have mattered: she was free.

Sometime in the months between her entry in the Baptist church records in November 1789 (her last recorded affiliation with the Townsend family) and the second half of 1790, she began work as a domestic servant—not a slave but a freewoman earning wages and owning herself—for the newly renamed David Richard Floyd-Jones and his young wife, Sarah, as they struggled to begin a family.

Erected in 1770 and overlooking the Great South Bay, the house itself was light and airy, despite its enormously thick walls "of strong oak frame, brick filled, well put together and of unusually durable construction," and described as "exceptionally large and well fitted for entertainment." Guests were greeted by six grand columns leading to a wide porch and, upon entering, found themselves in a spacious hall "thirty-six feet long by twenty-six wide" floored in pine, with fourteen-foot ceilings and immense windows. The large central staircase, "a puzzle to modern architects," was a conversation point, appearing to float as it reached up to the second floor.[1,2]

Here, Elizabeth worked alongside six enslaved people and thirteen other free people of color,[3] many of whom were small family groups, with the men working the land while the women and children maintained the house and extensive kitchens in the raised basement. In time, Elizabeth would have learned the quirks of the estate: the "Milk Room with its half brick, half wood floor and its tables suspended from the ceiling out of reach of the rats and mice," the water pump installed right in the kitchen, and the attic, which, for a time, was accessible only by a ladder lowered through a hatch door rather than stairs. She would have even learned to take the long way around "the Old Brick House," the original home of Thomas and Freelove Townsend Jones from 1692, which still stood a few miles away and was traditionally avoided by the estate's workers due to some long-forgotten superstition.[4]

The estate itself was quite prestigious, and any association with it bore a tremendous amount of social capital. The fact that it was staffed by so many paid staff rather than only by slaves added to its prestige among the service workers; it was considered quite an honor to be hired as part of the Floyd-Jones staff. That Elizabeth was now employed there as a freewoman was a mark of her good reputation, and she was likely hired on the Townsends' recommendation. The exact circumstances of how she was hired are unclear, but she does seem to be a part of the household by the summer of 1790.

Commencing on August 2, 1790, a national census was called throughout the new nation, in which households were to report the following demographic information for the sake of counting the population and ascertaining the nation's potential for military and economic power:

- Free white males aged sixteen and older
- Free white males under sixteen years
- Free white females
- All other free persons
- Slaves

In the Town of Oyster Bay, which stretched across Long Island from the north shore to the south shore, 366 slaves and 308 nonwhite free people were counted, Elizabeth included—the only free person of color by that name in the entire township. She is listed in the census as "Free Elizabeth," a single woman working for paid wages as a domestic servant at the prestigious Fort Neck House. She was, in fact, one of only two free African American women recorded with that name in all of Long Island. The other "Free Elizabeth" lived in the town of Jamaica, twenty-five miles from Oyster Bay, and was registered in the census as a mother of three living in the household of a man named John W. Wortman, who had no known connection to the Townsends.[5] Though admittedly circumstantial, the evidence indicates strongly that the "Free Elizabeth" of Oyster Bay was the same woman who appealed to Robert to allow her to stay in New York, who bore a child under his roof, and whom he pursued to South Carolina and back.

That child, however, now seven years old, remained the property of the Townsends.

With Samuel's passing, Robert took over the affairs of the Townsend estate, which continued running like a single, large company rather than being divided among the siblings. Though the shipping of goods from foreign ports had declined, the family still produced and sold large quantities of cider, wheat, corn, flaxseed, and oats. A flock of sheep was tended and sheared for wool, hogs and cattle were raised and butchered for meat, and monies were collected from neighbors for allowing their animals to pasture on Townsend land. Expenses for repairs to the house and outbuildings were accounted for "to make new cellar doors" or "to repair house and barn," and at regular intervals, Robert divided the profits equally among the six surviving children, with the notable exception of Solomon, whose continued slide toward insolvency left him perpetually owing money he had borrowed from the estate against his own dividends. For the first five years following Samuel's death, Robert accounted for the work of the family's slaves in the fields and orchards, at times paying other townspeople to send their enslaved field hands to help bring in the harvest too. He also hired more than twenty free people of color as laborers, some of whom had once been enslaved by his father and all of whom he paid standard wages.[6] In time, he came to have a reputation in town as a man who was not only willing to fairly employ African Americans but would also help manumit those who needed assistance navigating the complicated legal hoops. In one instance, Robert was asked by his cousin, a Quaker named Abraham Franklin, to assist in the manumission of a man named Edward, the grand-nephew of Jupiter Hammon. "My Black Man Edward will hand thee this letter, who is going up to purchase his freedom," Franklin began. "I have taken the liberty to apply to thee to assist him in the business & see that he gets a Proper discharge from the Estate to which he belongs."[7]

Through the 1790s, state laws placed age restrictions on when enslaved people could be freed, with a minimum age of twenty-one and a maximum age of fifty. Then in 1799, New York initiated the Gradual Emancipation Act, causing age restrictions to rise dramatically, with women not eligible for freedom until age twenty-five and men not until age twenty-eight. The law deemed all children in the state born after July 4 of that year as "free," but it also demanded that they live in slavery until they came of legal age.[8] Though the law mandated that they could not be sold out of their owner's estate, African American parents who had already been manumitted suffered an agonizing wait as their children grew into young adulthood, still trapped in bondage. But even with these legal restrictions, slavery was losing the power it once held in New York, and Robert was a recognized authority on the matter in Oyster Bay.

This meant, however, that Robert was finally forced to take a definitive stance with regard to his own family's culpability in terms of the institution, from his maternal uncle's involvement in the African slave trade to his father's position as one of the largest slaveholders in Queens County. Perhaps in response to this, Robert made a drastic decision in March 1796 to sell off most of the family's 350 acres of land, herds of animals, and agricultural accoutrements, as well as the excess household goods and luxuries acquired over the years, thanks to the importing business and merchant trade. The extensive records from the sale include eight tables, twenty-four chairs, thirty-six earthenware plates, four bedsteads, fourteen rugs, quilts and blankets, two spinning wheels, two wagons, two plows, three pitchforks, and much of the livestock; in short, well over three hundred items were inventoried and sold. Even "boxes of trumpery"—that is, collections of sundry knickknacks and small items that weren't worth itemizing—were purchased and carted off by locals. Robert's mother and sisters were listed among the buyers as well, each purchasing property and items they desired. Finally, with the estate very nearly liquidated, Robert distributed the earnings among his siblings.[9] Though he continued to maintain the remaining estate for another thirty years, he was able to settle down in the family home alongside Sally and Phebe for a life of relative calm.

Or such was his wish, but Robert had one more item of business to which he must attend: divesting himself of the Townsend family slaves. It is to this end that one of the most curious artifacts of Robert's life came into being.

The Townsend Slave Bible, created in one sitting, judging from the marginalia and the uniformity of the ink and pen strokes, records the names and birthdates of many of the slaves held by the family from 1769 to 1795 and notes on a second page that these were "colored people (slaves) belonging to the family of Samuel Townsend of Oyster Bay, Long Island, state of New York."[10]

Since birth records were accepted in lieu of ownership papers or sales receipts in order to grant manumission, Robert probably converted a Bible already in his father's library into this "family Bible" for a group of the African Americans owned by the estate, thereby providing all of the entrants with a kind of retroactive birth certificate and, thus, a means toward legal emancipation.

For Harry, however, Elizabeth's tenuous legal status presented a problem. Since the Townsends could not acknowledge that she had ever reentered the state without risking an astronomical fine and her return to Richard Palmes, she could not be anywhere recorded in association with the family except as an already emancipated woman. But this left Harry without a route to eventual, legitimate freedom in the eyes of the law. Robert circumnavigated this problem by some shrewd sleight of hand. He made Elizabeth disappear, while providing a partial genealogy for seventeen individuals owned by his father and Solomon: Hannah, Violet, two females named Susannah (one spelled "Susanah"), Jeffrey, Susan, Catherine, Lilly, Gabriel, Jane, Harry, Rachel, Maryann, Nancy, Kate, Jim, and Josh. If Elizabeth was not included in this ex post facto record, her current status could not be questioned should the Overseers of the Poor scrutinize the names, for who outside the family could possibly prove that the Townsends had ever owned a woman named Elizabeth who was now suddenly in their midst again? Outside family letters, there was no paper trail to prove she had ever been enslaved. In this one move, Robert both erased her identity and helped open a door that would allow Elizabeth to create a future on her own terms.

But even though Elizabeth's absence from this particular list of twenty-five years of Townsend slaves helped protect her freedom, it in turn created a problem for Harry, which Robert resolved by one more subtle act of creative reimagination: replacing Elizabeth's name with another. "Harry, the son of Jane the daughter of Susan was born on the 19th of Febry. 1783," reads the entry. By substituting Jane for Elizabeth, he granted Harry, now twelve, a claim to legitimacy that would not have necessitated further investigation, despite the fact that Jane and Gabriel had been given as a wedding present to Solomon, who lived many miles away, the year before he was born. No "Harry" appears in any of the other lists of Gabriel and Jane's children from Solomon's inventories and diaries, and the seven other children listed as being born to the couple all lived in Orange County (and later, Manhattan) with their biological family. Only Harry, the sole biracial slave owned by the family, resided in Oyster Bay, where he was singled out among the others to enjoy extra attention and small monetary gifts from Robert, as did Jeffrey, who had lost his mother Susannah to smallpox in 1779.

And so, with most of his father's estate liquidated, Robert began the slow, methodical process of manumitting his family's slaves outside the restraints of the legal system or selling off those he could not emancipate so that he would no longer be a slave owner. The process took over a decade, and even then it was incomplete, as Hannah, Lilly, and John appear never to have been freed prior to 1827. On August 21, 1804, Robert sold Harry (now 21) to Jotham Weekes, kin to schoolteacher and diarist Zachariah, who had so carefully chronicled Oyster Bay's pre-Revolutionary history.

Robert personally drew up the contract, called an "Instrument of Manumission," for Weekes to sign and explicitly stipulated that Harry was to
be freed on his twenty-fourth birthday, a full four years before the law
permitted, maybe in the hopes that the legal manumission ages would
be lowered in the meantime. Should Weekes fail to follow through with
the manumission, the contract stated, he was contractually bound to pay
Robert the staggering sum of $1,000. Perhaps reflecting on the breach of
contract that caused the boy's mother to be sold south nearly twenty years
prior, Robert was quite insistent that Harry should be freed at precisely
the time named and went to remarkable trouble to see it laid out in no
uncertain terms. The contract, in its entirety, reads thus:

> *Know all men by these presents, that I Jotham Weekes of the Town-
> ship of Oyster Bay, Queens County and the State of New York, am
> held and firmly bound unto Robert Townsend of the same Township,
> County, and State aforesaid in the sum of One thousand dollars, to be
> paid to the said Robert Townsend, or to his certain attorney, his Exec-
> utors, administrator or assigns, for which payment well and truthful
> to be made, I bind myself, my heirs, Executors and administrators
> firmly by these presents, sealed with my seal; Dated this twenty first
> day of August, one thousand, eight hundred and four: 1804.*
>
> *The condition of this obligation is such whereas the above bound
> Jotham Weekes has this day purchased from the above named Robert
> Townsend a Negro or Mulatto slave named Harry aged twenty one
> years, six months and two days, for the sum of One hundred and
> thirty seven dollars and one half of a Dollar, and has received a Bill of
> sale for said slave: But it is agreed and understood by the said Jotham
> Weekes and Robert Townsend that the said slave Harry is to serve
> the said Jotham Weekes no longer than until he attains the age of
> Twenty four years, which will be two years, five months and twenty
> nine days. If the above named slave Harry does continue with the said
> Jotham Weekes his heirs or assigns until he attains the age of twenty
> four years, then the aforesaid Jotham Weekes his heirs or assigns are
> to manumit the said Slave Harry: Now if the above bound Jotham
> Weekes his heirs or assigned do punctually and faithfully manumit*

*the said Slave Harry at the expiration of two years, five months and twenty nine days which will be the nineteenth day of February, in the year of our Lord, one thousand, eight hundred and seven then the above obligation to be void or else to remain in full force and virtue.*[11]

Unfortunately, Jotham Weekes died in 1807, just a few months after Harry's twenty-fourth birthday, and while there is no record to indicate that Harry was freed through legal channels, neither is there evidence that the contractual fine was paid to Robert to indicate Weekes's breach of the agreement. It is possible that Harry was casually rather than legally manumitted, as was becoming increasingly popular as the institution of slavery crawled toward its demise in New York. With the passage of a law in 1817 that sought to grant universal emancipation to all born before 1799 within a decade, the second great war for independence of Robert Townsend's life limped toward its feeble conclusion. And with it went any remaining zeal he harbored for changing the world. Robert had never possessed his father's fire or his older brother's frenetic energy, and now he slipped quietly into a life unmarked by passion, productivity, or purpose.

After divesting himself of his father's extensive business interests, he busied himself with reading things other than shop ledgers and inventories. In 1801, now in his mid-forties, he joined with David Richard Floyd-Jones and a few other local men to establish the Oyster Bay Academy but was otherwise largely retired from public life.

He copied essays and passages that caught his fancy, not only shedding light on his emotional state but also revealing a few prominent themes that seemed to occupy his thoughts, including solitude and regret. One such composition Robert duplicated in his personal notes states, "It is far easier for a man to live single than to be encumbered with the charge of a family, and to live altogether as he should do with his wife and children; whence we may conclude that celibacy is a state of more tranquility and ease than that of wedlock." Farther down, the essay praises reason and notes that a removal from society may be "occasioned by spite, love, or some other passion, which does not allow us time for reflection, but hurries us away, or bewilders us like an *ignis fatuus*, we know not whither. We fly from mankind, and endeavour to hide ourselves, thinking that the vexation and perplexity which prey upon us with such a weight, will quit us in solitude; but instead of subsiding, they pursue us with redoubled ardour; and at length we find too late, that we can expect no consolation from a mistaken course we took."[12]

A few years later, a distant cousin, the Reverend Joseph Townsend, published his reflections on his journey through Spain. Robert copied the following account of the narrator's farewell to his traveling companions in Madrid:

> *After my companions were dispersed, I took up my abode in solitude, with the reflection, painful for the moment, that I was come to my journey's end. It had been wearisome, and not altogether free from accidents and disagreeable adventures; but then, with an object constantly in view, everything may be endured. . . . [N]ow that our journey was at an end, the idea of dispersing to meet no more left a gloom which solitude was ill suited to relieve. At the end of a pursuit, a vacuum succeeds, which must be painful, till some new, some inter-esting object is in view, and gives fresh occupations to the mind.*[13]

"A vacuum succeeds," and so, it seems, was true for Robert's life. Having dedicated his years as a young man to leading a double life as a spy and his middle age to the complicated and still unresolved work of abolition—both on the individual and the collective levels—he now seemed without direction or purpose. The Americans won. Elizabeth was brought home. Slavery was being phased out. Samuel Townsend's estate was dissolved. And Robert no longer had a cause to which he could ded-icate himself with the singularity of focus that had defined his mode of being for so long.

Audrey's husband, Captain James Farley, noticed this aimlessness and wrote his brother-in-law a chiding letter, admonishing him for this apparent depression. Such a "dejected mind," Farley insisted, is "wilfully sinning against the Almighty Creator that gave you a being." Unfortu-nately, Farley's harsh attitude toward Robert reflects what was very much the prevailing view toward many mental health and emotional struggles in the late eighteenth and early nineteenth centuries—that such challenges were the result of a flaw in character, obstinate laziness, or sinful disobedience.

"Robert, in all my different letters from home," Farley begins, writing from his ship, anchored in Hull, England,

> they all mention that my Brother Robert Townsend is sunk under a low depressed and dejected state of mind, and yet has a tolerable good appetite and sleeps middling well. Excellent symptoms of health, and that he has lost all hope. This account gives me much pain to think that Robert Townsend has lost all his fortitude, why thus Robert,—a man in the prime of life, nobody to care for but himself (being a single man), blessed with more than common abilities and an ample sufficiency to support him in any way he should wish to live, makes me cry, Shame, Shame, Shame!—
>
> Robert, if you don't chose to marry (which was the grand intention of man's creation) so be it, yet you'r in duty bound to your maker to yourself and to your neighbor to do all the good you can in this life, so that you receive a good reward in the world to come, but this cannot be done in this state you are now in, therefore, don't keep your talents longer hid, bring them forward while it is still day for they are only lent. Arouse yourself up Robert. Shake off all these hypochondrial low-lived notions (for I hate them) take a horse and ride a few miles every day, put yourself in the way of good company but cheerful, at dinner afford yourself three glasses of good wine, till you shake off this slumber; go down to my house in the evening, but not with melancholy and either read a cheerful book or tell some pretty little stories to divert my poor complaining wife, whom I love, and sister Phebe who I suspect is there. These things would all be commendable even in the sight of God, who does not require dull servants.

Farley then suggests that if Robert wanted a diversion, he could oversee the clearing of one of his brother-in-law's fields and "at other leisure hours lay the foundation of a good plan that may have the appearance being productive to you and me."[14]

One can only imagine Robert's reaction upon receiving such a lecture—and it was not the only such letter he received from Farley on the subject. In fact, judging from some of Solomon's letters, too, Robert's disposition seems to have been a point of critique among several of the family members. But Robert was never one to bow to his family's sense of propriety and, in fact, may have even considered his melancholic state superior to the pitiable condition in which his older brother now found himself.

For years, Robert watched as Solomon overleveraged himself so completely that he eventually remained away from his home and family for months at a time both to avoid creditors and to avoid the shame of having to face their diminished circumstances. So desperate was Solomon that he did not even return home to be with his wife and three-year-old son when the latter contracted a terminal illness in 1804, instead recording his regrets in his pocket diaries but never summoning the will to set foot back in town until it was too late: "Got letter from New York—one from Brother William, informing me of the Death of my youngest little son Solomon who has been lying ill a long while, died the 1st instant at 2 o'clock in the afternoon. Poor little thing has suffered very much—is now no more and far from all his troubles. My absence from my family at this time of distress is a circumstance that adds to their trouble and to myself makes it doubly grievous. Have flattered myself that should see the poor little Babe again." Solomon then admitted to himself, "It has been a hard standing circumstance to reflect that I could not return home to my sick child without experiencing when I got there, such disagreeable summons in my business."[15]

It is not clear whether the breach between the oldest surviving Townsend brothers was ever fully mended, but one of Solomon's sons, Peter, grew up fascinated by his hermit-like Uncle Robert. As an adult, Peter became a doctor who was doubtlessly a very welcomed guest in a house of three aging people, and so he visited the Townsend home in Oyster Bay often to see his amiable aunts and to interview Robert on all matters of family history, local lore, and war stories. Despite the volumes of notes that Peter took from those interviews, Robert never breathed a word about his work as a spy.

The Townsends sent Oyster Bay tongues wagging yet again in 1808, when forty-five-year-old Phebe, the youngest of the Revolutionary-generation Townsends, married a man twenty years her junior, named Dr. Ebenezer Seeley, and moved her young husband into the family home with Sally and Robert. Peter described the "Doctor" as "a yankee deputy schoolmaster," complaining, "He never had money enough (except for my Aunt Phebe's) to jingle on a tombstone."[16] But by then, Robert was all but immune to family dramas; in fact, while the world around him was absorbed in Phebe's scandalous union, he quietly set up Polly Banvard's son, Robert Townsend Jr., now a young man in his early twenties, in training as a carpenter.[17]

Robert died in 1838 at the age of eighty-four. It is the job of a spy to be untraceable, and Robert Townsend played his part well—so well, in fact, that his wartime heroics were not uncovered until the 1920s.[18] His gradual conversion into an abolitionist was not brought to light until ninety years after that. Despite his significant and impactful efforts in a number of different causes, life was still something of a disappointment for Robert. He never achieved the satisfaction of seeing all his work brought about to the neat and satisfying conclusions he believed were the natural order of things.

Elizabeth's story, however, remained hidden even longer than Robert's. For a number of years, before all the extant Townsend records were discovered and placed in conversation with one another, it was believed that the "Liss" who disappeared with Colonel Simcoe was simply one of Samuel's dairy cows rather than a woman with her own deeply complex life.

There is something poignant about Elizabeth's disappearance from and eventual reemergence into the historical record. Her whole story, it seems, was a series of removals and returns. She escaped her master's house with the enemy only to reintroduce herself to her old master's son two years later, boldly asserting she had no desire to leave for Canada with her British owner. She was sold to Charleston only to be smuggled back to the state she considered home. She was left without any legal record on her return only to register her name in the Baptist church—free in the eyes of God, if not in the laws of man. And despite her omission from the Townsend Slave Bible—a smoothing over of the space she filled and the erasure of her identity, as if she had never existed—her name was listed in the 1790 census, where her status was not a mere descriptor of her condition but capitalized and placed before her name like a defiant title: "Free Elizabeth."

And this is the final record of her life. Whether she passed away during the following decade or married and was simply counted as a member of her husband's household in the census of 1800 remains unclear. She was likely buried either in the Fort Neck House cemetery or, perhaps, in the small Townsend family plot. When the Floyd-Jones cemetery was moved to make room for modern roadways, only the formal family headstones were relocated. However, the Townsend family graveyard still exists, behind the site of an old British fort, at the dead end of Simcoe Street in Oyster Bay. Right inside the gate of rusting chain link, within sight of Robert Townsend's grave, is a grouping of fieldstones, large, flat rocks in the general shape of headstones that were pulled from fields and stood up to mark the resting places of slaves of the household.

Though her fate cannot be established with absolutely certainty, it is important to acknowledge how much of Elizabeth's story is known. She was real. She had a name. She had an identity and ambitions. She had a child and a mind of her own. She had tremendous bravery and an extraordinary will. For a woman who had very little she could legally call her own, Liss—"Free Elizabeth"—was a woman who possessed quite a few things the prevailing culture insisted she could not have.

And now, at last, she also has a voice.

# "The Journey's End"

The lives of Robert and Liss intersected with those of countless others, many of whom went on to shape their community and their world in their own unique ways.

At least two members of the family of Tom Gall, the first African American freed on Long Island, moved to Canada at the end of the Revolution as part of a huge northward migration of approximately three thousand free people of color and escaped slaves.[1] Even so, many of his descendants continued to live in Pine Hollow until the 1950s, helping to establish that area of town as a community for African Americans for nearly three hundred years.[2] Prominent residents included Plato Gale (an alternate spelling of "Gall"), a founder of the AME Zion Church in Oyster Bay in 1848; the congregation is the oldest continuous religious body still meeting in its original structure in the town.[3] Another distinguished resident was David Carll, who served in an all-black unit in the Civil War. He used his enlistment bonus to purchase a sizable tract of land in Pine Hollow and eventually married a white woman named Mary Louisa Appleford in one of the earliest-known interracial marriages in Oyster Bay. One of David and Mary Louisa's descendants still lives in the family house, on a road now called Carll Hill, and another descendant, Vanessa Williams, attained worldwide fame when she became the first Miss America of African American descent in 1983.[4]

Jupiter Hammon, the enslaved poet, lived into his nineties, spending his final years with his grand-nephew Benjamin Hammon in nearby Huntington; their home was recently named a historic landmark.[5] No formal manumission record for Jupiter exists, but the Floyds do seem to have allowed him to live his final years away from their estate. For years, scholars regarded Hammon's poetry as problematic, since it seemed to take a positive view of enslavement; in early 2013, however, Dr. Cedrick May discovered a previously unknown 1786 poem by Jupiter Hammon in the Yale University archives that changed everything. Titled "An Essay on Slavery, with submission to Divine providence, knowing that God Rules over all things," the poem is the only one of Hammon's works to exist in his own handwriting and speaks out against the institution, encouraging fellow slaves to bear up under the yoke of oppression until the practice is abolished.[6] His masters likely withheld this poem from publication for fear that it seemed too radical, despite (or perhaps because of) its call for abolition in Christian terms.[7]

Among the Townsends' neighbors, only Thomas Buchanan enjoyed a marked improvement in his fortunes after the war. His political fence-sitting served him well; his public alignment with the Crown meant that his property was treated with extra respect during the British occupation of Long Island, but his private dealings in favor of the Patriot cause (such as his intervening during Samuel's arrest) meant that he was permitted to stay in America when many other wealthy Loyalists were driven out. He served as vice president of the Chamber of Commerce of New York from 1780 to 1783 and was a governor of the New York Hospital from 1785 to 1800. As he was one of the last great eighteenth-century shipping magnates in New York, his death in 1815 at age seventy-one marked the end of an era, including the waning years of slavery in New York, which was memorialized years later in dramatic fashion:

*There are no such funerals in these days. Grand old funerals—it was worth living in those times, just to have the pleasure of going to the stylish, comfortable funeral of an old Knickerbocker. Nothing of that kind can be got up now. In the first place, we lack the negroes. In those days the servants were all colored, and when their master was to be buried, they were dressed in black, with white towels on their arms. All the rooms in the house were flung open. Everybody received scarfs and gloves, and such wines!*

*There are no such wines now in existence as were to be had at an old Knickerbocker funeral. Thomas Buchanan had Madeira wine in his cellar one hundred years old. Dust, an inch thick, upon the bottles. All the friends went to such funerals. So did acquaintances, for it was only on such occasions that people could get wine to drink—the best, even in those days of cheapness, $10 per bottle. Could it be had now, it would be worth $100 per bottle; but it is not to be had. Such wine is not in existence. Thomas Buchanan was in business when this city had but 10,381 souls. He was here through all the dark hours of the Revolution, and he lived to see it grow to 120,000. He, modest merchant, little dreamed that it was he and such as he, kings of commerce, that had made it grow so greatly, and increase so vastly in wealth.*

*Where are your Clintons—your Tompkins, Jays—your Burrs, Hamiltons, and the names that adorn history—mere politicians or so-called statesmen, when compared with the creators of the wealth and the glory of the great commercial city.*[8]

Among Robert's compatriots in the Culper Ring, all did reasonably well for themselves following the war. Benjamin Tallmadge married Mary Floyd and partnered with Caleb Brewster on August 5, 1784, to purchase approximately 350 acres of confiscated Floyd family land.[9] Because of his assistance to the Culpers, Benjamin Floyd was allowed to stay in America and repurchase another large parcel of the Floyd estate for a third of its value. Austin Roe, meanwhile, ran a tavern where George Washington paid a visit during his 1790 tour of Long Island; he later served in the Suffolk County Militia.[10] Abraham Woodhull married Mary Smith and served as Suffolk County magistrate from 1799 to 1810; he was widowed in 1806 and was remarried eighteen years later to Lydia Terry.[11]

Colonel John Graves Simcoe, one of the Culpers' great antagonists, also did quite well for himself. In 1782, he married Elizabeth Posthumas Gwillum, herself a celebrated diarist and artist as well as an heiress with extensive landholdings in the southwest of England. The couple had five daughters before Simcoe was named the first lieutenant governor of Upper Canada in 1791 and established the city of York (now Toronto) two years later. The Simcoes had another daughter and two sons, and

Simcoe established himself as fierce abolitionist, succeeding in completely ending slavery in Upper Canada in 1810, fourteen years ahead of its abolition in Great Britain and decades ahead of America.[12] He continued to be an advocate for many of the African Americans who served under him, including helping B. E. Griffiths, the brave "Trumpeter Barney" from Simcoe's Virginia campaign, to secure a soldier's pension.

In 1797, Simcoe served briefly as the governor of Saint-Domingue in Britain's ultimately failed attempt to rule Haiti. Despite Simcoe's anti-slavery stance, he nevertheless acted to protect the Crown's interests and subsequently lost significant holdings to the slave revolts led by Toussaint Louverture. In 1806, though he was suffering from deteriorating health, Simcoe was appointed the commander in chief of the British army in India, but he passed away before he sailed. His legacy is preserved in Canada, where a nationwide public holiday on the first Monday of August is called "Simcoe Day" in Toronto.[13]

Of the people who were responsible for Elizabeth's nightmarish voyage and enslavement in Charleston, several of them did go on to noteworthy ends. Though nothing more of Ann Sharwin can be traced after her second marriage, Alexander Robertson busied himself in charitable work around the city, though still in the loud, boisterous style for which he was known. To celebrate the marriage of one of his daughters, for example, he ordered 150 loaves of bread, 300 pounds of beef, 130 pounds of cheese, 3 barrels of "strong ale," and 3 barrels of apples sent to the local alms house and debtors' prison.[14] In 1791, he donated two lots on King Street to the Scotch Presbyterian Church of New York to build a free school for poor children;[15] the Alexander Robertson School still exists on the Upper West Side, but now as an upscale private school rather than a charitable one.[16]

Alexander Shirras, who held Elizabeth's note, likewise took a turn toward benevolence. He established the Shirras Dispensary,[17] which operated as a clinic and pharmacy for the poor of Charleston, South Carolina, for over a century before merging with Roper Hospital in the 1920s.[18]

As for the two primary villains in Elizabeth's story, their stories intersected again. On September 1, 1789, two months before Elizabeth was registered in the Baptist church roll in Oyster Bay, Richard Palmes showed up in a legal advertisement, described as "an absent and nonresident debtor" of the city of New York and owing money to none other than "James Tinker, mariner." According to the notice, a judge ordered that all of Palmes's estate was to be seized and held: "Unless he the said Richard Palmes shall discharge his debts within one year after the publication of this notice, all his estate, real and personal, will be sold for the payment and satisfaction of his creditors."[19]

Tinker, meanwhile, began to expand his reach beyond the East Coast to international commerce. In early November 1793, he ran into some trouble on a voyage back from the Caribbean. The *New-York Daily Gazette*'s account read, "The sloop Free Mason, James Tincker, from Gaudaloupe for New-York, was first plundered by a Spanish privateer—afterwards taken by a Bermudian privateer—but meeting with a gale, sprung a-leek, doft her sails, and carried her prize-mailers and seven privateer-men into Wilmington, North Carolina, there to refit to proceed for New-York."[20] Five years later, Tinker and his brother-in-law both succumbed to an unknown illness en route from Charleston to L'Anceveau in what is now the Dominican Republic. After languishing for five weeks, Tinker finally died on February 28, 1798.[21]

Palmes met an even more dramatic fate. He eventually took to a life at sea, traveling frequently between Kingston, Jamaica, and New York. During one such voyage, the schooner he was on sprung a leak during a storm near Cape Hatteras, North Carolina, on the evening of April 29, 1802. The situation grew more perilous as the night wore on, so that by daybreak the crew loaded up the longboat with a compass, quadrant, and provisions and prepared to evacuate the ship. At 9 a.m. Palmes and the captain decided to make one last attempt to save the vessel by veering it toward land, but it turned too suddenly, capsized, and disappeared beneath the waves within two minutes. Six people onboard drowned, including Palmes. The remainder were spotted and rescued that afternoon adrift in the longboat.[22] Palmes would likely have taken comfort in the fact that the local paper near where he grew up ran a notice of his death "at sea, (drowned)," alongside the deaths of Charles Darwin and the queen of Sardinia, Naples, who both passed away that same spring.[23]

Richard Lushington, the conflicted Quaker and Robert's abolitionist friend, became a beloved figure in Charleston's political and benevolence circles. At his death from a sudden illness in June 1790, the *State Gazette of South-Carolina* ran a statement revealing that his concern for the plight of George Morris was quite typical of his character:

> *This gentleman's death may truly be considered, both as a public and private loss. His life was not unusefully spent—he filled the various public stations his fellow citizens had been pleased to place him in, with fidelity and integrity. He belonged to several charitable, incorporated societies in this city; in all of them he proved a most valuable member. . . . The widow and orphan supported by their bounty (and to whose complaints he was ever attentive) have cause to drop a tear for their departed friend;—he was hospitable, humane, and benevolent, possessed of a sympathetic heat that felt for others woes, and always found a secret satisfaction in relieving them.*[24]

Adam Gilchrist, meanwhile, found his gamble of moving to South Carolina paid off handsomely when he quickly grew his ventures to become a very wealthy merchant and served briefly in the South Carolina General Assembly. He is more notable, however, for his involvement in a case that went all the way to the Supreme Court in 1808. When President Thomas Jefferson enacted an all-encompassing embargo act that year forbidding any foreign trade, he encouraged inspectors to detain *all* ships for extra inspection. Gilchrist had a ship bound for Baltimore that was barred from sailing, despite any evidence it was headed overseas. Fighting the restrictions in court, *Gilchrist v. The Port of Charleston* asserted Jefferson's overreach of the executive branch. Despite being a Jefferson appointment, Charleston native Justice William Johnson agreed that the president was acting beyond his constitutional powers. The case was ultimately decided in favor of the plaintiffs, and Johnson earned the title of "First Dissenter" for demonstrating that the checks-and-balances system really did work, since justices could and would rule against the president who appointed them. Gilchrist passed away at the age of fifty-five on March 13, 1816.[25]

—❧—

At age seventy-six, Samuel's wife, Sarah, passed away on April 10, 1800, and was buried in the family plot. As for the subsequent generation of Townsends, Robert outlived all of his brothers. Following his return to Oyster Bay, William showed no inclination to settle down, never marrying or reviving his business career, and may have suffered from depression or other emotional struggles. He continued living at home, occasionally helping out with the family's remaining shipping concerns but never winning its confidence. On a bitterly cold day in March 1805, he went out with a crew to help a boat frozen in Oyster Bay Harbor. As they attempted to cut the vessel free, William stepped onto a cake of ice, slipped, and in seconds was trapped beneath the freezing water. A search for him continued until dark, with no success, but the next morning his body was found, still under the ice, at nearby Ship's Point. He was forty-seven.[26]

Solomon enjoyed some success as a New York assemblyman but was continually plagued by debt. He was serving in Albany at the statehouse when he suffered a cerebral hemorrhage in 1811 and died at age sixty-four. The entire Senate of New York attended his funeral, and he was buried in Albany, though many years later his body was returned to the family graveyard in Oyster Bay.[27]

Back in Chester, his widow, Anne, was left bankrupt and had to liquidate all of the family's holdings in order to pay their creditors.[28] The Jefferson Trade Embargo had decimated Solomon's anchor business, and the US Navy, which had given him the contract to outfit the frigate *President* with ironwork, had never paid. Decades after his death, the navy finally agreed to pay a settlement to the family.

Audrey, who became blind at the end of her life, outlived her lecturing husband, James Farley, by nineteen years, passing away on November 28, 1829. They had no children of their own, though Audrey raised two daughters from Farley's first marriage. Phebe's much younger husband, Ebenezer Seeley, remarried within six months of Phebe's death in 1841 and moved his new wife into the Townsend family house. "Disgusted with the indecent haste" of her brother-in-law's actions, Sally took a steamboat out of Oyster Bay on the same day as the couple's marriage and went to visit her nephew Peter, Solomon's son, in Manhattan.[29] Sally passed away the following year; she never married, despite the compliments she received as a young woman in Simcoe's poem and McGill's etched windowpane.

In 1807, Polly Banvard's son Robert Townsend Jr. joined a committee tasked with creating a dignified resting place for the bones of Patriot martyrs of the British prison ships. In May 1808, when the tomb was completed, he marched in a grand procession through lower Manhattan with thirteen coffins full of skeletal remains to the vault located across the East River in Brooklyn. In his final years, Robert Jr. again advocated for the dignity of the deceased, railing against the Common Council of New York City, which proposed exhuming the bodies in the graveyard of Trinity Church in 1860, so that the land could be developed. Both his first wife and a daughter were buried at Trinity, and he accused the council of being "unconcerned of the dust of the beloved dead." He died two years later, on March 20, 1862, at age seventy-eight, and found his own final resting place in Sleepy Hollow, New York.[30]

In the 1850s, Solomon's youngest son, Solomon II, bought the Townsend family home back from Ebenezer Seely and greatly expanded it into a rambling Victorian mansion. He also maintained a residence in Manhattan and wrote to his uncle Robert in 1833 to recommend "a colored boy" to work as his servant there. The elder Robert reached out to a local man named James Gaul, who had a son that he attested was "a very smart boy and having been much used to horses, I have no doubt would answer every purpose you want a boy for." But on July 26, 1833, Robert replied to his nephew that James Gaul "last evening called to inform me" that he "could not part with him."[31] The descendants of Tom Gall remained fixed on their land and their freedom for generations.

As for the African Americans enslaved by the Townsend family, the fates of many of them have been lost to history, though their existence is marked by their names in family documents, like the Townsend Slave Bible, and the crude fieldstones clustered at one end of the small

Townsend family cemetery in Oyster Bay. A large community of free African Americans living in Oyster Bay chose the last name Townsend, but because so many white slave-owning families named Townsend lived in Oyster Bay, and because the reasons for a freed person's choice of last name may not be known, connecting these free Townsends to previously enslaved individuals proves to be extremely difficult.

As for Gabriel and Jane, by the mid-1790s, Gabriel was a freeman, though Jane and the children were still enslaved. They lived together in the cellar of Solomon's anchor shop in Manhattan and one by one gained their emancipation through the "gradual abolition" laws of early-nineteenth-century New York. In March 1796, the anchor shop ledger listed Gabriel with a full name: Gabriel Parker.[32] The New York City household of "Gabriel Parker, a Black" appears in the 1800 Census living in the 7th Ward. According to her manumission certificate, Gabriel and Jane's daughter Rachel also took the last name "Parker" upon her freedom, though no reason is known for her choosing that name.[33]

Hannah's daughter and Elizabeth's niece, Violet, died tragically at the age of seven, but the fate of Elizabeth's son remains unclear. Harry was not formally manumitted by Jotham Weekes on his twenty-fourth birthday in 1807, despite the contract between Weekes and Robert. While this lack of a record may indicate a more casual emancipation, since no £1,000 payment shows up in Robert's account books and it seems unlikely he would have let such an obligation pass, there is the possibility that Harry remained enslaved.[34] Records do show that a cousin, Richard Townsend, freed a slave named Harry in 1818. If this was the same man, it means Elizabeth's son was enslaved until age thirty-five.[35]

As frustrating as the lack of records can be at times, it is also remarkable that the documents that survive provide us with enough of a glimpse into so much minutiae of life—the daily activities, concerns, purchases, and ambitions that fill the time between the dates in documents, if not on headstones. The story reconstructed in these pages was likely just a small, largely forgotten series of incidents for most of the people involved. But it was of central importance for Robert and even more so for Liss. Robert Townsend lived by his own strict moral code: complex, imperfect, but also changeable as his own sense of justice and liberty grew. Elizabeth's assertion of her own will in running away with the British, her intrepid petitions to control her own fate, the denials of her basic humanity, and her ultimate triumph in the face of repeated tragedy and injustice make her a symbol of enduring bravery and of the promise that when voices are raised, minds can change. Robert and Elizabeth's story stands as a testament to the marginalized people whose lives, courage, and blood are a part of the very fabric of our nation.

# Acknowledgments

A research project of this magnitude would not have been possible without the efforts of countless people.

To the tremendous staff, Board of Directors, and both Sarah Abruzzi and Harriet Gerard-Clark (the museum director from the Raynham Hall Museum when the hunt for Liss began and the present director, respectively), we cannot thank you enough for your support and encouragement.

We would also like to extend our appreciation to the countless historians and archivists who helped point the way towards the crumbs of evidence that together helped form a fuller picture, including (but in no way limited to) Andrea Meyer at the Long Island Collection of the East Hampton Free Library; John Hammond, Town of Oyster Bay Historian; Denise Evans Sheppard of the Oyster Bay Historical Society; Dr. Cedrick May, assistant professor of African American Literature at the University of Texas at Arlington and expert on Jupiter Hammon; Thomas Hogan and Andrew Way, researchers of the *Glasgow*; journalist Bill Bleyer of *Newsday*; the staff at the Patricia D. Klingenstein Library at the New York Historical Society; Nic Butler, historian at the Charleston County Public Library; the staff at the South Carolina Department of Archives and History; the staff of the Archives of Ontario; the staff of the William L. Clements Library in Ann Arbor, Michigan; and many, many others. We cannot thank you enough for your dedication to preserving the records of our past and your willingness to help resurrect voices that have been kept in silence too long.

We would be remiss if we did not recognize the amazing Lindsay Levine whose research and incredible artistic abilities created the beautiful rendering of Liss featured on the cover of this book. Thank you for sharing your tremendous talents with us.

Special thanks to Alexander Rose, Brian Kilmeade, and Don Yaeger whose interest in Robert Townsend and the Culper spies led them to share the story of both with a broader audience.

To Eric Myers of Myers Literary Management, a wonderful and supportive agent whose enthusiasm for this project breathed new life into it—thank you for believing in Robert and Liss, and for advocating for us.

To the editorial staff at Lyons Press—Stephanie Scott, who first championed this book; Rick Reinhart, who expertly steered us through the editing process and answered dozens of panicked emails that calmed our fears about the impact of COVID-19 on the production schedule; Kristen Mellitt and Jennifer Kelland, who took on the monumental task of copyediting this manuscript and preparing it for publication—we could not have asked for a better team. Thank you for your expertise, professionalism, and everything you did to help us tell this story in the most impactful way possible. You are amazing.

To the unparalleled Vanessa Williams, who listened to Liss's story, connected with her humanity, and lent her powerful voice to this book: You are a national treasure, and we will be forever humbled that you took an interest in our project. Thank you, thank you, thank you.

And finally, to our families: thank you for all you did to make this book a reality. (From Claire) To my wonderful husband, Chris, whose loving support never wavered and who proved a tremendous research partner over this sixteen-year journey—there will never be words sufficient to express my love and appreciation. To my amazing kids, Karl and Charlotte Beller-jeau, who grew up alongside Liss's story and learned about every discovery in real time, thank you for your support and interest and for growing up to be such incredible adults; I am in awe of you. (From Tiffany) To my history-teacher mom, thank you for fostering a love for untold stories from America's past. To my husband, who encouraged me to embrace this project and cheered me on when I needed it, I am eternally grateful. And to Bridget, who was barely four months old when I took the first phone call from Claire asking if I'd be interested in partnering on an intriguing story she was researching—may you grow up to be as brave and bold as Liss and as unconcerned about other people's judgments as Robert Townsend.

# Sources

## Chapter 1: Merchants and Masters

1. Henry Louis Gates Jr., *The African Americans: Many Rivers to Cross* (Carlsbad, CA: Smiley Books, 2013).

2. John Thorton, "The African Experience of the '20. and Odd Negroes' Arriving in Virginia in 1619," *William and Mary Quarterly* 55, no. 3 (July 1998): 421–34.

3. Michael Guasco, *Slaves and Englishmen: Human Bondage in the Early Modern Atlantic World* (Philadelphia: University of Pennsylvania Press, 2014), 155–94.

4. David N. Gellman, *Emancipating New York: The Politics of Slavery and Freedom, 1777–1827* (Baton Rouge: Louisiana State University Press, 2006), 4.

5. *History of Queens County, New York, with Illustrations, Portraits & Sketches of Prominent Families and Individuals* (New York: W. W. Munsell & Co., 1882), 49–55.

6. John Brown Dillon, *Oddities of Colonial Legislation in America: As Applied to the Public Lands, Primitive Education, Religion, Morals, Indians, Etc., with Authentic Records of the Origin and Growth of Pioneer Settlements, Embracing Also a Condensed History of the States and Territories* (Indianapolis: Robert Douglass, Publisher, 1879), 243.

7. John Cox Jr., ed., *Oyster Bay Town Records* (New York: Tobias A. Wright, 1916).

8. John E. Hammond, "The Early Settlement of Oyster Bay," *The Freeholder* 7, no. 4 (Spring 2003): 3–9, 18–19.

9. James C. Townsend, *A Memorial of John, Henry and Richard Townsend and Their Descendants* (New York: W. A. Townsend, 1865), 81–84.

10. "Remonstrance of the Inhabitants of Flushing against Anti-Quaker Laws," *Ecclesiastical Records of the State of New York*, published by the State under the supervision of Hugh Hastings, State Historian (Albany, NY: James B. Lyon, State Printer, 1901), 412, 413.

11. Kenneth T. Jackson, "A Colony with a Conscience," *New York Times*, December 27, 2007.

12. Dr. Peter Townsend, Notebook, F89.11.9, Collection of Friends of Raynham Hall Museum, 73–74.

13. John Cox Jr., ed., *Oyster Bay Town Records* (New York: Tobias A. Wright, 1916).

14. George Weekes, Account Book, Oyster Bay, 1753–1773, Collection of Friends of Raynham Hall Museum.

15. McCoun Family Account Book, 1793–1809, Collection of Friends of Raynham Hall Museum.

16. Lewis Morris to Richard Crabb, Transfer of slave Owah, November 26, 1673, Oyster Bay Town Records.

17. *The Wright Family of Oysterbay, L.I. with the Ancestry and Descent from Peter Wright and Nicholas Wright, 1423–1923* (North Clarendon, VT: Tuttle Antiquarian Books, 1923), 65.

18. Will of Alice Crabb, Oysterbay, April 1685, proved October 13, 1685, Oyster Bay Town Records.

19. Vivienne L. Kruger, Slow Growth of a Free Black Community, 1644 Until the American Revolution, http://newyorkslavery.blogspot.com/

20. "Pine Hollow Land Survey including Naomi Gaul and Plato Gale properties," private collection of Denise Evans-Sheppard, 1959.

21. Stanley A. Ransom, *America's First Black Poet: Jupiter Hammon of Long Island.* (Denver: Outskirts Press, 2020), 15–23.

22. Cedrick May and Julie McCowen, "'An Essay on Slavery': An Unpublished Poem by Jupiter Hammon," *Early American Literature* 48, no. 2 (2013): 457–71.

23. Cedrick May, *The Collected Works of Jupiter Hammon* (Knoxville: University of Tennessee Press, 2017), xxxv-xxxvi.

24. Charla E. Bolton and Reginald H. Metcalf Jr., "The Migration of Jupiter Hammon and His Family: From Slavery to Freedom and Its Consequences," *Long Island History Journal* 23, no. 2 (2013): 3.

25. Letter, Henry Lloyd to Samuel Clowes, September 23, 1728, in *Papers of the Lloyd Family of the Manor of Queens Village, Lloyd's Neck, Long Island, New York, 1654–1826,* ed. Dorothy C. Barck. Collections of the New-York Historical Society, 2 vols. (New York: J. J. Little & Ives Co. for the New-York Historical Society, 1926–1927), 302–3, Volume I.

26. Account book of Jacob Townsend, 1715–1730, East Hampton Library, Long Island Collection.

27. Geoffrey L. Rossano, "Prosperity on the Ways: Shipbuilding in Colonial Oyster Bay, 1745–1775," *Long Island Historical Journal* 2, no. 1 (fall 1989): 21–28.

28. Benjamin F. Thompson, *History of Long Island; Containing an Account of the Discovery and Settlement; with Other Important and Interesting Matters to the Present Time,* 3 vols. (New York: E. French Publishing Co., 1839), 3: 429–30.

29. Advertisement, "For Sale, the Following Houses and Tracts of Land," *Aurora (New York) General Advertiser,* February 26, 1796, 1.

30. Paul Bailey, *Long Island; a History of Two Great Counties, Nassau and Suffolk,* vol. 1 (New York: Lewis Historical Publishing Company, 1949), 84.

31. Livingston Rowe Schuyler, *The Liberty of the Press in the American Colonies before the Revolutionary War; with Particular Reference to Conditions in the Royal Colony of New York* (New York: Wentworth Press, 1905), 59–60.

32. Dr. Peter Townsend, Notebook, F89.11.9, Collection of Friends of Raynham Hall Museum, 92.

33. Zachariah Weekes, Diary, March 27, 1758, Collection of Friends of Raynham Hall Museum.

34. "Slavery at the Townsends'," Raynham Hall Museum. https://raynhamhallmuseum
.org/history/1740–1776–before-the-revolution.

35. Receipt book of Samuel Townsend, 1748–49, Collection of Friends of Raynham
Hall Museum.

36. Advertisement, "To Be Sold at Publik Vendue," *New-York Gazette, or Weekly Post-Boy* (New York, NY), September 26, 1748.

37. Ship news, "Capt. Troup, Being on a Cruize," *New-York Gazette*, March 23, 1747.

38. "Samuel Townsend Purchase of Jacob from Thomas Seaman of Hempstead," May 1,
1767, Townsend Family Papers, New-York Historical Society.

39. Advertisement, "A few healthy young Negro Slaves," *New-York Mercury* (New York,
NY), July 22, 1765.

40. Letter, Robert Townsend to Samuel Townsend, December 14, 1781, Townsend
Papers, East Hampton Library, Long Island Collection.

41. Account book of Samuel Townsend, merchant, 1781–1788, Townsend Papers, East
Hampton Library, Long Island Collection, 60.

42. "Negro Ledger," Townsend Family Papers, New-York Historical Society.

43. Henry Onderdonk, *Queens County in Olden Times: Being a Supplement to the Several
Histories Thereof* (Jamaica, NY: Charles Welling, Publisher, 1865), 44.

44. Samuel Townsend Jr., Waste Book: May 12, 1772–June 25, 1772, Collection of
Friends of Raynham Hall Museum.

45. "Voyages: The Trans-Atlantic Slave Trade Database," https://www.slavevoyages.org.

46. Ship news. "Newport. March 10th," Boston News-Letter, April 2, 1766, 2.

47. "Voyages: The Trans-Atlantic Slave Trade Database," https://www.slavevoyages.org.

48. *Joseph Lawrence Ledger, 1762–1808*, Lawrence Family Papers, Brooklyn Historical
Society.

49. Advertisement, "A Likely, handy Negro girl, about nine years of age," *New-York
Gazette and the Weekly Mercury*, April 3, 1775, 3.

## Chapter 2: Congressman and Commissary

1. James Bowdoin et al., *A Short Narrative of the Horrid Massacre in Boston* (New York:
J. Doggett, Jr., 1849), 71.

2. *Boston Evening-Post*, March 12, 1770.

3. "An Alphabetical List of the Sons of Liberty who din'd at Liberty Tree, Dorchester,
Aug. 14th 1769," Massachusetts Historical Society, http://www.masshist.org/objects/
cabinet/august2001/sonsoflibertyfull.htm.

4. *Boston Gazette*, January 30, 1775.

5. John Cox Jr., ed., *Oyster Bay Town Records, Volume 7* (New York: Tobias A. Wright,
1916), 55.

6. Samuel Townsend, Jr. *Waste Book: May 12, 1772–June 25, 1772*, Collection of
Friends of Raynham Hall Museum.

7. Henry Onderdonk, *Documents and Letters Intended to Illustrate the Revolutionary
Incidents of Queens County: With Connecting Narratives, Explanatory Notes, And Additions*
(New York: Leavitt, Trow and Company, 1846), 55.

8. New York (Colony) et al., *Journals of the Provincial Congress, Provincial Convention, Committee of Safety and Council of Safety of the State of New-York: 1775–1776–1777* (Albany: Printed by Thurlow Weed, printer to the State, 1842), 9.

9. Ibid., 63, 117.

10. Ibid., 40.

11. Ibid., 116–18.

12. Ibid., 125.

13. Ibid., 428.

14. Cedrick May, *The Collected Works of Jupiter Hammon* (Knoxville, TN: University of Tennessee Press, 2017), 3–6.

15. New York (Colony). Provincial Congress, et al. *Journals of the Provincial Congress*, 515.

16. Ibid., 529.

17. Andrew Way, "The Last Migration," *The Stewarts*, Volume 23, no. 2 (2009): 137–66 and Volume 23, no. 3 (2010): 180–218.

18. Alexander McDonald, *Letter-book of Captain Alexander McDonald of the Royal Highland Emigrants, 1775-1779*. Published by the New York Historical Society (New York, NY, 1883), 254.

19. Silas Wood, *A Sketch of the First Settlement of the Several Towns on Long Island: With Their Political Condition, to the End of the American Revolution*. Printed by Alden Spooner (Brooklyn, NY, 1828), 125–36.

20. Benson J. Lossing, *The Pictorial Field-book of the Revolution: Or, Illustrations, by Pen and Pencil, of the History, Biography, Scenery, Relics, and Traditions of the War for Independence*, Volume 2 (New York: Harper & Brothers, 1859), 833–34.

21. New York (Colony). Provincial Congress, et al. *Journals of the Provincial Congress*, 599–601.

22. Henry Onderdonk, *History of Queens County with illustrations, Portraits & Sketches of Prominent Families and Individuals* (New York: W.W. Munsell & Co., 1882), 115.

23. Townsend II, Solomon (1805–1880). Undated Typescript, "Town of Oyster Bay Centennial 1876, Letter to the Editor of the Glen Cove Gazette," Collection of Friends of Raynham Hall Museum.

## Chapter 3: Oyster Bay Occupied

1. Susan Emma Woodruff Abbott, *Woodruff Genealogy, Descendants of Mathew Woodruff of Farmington, Connecticut* (New Haven: Hardy Press, 1963), 76–77.

2. "A List of the Unfortunate Prisoners," *Connecticut Journal*, February 19, 1777.

3. Letter copy book of Solomon Townsend, 1777–1778, Townsend Papers, East Hampton Library, Long Island Collection.

4. Solomon Townsend, Day Book, Ship Glasgow, 1776–1778, Townsend Family Papers, New-York Historical Society.

5. Dr. Peter Townsend, Notebook, Collection of Townsend Society of America, 5.

6. John Hannibal Sheppard, *The Life of Samuel Tucker, Commodore in the American Revolution* (Boston: Alfred Mudge and Son, Publisher, 1868), 94–95, 304–5.

7. J. Doggett et al., *A Short Narrative of the Horrid Massacre in Boston: Perpetrated in the Evening of the Fifth Day of March, 1770, by Soldiers of the 29th Regiment, Which with the 14th Regiment Were Then Quartered There: With Some Observations on the State of Things Prior to That Catastrophe* (New York: Reprinted by J. Doggett, Jr. 1849), 70–72.

8. Dr. Peter Townsend, Notebook, Collection of Townsend Society of America, 5.

9. Benjamin Franklin to Solomon Townsend, June 27, 1778, *The Papers of Benjamin Franklin*, Digital Edition, Vol. 26. https://franklinpapers.org/framedVolumes.jsp

10. Letter, Captain Abraham Whipple to Solomon Townsend, November 28, 1778, Collection of Friends of Raynham Hall Museum.

11. "Portsmouth, Oct. 19th: Thursday the 15th Instant, Arrived Here from France," *Boston Gazette*, November 2, 1778, 2.

12. Diary of Solomon Townsend, 1778–1779, Collection of Townsend Society of America.

13. Letter, Robert Townsend to Samuel Townsend, February 1, 1779, New-York Historical Society, Townsend Family Papers, Box 1.

14. Ira Morris, *Morris's Memorial History of Staten Island, New York*, vol. 2 (Staten Island, NY: Published by the Author, 1900), 181.

15. Donald Gara, *The Queen's American Rangers* (Yardley, PA: Westholme Publishing, 2015).

16. Ibid., 86–88.

17. John Graves Simcoe, *A Journal of the Operations of the Queen's Rangers from the End of 1777 until the Conclusion of the Revolutionary War* (Exeter, 1787), reprinted New York in 1844, 1961, and 1969 in different editions, 28.

18. Junius Rodriguez, *Encyclopedia of Emancipation and Abolition in the Transatlantic World* (New York: Routledge, 2007), 478.

19. Benson J. Lossing, *The Pictorial Field-book of the Revolution: Or, Illustrations, by Pen and Pencil, of the History, Biography, Scenery, Relics, and Traditions of the War for Independence*, vol. 2 (New York: Harper & Brothers, 1859), 627.

20. "Sketch of the Samuel Townsend Family," Raynham Hall Museum, https://raynham hallmuseum.org/history/the-townsends.

21. "Slavery at the Townsends'," Raynham Hall Museum. https://raynhamhallmuseum .org/history/1740-1776-before-the-revolution.

22. John Graves Simcoe, *A Journal of the Operations of the Queens Rangers from the End of 1777 until the Conclusion of the Revolutionary War*. Exeter, 1787, reprinted New York in 1844, pp. 93–101.

23. Stephen Jarvis, "An American's Experience in the British Army: Manuscript of Colonel Jarvis," *Connecticut Magazine* 11 (1907): 208–11.

24. William Kelby, *Orderly Book of the Three Battalions of Loyalists Commanded by Brigadier Oliver DeLancey, 1776–1778* (New York: New-York Historical Society, 1917).

25. Genealogy of John Greene (c. 1716–1798), WikiTree.com, https://www.wikitree .com/wiki/Greene-4887

26. Kelby, 39.

27. Account book of Israel Underhill of Oyster Bay, 1768, New-York Historical Society, Townsend Family Papers, Box 1.

28. Ledger, "Marriages in Oyster Bay by Hempstead Rectors, 1726–1845," Oyster Bay Historical Society.

29. Account book of Samuel Townsend, 1774–1781, East Hampton Library, Long Island Collection.

30. King's American Regiment orderly book, 1776–1777, William L. Clements Library, University of Michigan.

31. Henry Onderdonk, *History of Queens County, New York, with Illustrations, Portraits & Sketches of Prominent Families and Individuals* (New York: W. W. Munsell & Co., 1882), 469–576.

32. Account book of Samuel Townsend, 1774–1781, East Hampton Library, Long Island Collection.

33. Three glass windowpanes with etching, TX114.1-3. Collection of Friends of Raynham Hall Museum.

34. "America's First Valentine," Raynham Hall Museum, https://raynhamhallmuseum.org/history/first-valentine.

35. Poem, John Graves Simcoe, "Boston Camp 1775, Sacred to the Memory of _____," Simcoe Family Fonds, ca. 1750–1918, Archives of Ontario.

36. "Voyages: The Trans-Atlantic Slave Trade Database," https://www.slavevoyages.org

37. John Russell Bartlett, ed. *State of Rhode Island and Providence Plantations in New England* (Providence: Providence Press Company, 1865), 47–48.

38. Letter, Robert Townsend to Robert Stoddard, February 1, 1779, New-York Historical Society, Townsend Family Papers, Box 1.

39. "Correspondence from brothers Solomon and Robert Townsend, merchants of New York, N.Y. and Oyster Bay, N.Y., to merchants Lushington & Kirk, at Charleston, South Carolina," January 17, 1787, East Hampton Library, Long Island Collection.

40. Winthrop Sargent, *The Life of Major John André, Adjutant-General of the British Army in America* (New Jersey: D. Appleton Publishers, Harvard University, 1871).

41. Robert McConnell Hatch, *Major John André: A Gallant in Spy's Clothing* (New York: Houghton Mifflin Harcourt Publishing Company, 1986).

42. Letter, John André to John Graves Simcoe, February 29, 1779, Simcoe Papers, Microfilm Reel MS 1803, Ontario Archives in Toronto, Ontario.

43. Carl Leopold Bauermeister, *Revolution in America: Confidential Letters and Journals 1776–1784 of Adjutant General Major Bauermeister of the Hessian Forces*, trans. B. A. Uhlendorf (New Brunswick, NJ: Rutgers, 1957), 265.

44. Letter, John André to Sir Henry Clinton, March 20, 1779, Henry Clinton Papers, 1736–1850, John André's Letter Book, 1770–1780, vol. 275, William L. Clements Library, University of Michigan, Ann Arbor, Michigan.

45. Partial transcription of letter, John André to John Graves Simcoe, April 6, 1779, in *Bibliotheca Americana et Philippina*, Catalogue No. 429 (London: Maggs Bros., 1922), 391.

46. Willard Sterne Randall, *Benedict Arnold: Patriot and Traitor* (New York: William Morrow & Co, 1990).

47. Letter, John André to Sir Henry Clinton, May 20, 1779, Henry Clinton Papers, 1736–1850, John André's Letter Book, 1770–1780, vol. 275, William L. Clements Library, University of Michigan, Ann Arbor, Michigan.

48. Ledger, "Marriages in Oyster Bay by Hempstead Rectors, 1726–1845," Oyster Bay Historical Society.

49. Letter, Robert Townsend to Samuel Townsend, May 26, 1779, Townsend Family Papers, Collection of Friends of Raynham Hall Museum.

## Chapter 4: "No Probability of Your Getting Her Again"

1. *Holy Bible* (Edinburgh: Printed by Alexander Kincaide, 1771), Collection of the Friends of Raynham Hall Museum. Handwritten inscription on front pastedown reads, "Bible for the Servants in the House of Samuel Townsend, Oyster Bay Long Island"; handwritten inscriptions at the end of the volume give dates of births and deaths and partial history of Townsend slaves from 1769 to 1795.

2. Elizabeth Fenn, *Pox Americana: The Great Smallpox Epidemic of 1775–82* (New York: Farrar, Straus and Giroux, 2002).

3. Advertisement, "To Be Sold, a Young Negro Wench," *New-York Gazette and the Weekly Mercury*, January 3, 1780, 3.

4. Account book of Samuel Townsend, 1774–1781, East Hampton Library, Long Island Collection.

5. John Graves Simcoe, *A Journal of the Operations of the Queen's Rangers from the End of 1777 until the Conclusion of the Revolutionary War* (Exeter, 1787), reprinted New York in 1844, 101.

6. Letter, Robert Townsend to Samuel Townsend, May 26, 1779, Townsend Family Papers, Collection of Friends of Raynham Hall Museum.

7. S. R. Mealing, "Simcoe, John Graves," *Dictionary of Canadian Biography*, vol. 5, University of Toronto/Université Laval, 2003–, accessed November 9, 2014, http://www.biographi.ca/en/bio/simcoe_john_graves_5E.html.

8. Graham Russell Gao Hodges, *Root and Branch: African Americans in New York and East Jersey, 1613–1863* (Chapel Hill: University of North Carolina Press, 2005), 139–40.

9. "Proclamation by His Excellency Sir Henry Clinton," *Royal American Gazette* (New York, July 22, 1779), 1.

10. Letter, Simcoe to André, no date, c. May 1780, Sir Henry Clinton Papers, vol. 95, item 57, William L. Clements Library, University of Michigan.

11. Letter, Simcoe to André, no date, c. May 1780, Sir Henry Clinton Papers, vol. 95, item 58, William L. Clements Library, University of Michigan.

12. Henry A. M. Smith, "Charleston and Charleston Neck: The Original Grantees and the Settlements along the Ashley and Cooper Rivers," *South Carolina Historical and Genealogical Magazine* (South Carolina Historical Society) 19, no. 1 (January 1918): 43–45.

13. John Graves Simcoe, *A Journal of the Operations of the Queen's Rangers from the End of 1777 until the Conclusion of the Revolutionary War* (Exeter, 1787), reprinted New York in 1844, 228.

14. Todd W. Braisted, "Bernard E. Griffiths: Trumpeter Barney of the Queen's Rangers, Chelsea Pensioner—and Freed Slave," *Journal of the American Revolution*, February 21, 2019, https://allthingsliberty.com/2019/02/bernard-e-griffiths-trumpeter-barney-of-the -queens-rangers.

15. "Yesterday a party of the enemy, consisting of Ty[e] with 30 blacks," *New-Jersey Gazette*, June 28, 1780, 3.

16. Steven Jarvis, "An American's Experience in the British Army: Manuscript of Colonel Jarvis," *Connecticut Magazine* 11 (1907): 208–11.

17. "One Guinea Reward, Run away," *New-York Gazette and Weekly Mercury*, April 12, 1779, 2.

18. "Two Guineas Reward, Run away," *New-York Gazette and the Weekly Mercury*, August 9, 1779, 3.

19. "Five Pounds Reward, Run Away," *New-York Gazette and the Weekly Mercury*, September 6, 1779, 2.

20. "Four Dollars Reward, Run Away," *New-York Gazette and the Weekly Mercury*, January 4, 1779, 4.

21. "A Negro Run away," *Royal Gazette*, May 1, 1779, 3.

22. "One Guinea Reward, Run away," *Royal Gazette*, May 29, 1779, 2.

23. Willard Sterne Randall, *Benedict Arnold: Patriot and Traitor* (New York: William Morrow & Co, 1990).

24. Lincoln Diamant, *Chaining the Hudson: The Fight for the River in the American Revolution* (New York: Fordham University Press, 2004).

25. Henry Phelps Johnston, *The Storming of Stony Point on the Hudson, Midnight, July 15, 1779* (New York: James T. White & Company, 1900), 29.

26. John Graves Simcoe, *A Journal of the Operations of the Queen's Rangers* (New York: Bartlett and Welford, 1844), 107.

27. Letter, Robert Townsend to Benjamin Tallmadge, June 29, 1779, George Washington Papers, Manuscript Division, Library of Congress, Washington, DC.

## *Chapter 5: Spies and Traitors*

1. Hannah Adams, *A Summary History of New-England, from the First Settlement at Plymouth, to the Acceptance of the Federal Constitution. Comprehending a General Sketch of the American War* (Dedham, MA: H. Mann & J. H. Adams, 1799), 358.

2. "Who has not pitied Major Andre?," *Albany (New York) Argus*, November 29, 1816, 2.

3. "Pensioner's Muster," *Connecticut Mirror*, August 7, 1820, 3.

4. Letter, Ebenezer Seeley to Henry Onderdonk, September 30, 1846, Henry Onderdonk Correspondence, Brooklyn Historical Society.

5. Letter, Ebenezer Seeley to Henry Onderdonk, February 2, 1848, Henry Onderdonk Correspondence, Brooklyn Historical Society.

6. Master's log of the *Halifax*, by Captain Quarme, November 11, 1775–June 22, 1778, 46–48. The National Archives of the United Kingdom.

7. Henry Onderdonk, *Revolutionary Incidents of Suffolk and Kings Counties: With an Account of the Battle of Long Island and the British Prisons and Prison-ships at New York* (New York: Leavitt & Company, 1849), 52.

8. Letter, Ebenezer Seeley to Henry Onderdonk, September 30, 1846, Henry Onderdonk Correspondence, Brooklyn Historical Society.

9. "Monthly List of Prisoners Confined in the Provost," *Royal Gazette* (New York), February 1, 1783, 3.

10. "A General Court-Martial," *Royal Gazette* (New York), February 5, 1783, 2.

11. Dorothy Verrill, Maltby-Maltbie Family History (Newark, NJ: B. L. Maltbie, by the authority of the Maltby Associates, 1916), 387–88.

12. Letter, George Washington to Caleb Brewster, August 8, 1778, George Washington Papers, Manuscript Division, Library of Congress, Washington, DC.

13. Letter, George Washington to Benjamin Tallmadge, August 25, 1778, George Washington Papers, Manuscript Division, Library of Congress, Washington, DC.

14. Letter, Abraham Woodhull to Brigadier General Charles Scott, October 31, 1778, George Washington Papers, Manuscript Division, Library of Congress, Washington, DC.

15. Letter, George Washington to Benjamin Tallmadge, March 21, 1779, George Washington Papers, Manuscript Division, Library of Congress, Washington, DC.

16. Letter, Abraham Woodhull to Benjamin Tallmadge, April 10, 1779, George Washington Papers, Manuscript Division, Library of Congress, Washington, DC.

17. Letter, Abraham Woodhull to Benjamin Tallmadge, June 5, 1779, George Washington Papers, Manuscript Division, Library of Congress, Washington, DC.

18. Letter, Abraham Woodhull to Benjamin Tallmadge, June 20, 1779, George Washington Papers, Manuscript Division, Library of Congress, Washington, DC.

19. Advertisement. "Just Imported and to be Sold by Oakman and Townsend," *Royal American Gazette* (New York, NY), 4.

20. Letter, George Washington to Benjamin Tallmadge, July 5, 1779, George Washington Papers, Manuscript Division, Library of Congress, Washington, DC.

21. Culper Code Book: Created by Col. Benjamin Tallmadge, 1779, edited and transcribed by Michael Godket, https://raynhamhallmuseum.org/programs/distance-learning/

22. Letter, Abraham Woodhull to Benjamin Tallmadge, August 15, 1779, George Washington Papers, Manuscript Division, Library of Congress, Washington, DC.

23. Letter, John Jay to George Washington, November 19, 1778, George Washington Papers, Manuscript Division, Library of Congress, Washington, DC.

24. Letter, John André to Joseph Stansbury, May 10, 1779, Henry Clinton Papers, 1736–1850, John André's Letter Book, 1770–1780, vol. 275, William L. Clements Library, University of Michigan, Ann Arbor, Michigan.

25. Letter, Benjamin Tallmadge to George Washington, July 25, 1779, George Washington Papers, Manuscript Division, Library of Congress, Washington, DC.

26. Letter, George Washington to Benjamin Tallmadge, September 24, 1779, George Washington Papers, Manuscript Division, Library of Congress, Washington, DC.

27. Letter, Robert Townsend to Benjamin Tallmadge, July 29, 1779, George Washington Papers, Manuscript Division, Library of Congress, Washington, DC.

28. Letter, Robert Townsend to Benjamin Tallmadge via James Townsend, March 23, 1780, George Washington Papers, Manuscript Division, Library of Congress, Washington, DC.

29. Letter, John Deausenberry to George Washington, March 23, 1780, George Washington Papers, Manuscript Division, Library of Congress, Washington, DC.
30. Letter, Abraham Woodhull to Benjamin Tallmadge, February 26, 1779, George Washington Papers, Manuscript Division, Library of Congress, Washington, DC.
31. Letter, Abraham Woodhull to Benjamin Tallmadge, October 29, 1779, George Washington Papers, Manuscript Division, Library of Congress, Washington, DC.
32. Letter, Benjamin Tallmadge to George Washington, November 1, 1779, George Washington Papers, Manuscript Division, Library of Congress, Washington, DC.
33. Letter, Benjamin Tallmadge to George Washington, July 22, 1780, George Washington Papers, Manuscript Division, Library of Congress, Washington, DC.
34. Letter, Robert Townsend to Col. Richard Floyd, July 20, 1780, George Washington Papers, Manuscript Division, Library of Congress, Washington, DC.
35. Letter, Robert Townsend to Col. Richard Floyd, August 6, 1780, George Washington Papers, Manuscript Division, Library of Congress, Washington, DC.
36. Account book of Robert Townsend, November 23, 1779–March 29, 1781, East Hampton Library, Long Island Collection.
37. Letter, Robert Townsend to Hercules Mulligan, February 24, 1783, New-York Historical Society, Townsend Family Papers.
38. Thomas Buchanan, "Diary Kept by Thomas Buchanan During the Year 1780," unpublished typescript, New York Historical Society.
39. Dr. Peter Townsend (c. 1845 note at bottom), document in the handwriting of Robert Townsend regarding formation of New York City Volunteer Company, New-York Historical Society, Townsend Family Papers, Box 1, Folder 4.
40. Account book of Robert Townsend, 1781–1785, East Hampton Library, Long Island Collection.
41. Dr. Peter Townsend (c. 1845 note at bottom), document in the handwriting of Robert Townsend regarding formation of New York City Volunteer Company, New-York Historical Society, Townsend Family Papers, Box 1, Folder 4.
42. Letter, John André to Sir Henry Clinton, March 20, 1779, Henry Clinton Papers, 1736–1850, John André's Letter Book, 1770–1780, vol. 275, William L. Clements Library, University of Michigan, Ann Arbor, Michigan.
43. James A. Knauss, "Christopher Saur the Third," *Proceedings of American Antiquarian Society* 41 (1931): 235–53.
44. "Sale of Forfeited Estates," *Pennsylvania Packet* (Philadelphia, PA), August 27, 1779, 1.
45. Winthrop Sargent, *The Life of Major John André, Adjutant-general of the British Army in America* (New York: D. Appleton Publishers, Harvard University, 1871).
46. Robert McConnell Hatch, *Major John André: A Gallant in Spy's Clothing* (New York: Houghton Mifflin Harcourt Publishing Company, 1986).
47. Simcoe, *A Journal*, 150–52.
48. Letters, John André to John Graves Simcoe, August 29, 1780 and September 12, 1780, Henry Clinton Papers, 1736–1850, John André's Letter Book, 1770–1780, vol. 275, William L. Clements Library, University of Michigan, Ann Arbor, Michigan.

49. Letter, Abraham Woodhull to Benjamin Tallmadge, November 12, 1780, George Washington Papers, Manuscript Division, Library of Congress, Washington, DC.
50. Letter, Abraham Woodhull to Benjamin Tallmadge, January 14, 1781, George Washington Papers, Manuscript Division, Library of Congress, Washington, DC.
51. Lease agreement, Robert Townsend to Hannah Cockle, March 28, 1781, Manuscripts Collection, G. W. Blunt White Library, Mystic Seaport Museum.
52. Solomon Townsend II, *Scrapbook of Solomon Townsend* (Oyster Bay, NY: Raynham Hall Museum, 1846).
53. Account book of Robert Townsend, 1781–1785, East Hampton Library, Long Island Collection.
54. Ibid.
55. "Correspondence from brothers Solomon and Robert Townsend, merchants of New York, N.Y. and Oyster Bay, N.Y., to merchants Lushington & Kirk, at Charleston, South Carolina," January 17, 1787, East Hampton Library, Long Island Collection.
56. Account book of Samuel Townsend, 1781–1788, East Hampton Library, Long Island Collection, 29.

## Chapter 6: "A Child with Her Then Master"

1. "It is earnestly recommended. . .," *New-York Gazette and the Weekly Mercury*, August 7, 1782, 1.
2. "Public Auction To-morrow—The Effects of Officers Going to England," *New-York Gazette and the Weekly Mercury*, August 7, 1782, 3.
3. Benjamin Quarles, *The Negro in the American Revolution* (Chapel Hill: Published for the Institute of Early American History and Culture, Williamsburg, VA, by the University of North Carolina Press, 1916), 175–78.
4. Advertisement, "Public Auction," *Royal Gazette* (New York, NY), October 19, 1782, 2.
5. Ira Berlin and Leslie M. Harris, eds., *Slavery in New York* (New York: The New Press, 2005), 101–9.
6. Letter, Robert Townsend to Benjamin Tallmadge, November 14, 1782, George Washington Papers, Manuscript Division, Library of Congress, Washington, DC.
7. Brian Kilmeade and Don Yaeger, *George Washington's Secret Six: The Spy Ring That Saved the American Revolution* (New York: Sentinel, 2013), 193–95.
8. Carl Leopold Bauermeister, *Revolution in America: Confidential Letters and Journals 1776–1784 of Adjutant General Major Bauermeister of the Hessian Forces*, trans. B. A. Uhlendorf (New Brunswick, NJ: Rutgers, 1957), 528.
9. Dr. Peter Townsend (c. 1845 at bottom), document in the handwriting of Robert Townsend regarding formation of New York City Volunteer Company, New-York Historical Society, Townsend Family Papers, Box 1, Folder 4.
10. *Holy Bible* (Edinburgh: Printed by Alexander Kincaide, 1771), Collection of the Friends of Raynham Hall Museum. Handwritten inscription on front pastedown reads, "Bible for the Servants in the House of Samuel Townsend, Oyster Bay Long Island"; handwritten inscriptions at the end of the volume give dates of births and deaths and partial history of Townsend slaves from 1769 to 1795.

11. Solomon Townsend to Samuel Townsend, August 24, 1788, New-York Historical Society, Townsend Family Papers, Box 1, Folder 5.

12. Account book of Robert Townsend, 1781–1785, East Hampton Library, Long Island Collection, 3, 31.

13. Cash book of Robert Townsend, entry for September 30, 1782, New-York Historical Society, Townsend Family Papers, 19.

14. "Correspondence from brothers Solomon and Robert Townsend, merchants of New York, N.Y. and Oyster Bay, N.Y., to merchants Lushington & Kirk, at Charleston, South Carolina," January 17, 1787, East Hampton Library, Long Island Collection.

15. "Correspondence from brothers Solomon and Robert Townsend, merchants of New York, N.Y. and Oyster Bay, N.Y., to merchants Lushington & Kirk, at Charleston, South Carolina," March 22, 1787, East Hampton Library, Long Island Collection.

16. Bill of Sale from Robert Townsend to Jotham Weekes, "Obligation from Jotham Weekes to Manumit Harry," August 21, 1804, Townsend Family Papers, New-York Historical Society.

17. Obituary, *Connecticut Gazette* (New London, CT), August 8, 1783, 2.

18. Advertisement, *Royal Gazette*, July 30, 1783, 2.

19. Berlin and Harris, *Slavery in New York*, 121–26.

20. "Correspondence from brothers Solomon and Robert Townsend, merchants of New York, N.Y. and Oyster Bay, N.Y., to merchants Lushington & Kirk, at Charleston, South Carolina," January 17, 1787, East Hampton Library, Long Island Collection.

21. Account book of Robert Townsend & Co., Parts A & B, May 18, 1781–August 1, 1783, East Hampton Library, Long Island Collection, 39.

22. Advertisement, *New-York Packet,* May 17, 1784, 3.

23. "A Gentleman of this City . . .]," *New-York Journal* (New York, NY), July 6, 1769, 3.

24. Obituary, *New-York Packet* (New York, NY), July 12, 1784, 3.

25. Harry Macy Jr., "Robert Townsend Jr., of New York City," *New York Genealogical and Biographical Record* 126 (1995): 29.

## *Chapter 7: "Ensnared into Bondage"*

1. Solomon Townsend II, *Scrapbook of Solomon Townsend* (Oyster Bay, NY: Raynham Hall Museum, 1846), 35–36.

2. Pocket diary of Solomon Townsend, entry for March 6, 1805, New-York Historical Society.

3. Harry Macy Jr., "Robert Townsend Jr., of New York City," *New York Genealogical and Biographical Record* 126 (1995).

4. "Minutes of the New York Manumission Society (January 5, 1785).

5. Walter Stahr, *John Jay: Founding Father* (New York: Hambledon Continuum, 2006).

6. "Extract of a Letter from a Gentleman in Charleston, to His Friend in This City," *New York Packet* (New York, NY), March 13, 1786, 3.

7. "A Hint—Now riding in this harbor," *Independent Ledger* (Boston, MA), April 10, 1786.

8. Jacob R. Marcus, "Jews and the American Revolution: A Bicentennial Documentary," *American Jewish Archives* 27, no. 2 (November 1975): 108.

9. Estate of Richard Lushington, deceased, *U.S., Quaker Meeting Records, 1681–1935 Philadelphia Monthly Meeting Minutes, 1789–1840*, Ancestry.com, https://www.ancestry.com/imageviewer/collections/2189/images/42060_1821100519_3627-000 90?treeid=&personid=&hintid=&queryId=6a26e8bf3f986674e78b2cf2faeafc9b&usePUB=true&_phsrc=tin328&_phstart=successSource&usePUBJs=true&pId=1100485729

10. J. Hector St. John de Crèvecoeur, *Letters from an American Farmer: Describing Certain Provincial Situations, Manners, and Customs, Not Generally Known; . . . By J. Hector St. John* (Dublin: printed by John Exshaw, 1782).

11. Letter, Richard Lushington to John Jay, February 22, 1786, Papers of John Jay, Rare Book and Manuscript Library, Columbia University.

12. S. Foster Damon, "The History of Square Dancing," *Proceedings of the American Antiquarian Society*, April 1952, Vol. 62, Part 1, 74–75.

13. "This evening Mr. Griffiths will have a Grand Ball," *Loudon's New-York Packet*, February 20, 1786.

14. Letter, Richard Lushington to John Jay, February 22, 1786.

15. William Jay, *The Life of John Jay with Selections from His Correspondence* (New York: J. & J. Harper, 1833), 181–82.

16. "Mr. Printer, the Many Affecting Instances of Injustice," *Independent Journal* (New York, NY), March 15, 1786, 2.

17. Letter copy book of Solomon Townsend, 1786–1791, Collection of Friends of Raynham Hall Museum.

18. "Died, last Wednesday evening," *New York Packet* (New York, NY), July 12, 1784, 3.

19. "New York, December 25," *Independent Journal* (New York, NY), December 25, 1784, 2.

20. "Correspondence from brothers Solomon and Robert Townsend, merchants of New York, N.Y. and Oyster Bay, N.Y., to merchants Lushington & Kirk, at Charleston, South Carolina." New York, NY: East Hampton Library, Long Island Collection, January 17, 1787.

## Chapter 8: "A Townsman with a Cudgel"

1. James Savage, *A Genealogical Dictionary of the First Settlers in New England* (Boston, 1860), 343.

2. Joseph James Muskett, *Evidences of the Winthrops of Groton, Co. Suffolk, England, and of Families in and Near That County, with Whom They Intermarried* (Private printing, 1896), 27.

3. Benjamin Trumbull, *A Complete History of Connecticut, Civil and Ecclesiastical, from the Emigration of Its First Planters, from England, in the Year 1630, to the Year 1764* (New Haven, CT: Maltby, Goldsmith and Company and Samuel Wadsworth, 1818), 410–19.

4. "We, the Subscribers," *Connecticut Gazette*, May 8, 1767.

5. "This is to Notify the creditors," *Connecticut Gazette*, April 15, 1768, 4.

6. "Just Imported, and to be Sold by Richard Palmes," *New London Summary*, September 16, 1763.

7. "To Be Sold by Richard Palmes," *Boston News-Letter*, May 16, 1765.

8. Edward Lillie Pierce, *Major John Lillie, 1755–1801: The Lillie Family of Boston, 1663–1896* (Cambridge, MA: J. Wilson & Son, 1896), 72–79.

9. "Richard Palmes, late of Boston," *Boston News-Letter*, December 6, 1765, 4.

10. "On Wednesday, the 18th Instant," *Boston News-Letter*, June 12, 1766, 2.

11. Col. William Palfrey, in "An Alphabetical List of the Sons of Liberty who din'd at Liberty Tree, Dorchester, Aug. 14th 1769," Massachusetts Historical Society, http://www.masshist.org/objects/cabinet/august2001/sonsoflibertyfull.htm.

12. Lithograph, William L. Champney, "Boston Massacre, March 5th, 1770," Boston, published by Henry Q. Smith, 1856.

13. "Extract of a Letter from Boston," *London Magazine, Or, Gentleman's Monthly Intelligencer* 39 (1770): 222.

14. "Please to give the following a place in your useful paper," *Boston Gazette*, April 22, 1771.

15. L. Kinvin Wroth and Hiller B. Zobel, eds., "The Boston Massacre Trials," Cases 63 and 64, in *The Adams Papers, Legal Papers of John Adams*, vol. 3 (Cambridge, MA: Harvard University Press, 1965), 62–81.

16. Wroth and Zobel, "The Boston Massacre Trials," Cases 1–30, 1: 31–86.

17. Palmes vs. Greenleaf, "The Pleadings Book: 1771–1773," Founders Online, National Archives, https://founders.archives.gov/documents/Adams/05-01-02-0002-0001-0002. [Original source: *The Adams Papers, Legal Papers of John Adams*, vol. 1, Cases 1–30, ed. L. Kinvin Wroth and Hiller B. Zobel (Cambridge, MA: Harvard University Press, 1965), 31–86.]

18. "Whereas I the Subscriber, being in a Passion," *Boston Gazette*, April 12, 1773.

19. Christian DiSpigna, *Founding Martyr: The Life and Death of Joseph Warren, the American Revolution's Last Hero* (New York: Crown, 2018), 262.

20. Charles Richard Smith, *Marines in the Revolution: A History of the Continental Marines in the American Revolution, 1775–1783* (Washington, DC: History and Museums Division, Headquarters, U.S. Marine Corps, 1975), 79, 462.

21. Ibid., 729.

22. Naval Documents of the American Revolution, vol. 9 (Washington, DC: Naval History Division, Department of the Navy, 1964), 900.

23. Ibid., 732, 804.

24. Smith, 115.

25. John Hannibal Sheppard, *The Life of Samuel Tucker: Commodore in the American Revolution* (Boston: Alfred Mudge and Son, Publisher, 1868), 94–95, 305.

26. Smith, 462.

27. "To Be Let, An airy and commodious House, Without the City," *Columbian Herald* (Charleston, SC), January 4, 1787.

28. Papers of the Continental Congress, Petitions Address to Congress, 1775–89, The National Archives Collection, vol. 8, 295.

29. "Auction and Commission Store," *Independent Journal* (New York, NY), April 3, 1784.

30. "A large quantity of the best English Cheese," *Independent Journal* (New York, NY), April 24, 1784.

31. "The House of Parker, Hopkins, and McClane, being dissolved," *Independent Journal* (New York, NY), February 9, 1785, 3.

32. "In the Brig Lucretia, from New York, came passengers," *South-Carolina Gazette and General Advertiser* (Charleston, SC), January 25, 1785, 3.

33. "Two Guineas Reward, and all charges paid," *South-Carolina Advertiser* (Charleston, SC), June 24, 1785.

34. "Correspondence from brothers Solomon and Robert Townsend, merchants of New York, N.Y. and Oyster Bay, N.Y., to merchants Lushington & Kirk, at Charleston, South Carolina," January 17, 1787, East Hampton Library, Long Island Collection.

35. "New York and Charleston Packet, Brigantine Lucretia, James Tinker, Master," *South-Carolina Gazette and General Advertiser*, January 31, 1785.

## Chapter 9: "Derangement and Separation"

1. Letter (partial), undated, Robert Townsend about Henry Oakman, East Hampton Library, Long Island Collection.

2. Photocopy of letter, Robert Townsend to Thomas Stewart, September 8, 1784, Collection of Friends of Raynham Hall Museum.

3. Joan Baldwin and Geoffrey Rossano, *Clan and Commerce: The Townsend Family of Oyster Bay* (unpublished thesis, 1986), 151–57, Collection of Friends of Raynham Hall Museum.

4. Letter, Ancrum, Forster, and Brice to Robert Townsend, April 10, 1776, Townsend Family Papers, New-York Historical Society.

5. H. Bacon McKoy, *The McKoy Family of North Carolina and Other Ancestors Including Ancrum, Berry, Halling, Hasell [and] Usher* (Greenville, SC, 1955), 54–55.

6. Letters, Robert Townsend to Mr. Frances Brice, February 12 & May 25, 1784, East Hampton Library, Long Island Collection.

7. Letter, Robert Townsend to Henry Toomer, September 8, 1784, East Hampton Library, Long Island Collection.

8. Account book of Robert Townsend & Co., 1781–1785, East Hampton Library, Long Island Collection.

9. Quote by Junius (anonymous essayist) in the handwriting of Robert Townsend, undated, East Hampton Library, Long Island Collection.

10. Letter, John Townsend to Robert Townsend, April 7, 1792, East Hampton Library, Long Island Collection.

11. Essay, "On the Advantages and Inconveniences of a Retired Life," in the handwriting of Robert Townsend, undated, Townsend Family Papers, New-York Historical Society.

12. "And the same evening was married Mr. Alexander Robertson," *Independent Journal* (New York), December 25, 1784, 2.

13. Henry James, *A Small Boy and Others: A Critical Edition* (Charlottesville: University of Virginia Press, 2011), 9.

14. "Alexander Robertson & Co," *New-York Packet*, July 4, 1785.

15. William M. MacBean, *Biographical Register of Saint Andrew's Society of the State of New York, 1756–1806*, vol. 2 (New York: Printed for the Society of Saint Andrews, 1922), 22.

16. "Correspondence from brothers Solomon and Robert Townsend, merchants of New York, N.Y. and Oyster Bay, N.Y., to merchants Lushington & Kirk, at Charleston, South Carolina," January 17, 1787, East Hampton Library, Long Island Collection.

17. "List the Hon., the Senators, for the present Year," *Daily Advertiser* (New York, NY), January 15, 1787, 2.

18. "Yesterday the winds began to blow very hard," *Independent Journal* (New York, NY), November 12, 1785, 2.

19. "Charleston," *New York Independent Journal*, December 10, 1785, 2.

20. "For Savannah, the Schooner Sally," *Charleston Evening Gazette*, January 24, 1786, 3.

21. "For George-Town, the Schooner Sally," *Charleston Evening Gazette*, November 29, 1785, 2.

22. Purchase agreement, Schooner Sally, Charleston District, South Carolina Estate Inventories and Selected Bills of Sale, 1732–1872, South Carolina Department of Archives and History, 504.

23. "For Sale, the Schooner Sally," *Charleston Morning Post* (Charleston, SC), May 5, 1787, 2.

24. "Correspondence from brothers Solomon and Robert Townsend, merchants of New York, N.Y. and Oyster Bay, N.Y., to merchants Lushington & Kirk, at Charleston, South Carolina," January 17, 1787, East Hampton Library, Long Island Collection.

## Chapter 10: "Principled against Selling Slaves"

1. Letter copy book of Solomon Townsend, 1786–1791, Collection of the Friends of Raynham Hall Museum.

2. "A Caution: The Free Negroes in this city are desired to be very careful," *Daily Advertiser* (New York, NY), February 20, 1787, 2.

3. "To the Impartial Public," *Daily Advertiser* (New York, NY), February 23, 1787, 2.

4. "Minutes of the New York Manumission Society, February 15, 1787," The Papers of John Jay, Columbia University Libraries: A Project of Columbia University Libraries Digital Program.

5. "A Hint," *New-York Packet* (New York, NY), March 16, 1786, 3.

6. "Mr. Printer," *Freeman's Journal* (Philadelphia, PA), September 6, 1786, 3.

7. "Runaway from my Plantation," *State Gazette of South-Carolina* (Charleston, SC), September 15, 1785.

8. Find a Grave memorial page for Maurice Simons (January 23, 1744–November 12, 1785), Find a Grave Memorial ID 49944179, citing Saint Philip's Episcopal Church Cemetery, Charleston, Charleston County, South Carolina, USA; maintained by Susan Bowman (contributor 47065755), https://www.findagrave.com/memorial/49944179/maurice-simons (accessed March 8, 2020).

9. "Yesterday evening the declaration was made of the ballot," *South Carolina Weekly Gazette* (Charleston, SC), December 4, 1784.

10. Henry Laurens, David Chesnutt, and C. Taylor, *The Papers of Henry Laurens*, vol. 16: September 1, 1782–December 17, 1792 (Columbia: University of South Carolina Press for the South Carolina Historical Society, 2003).

11. "The dismal story and good character of Colonel Maurice Simons," *Boston American Recorder*, December 23, 1785.

12. "Ten Dollars Reward," *Charleston Morning Post* (Charleston, SC), June 23, 1786, 3.

13. Leo H. Hirsch, "The Slave in New York," *Journal of Negro History* 16, no. 4 (1931): 387.

14. John Cox Jr., ed., *Oyster Bay Town Records* (New York: Tobias A. Wright, 1916).

15. "Correspondence from brothers Solomon and Robert Townsend, merchants of New York, N.Y. and Oyster Bay, N.Y., to merchants Lushington & Kirk, at Charleston, South Carolina," March 22, 1787, East Hampton Library, Long Island Collection.

16. Henry Onderdonk, *Queens County in Olden Times: Being a Supplement to the Several Histories Thereof* (Jamaica, NY: Charles Welling, Publisher, 1865), 115.

17. "Correspondence from brothers Solomon and Robert Townsend, merchants of New York, N.Y. and Oyster Bay, N.Y., to merchant Adam Gilchrist, at Charleston, South Carolina," March 22, 1787, East Hampton Library, Long Island Collection.

## Chapter 11: "Obtain the Wench from Him"

1. "Twenty Shillings Reward, Run away," *New-York Gazette and the Weekly Mercury*, July 27, August 3, 10, and 24, and September 9, 1772.

2. William MacBean, *Biographical Register of Saint Andrew's Society of the State of New York, 1756–1806*, vol. 2 (New York: Printed for the Society of Saint Andrews, 1922), 164–65.

3. New York (State) et al., *New York in the Revolution as Colony and State: Supplement* (Albany: O. A. Quayle, 1901), 78.

4. "Southern Campaign American Revolution Pension Statements and Rosters: American Officers Imprisoned at New York City and Long Island NY, 1776–1780," transcribed and annotated by C. Leon Harris, Southern Campaigns Revolutionary War Pension Statements & Rosters, https://www.revwarapps.org/b220.pdf, 18.

5. Edwin G. Burrows, *Forgotten Patriots: The Untold Story of American Prisoners during the Revolutionary War* (New York: Basic Books, 2008), 64.

6. Oath of Allegiance of Adam Gilchrist, "Numbered Records Books Concerning Military Operations and Service Pay and Settlement of Account: War Department," Fold3, 117.

7. "Papers of the Continental Congress, Prisoners Released," February 17, 1779, Fold3, 59.

8. "For Sale at the store of Adam Gilchrist & Co," *New-York Packet* (New York, NY), May 20, 1784, 2.

9. "The committee will proceed," *Columbian Herald*, November 23, 1784, 4.

10. "That your memorialists being deeply affected," *Loudon's New-York Packet*, March 13, 1786, 3.

11. "The Co-partnership of Adam Gilchrist and Company being Dissolved," *New-York Packet* (New York, NY), March 21, 1785.

12. Letter copy book of Solomon Townsend, 1786–1791, Collection of the Friends of Raynham Hall Museum.

13. "Correspondence from brothers Solomon and Robert Townsend, merchants of New York, N.Y. and Oyster Bay, N.Y., to merchant Adam Gilchrist, at Charleston, South Carolina," March 22, 1787, East Hampton Library, Long Island Collection.

14. Letter copy book of Solomon Townsend, 1786–1791, Collection of the Friends of Raynham Hall Museum.

15. Letter, Adam Gilchrist to Robert Townsend, April 12, 1787, Townsend Family Papers, New-York Historical Society.

16. Robert Behre, "Hotel construction unearths piece of wall that surrounded Charleston in the early 1700s," *Post and Carrier* (Charleston, SC), February 22, 2019, https://www.postandcourier.com/news/hotel-construction-unearths-piece-of-wall-that-surrounded-charleston-in/article_dd9dac08-3613-11e9-a877-e3dec3039f8a.html.

17. Nic Butler, "The Earliest Fortifications at Oyster Point," *Rediscovering Charleston's Colonial Fortifications,* January 26, 2019, https://walledcitytaskforce.org.

18. "To Be Let, An airy and commodious House, Without the City," *Columbian Herald* (Charleston, SC), January 4, 1787.

19. "Needle worked Lawn Aprons," *Charleston Evening Gazette*, May 11, 1786.

20. "For Sale, at our store, by the package," *City Gazette* (Charleston, SC), May 3, 1788.

21. "For Sale, A tract of land," *City Gazette and Daily Advertiser* (Charleston, SC), September 23, 1795.

22. "For Sale, a likely young Mulatto woman," *Charleston Evening Gazette*, February 7, 1786.

23. Alice and Daniel Huger-Smith, *The Dwelling Houses of Charleston, South Carolina* (Philadelphia and London: J. B. Lippincott, 1917), 293.

24. Thomas Cooper and David James McCord, *The Statutes at Large of South Carolina: Acts, 1787–1814* (Columbia, SC: A. S. Johnston, 1839), 36–38.

25. Letter copy book of Solomon Townsend, 1786–1791, Collection of the Friends of Raynham Hall Museum.

26. "For Sale, the Schooner Sally," *Charleston Evening Post*, May 8, 1787.

27. "Tomorrow will be Sold, by David Denoon," *Columbian Herald* (Charleston, SC), October 29, 1787, 3.

28. Letter copy book of Solomon Townsend, 1786–1791, Collection of the Friends of Raynham Hall Museum.

29. "Arrivals since our last," *Charleston Independent Journal*, April 28, 1787.

30. "Inward Entries," *Maryland Journal*, April 10, 1787, 2.

31. "For Philadelphia, the Sloop Betsy," *Massachusetts Centinel*, May 26, 1787.

32. *Richard Palmes v. Robert Smither*, Judgment Roll, 1787, Judgment Rolls (Court of Common Pleas), Box 135A Item 0237A (S136002), South Carolina Department of Archives and History.

### Chapter 12: "Elizabeth, a Black Woman"

1. *Holy Bible* (Edinburgh: Printed by Alexander Kincaide, 1771).

2. *The New York Genealogical and Biographical Record* (quarterly) (New York: New York Genealogical and Biographical Society, selected extracts 1881), 36. Ancestry.com,

https://search.ancestry.com/cgi-bin/sse.dll?indiv=1&dbid=7854&h=119876&tid=&pid=
&queryId=d019280600b01db0d6ce55f9a52f5d94&usePUB=true&_phsrc=tin330&_
phstart=successSource

3. "An Act Concerning Slaves," *New York Packet* (New York, NY), April 25, 1788, 2.

4. Dr. Peter Townsend, Notebook, F89.11.9, Collection of the Friends of Raynham Hall Museum, 92.

5. "Sketch of the Samuel Townsend Family," Raynham Hall Museum, https://raynham hallmuseum.org/history/the-townsends.

6. Letter, Solomon Townsend to Samuel Townsend, August 24, 1788, Townsend Family Papers, New-York Historical Society.

7. Members of the Baptist Church of Oyster Bay, New York, November 16, 1789, Office of the Town Clerk, Town of Oyster Bay.

8. "A Bill to enable David Richard Floyd to add Jones to his surname," *Daily Advertiser* (New York, NY), March 21, 1788, 2.

9. New York (State), *Laws of the State of New York: Passed at the Sessions of the Legislature Held in the Years 1777–1801, Being the First Twenty-Four Sessions*, vol. 3 (Albany: Weed, Parsons, 1887), 116.

10. "Saturday night last, Brigadier General Silliman, and his son," *Connecticut Journal* (New Haven, CT), May 5, 1779, 2.

11. Benson J. Lossing, *The Pictorial Field-book of the Revolution: Or, Illustrations, by Pen and Pencil, of the History, Biography, Scenery, Relics, and Traditions of the War for Independence*, vol. 2 (New York: Harper & Brothers, 1859), 646.

12. Blake Bell, "Exchange of Prisoners in the Waters Off the Manor of Pelham during the Revolutionary War," *Historic Pelham*, May 25, 2007, http://historicpelham.blogspot.com/2007/05/exchange-of-prisoners-in-waters-off.html.

13. Dr. Peter Townsend, Notebook, F89.11.9, Collection of the Friends of Raynham Hall Museum.

14. Benson John Lossing, *The Diary of George Washington, from 1789 to 1791: Embracing the Opening of the Frst Congress, and His Tours through New England, Long Island, and the Southern States* (Richmond: Press of the Historical Society, 1861), 120–26.

15. Obituary, "On the 24th, at Oyster-Bay on Long Island," *Albany Register* (Albany, NY), December 6, 1790, 3.

### *Chapter 13: Uncle Robert and "Free Elizabeth"*

1. John Henry Jones, *The Jones Family of Long Island: Descendants of Major Thomas Jones (1665–1726) and Allied Families* (New York: T. A. Wright, 1907), 93.

2. William Dewey Foster, *Historic American Buildings Survey, Fort Neck House (Tryon Hall)* (Massapequa, NY: Historical Society of the Massapequas, 1936).

3. First Census of the United States, 1790 (NARA microfilm publication M637, 12 rolls), Records of the Bureau of the Census, Record Group 29, National Archives, Washington, DC.

4. Thomas Floyd-Jones, *Thomas Jones: Fort Neck, Queens County, Long Island, 1695 and His Descendants the Floyd-Jones Family: With Connections from the Year 1066* (New York: n.p., 1906), 19.

5. First Census of the United States, 1790 (NARA microfilm publication M637, 12 rolls), Records of the Bureau of the Census, Record Group 29, National Archives, Washington, DC.

6. Account book of Robert Townsend, 1791–1827, East Hampton Library, Long Island Collection.

7. Letter, Abraham Franklin to Robert Townsend, June 2, 1795, East Hampton Library, Long Island Collection.

8. "An Act for the Gradual Abolition of Slavery," March 29, 1799, New York State Archives, http://digitalcollections.archives.nysed.gov/index.php/Detail/objects/10815. Source: New York (State), Department of State, Bureau of Miscellaneous Records. Enrolled acts of the State Legislature. Series 13036–78, Laws of 1799, Chapter 62.

9. Account book of Robert Townsend, 1791–1827, East Hampton Library, Long Island Collection.

10. *Holy Bible* (Edinburgh: Printed by Alexander Kincaide, 1771).

11. Bill of Sale from Robert Townsend to Jotham Weekes, "Obligation from Jotham Weekes to Manumit Harry," August 21, 1804, Townsend Family Papers, New-York Historical Society.

12. Photocopy of essay, "With regard to the constitution of the mind," in the handwriting of Robert Townsend, Collection of the Friends of Raynham Hall Museum.

13. Copy of "Extract of a Journey through Spain by the Rev. Joseph Townsend" in the handwriting of Robert Townsend, Townsend Family Papers, New-York Historical Society.

14. Letter, James Farley to Robert Townsend, April 9, 1800, East Hampton Library, Long Island Collection.

15. Solomon Townsend, Pocket Diaries, 1803–1804, New-York Historical Society.

16. Typescript of "From my Aunt Sarah T. 1842" from the notebook of Dr. Peter Townsend, Collection of the Friends of Raynham Hall Museum.

17. Harry Macy Jr., "Robert Townsend Jr., of New York City," New York Genealogical and Biographical Record 126 (1995).

18. "Sketch of the Samuel Townsend Family," Raynham Hall Museum, https://raynham hallmuseum.org/history/the-townsends.

## *Epilogue: "The Journey's End"*

1. "Book of Negroes," 1783, Nova Scotia Archives, Halifax, Nova Scotia, Canada, 111.

2. "Pine Hollow Land Survey including Naomi Gaul and Plato Gale properties," private collection of Denise Evans-Sheppard, 1959.

3. John Jamison Moore, *History of the A. M. E. Zion Church in America. Founded in 1796, in the City of New York* (York, PA: Teachers Journal Office, 1884), 223.

4. Denise Evans-Sheppard and Francis S. Carl, *Footsteps of a Forgotten Soldier: The Life and Times of David Carll* (Scottsdale, AZ: Bookpatch, 2015).

5. Nicholas Wieland, "Huntington Unveils Historic Marker at Jupiter Hammon House," *The Huntingtonian*, December 11, 2015, https://thehuntingtonian .com/2015/12/11/huntington-unveils-historic-marker-at-jupiter-hammon-house.

6. Cedrick May and Julie McCowen, "'An Essay on Slavery': An Unpublished Poem by Jupiter Hammon," *Early American Literature* 48, no. 2 (2013): 457–71.

7. Cedrick May, *The Collected Works of Jupiter Hammon* (Knoxville: University of Tennessee Press, 2017).

8. "John B. Coles," in Walter Barrett, *The Old Merchants of New York City, Second Series* (New York: Thomas R. Knox & Co., 1863), http://bklyn-genealogy-info.stevemorse.org/Business/Merchant/Coles.html.

9. Matthew Montelione, "Richard Floyd IV: Long Island Loyalist," *Long Island History Journal*, https://lihj.cc.stonybrook.edu/2015/articles/richard-floyd-iv-long-island-loyalist.

10. Alexander Rose, *Washington's Spies: The Story of America's First Spy Ring* (New York: Bantam Books, 2006), 174.

11. Michael Schellhammer, "Abraham Woodhull: The Spy Named Samuel Culper," *Journal of the American Revolution*, May 19, 2014, https://allthingsliberty.com/2014/05/abraham-woodhull-the-spy-named-samuel-culper.

12. "John Graves Simcoe," Historical Narratives of Early Canada, http://www.uppercanadahistory.ca/simcoe/simcoe1.html.

13. Todd W. Braisted, "Bernard E. Griffiths: Trumpeter Barney of the Queen's Rangers, Chelsea Pensioner—and Freed Slave," *Journal of the American Revolution*, February 21, 2019, https://allthingsliberty.com/2019/02/bernard-e-griffiths-trumpeter-barney-of-the-queens-rangers.

14. "Alexander Robertson, Esq., Merchant of the city, has made a donation," *New-York Daily Gazette*, February 25, 1791.

15. William M. MacBean, *Biographical Register of Saint Andrew's Society of the State of New York, 1756–1806*, vol. 2 (New York: Printed for the Society of Saint Andrews, 1922), 13.

16. "Admissions," Alexander Robertson School, https://www.alexanderrobertson.org/admissions.

17. "An Ordinance to Aid the establishment of Shirras Dispensary," *City Gazette* (Charleston, SC), November 8, 1813.

18. "Dispensary at Roper Hospital," *Evening Post* (Charleston, SC), January 4, 1922.

19. "Notice is hereby given to Richard Palmes," *New-York Daily Gazette*, October 6, 1789.

20. "The sloop Free Mason," *New York Daily Gazette* (New York, NY), November 11, 1793, 3.

21. "Capt. Tinker of the Sloop Romeo," *Spectator* (New York, NY), March 28, 1798, 3.

22. "Some account of the loss of the Schooner Eliza," *Alexandria Times* (Alexandria, VA), May 18, 1802.

23. Obituary, "At sea (drowned)," *Norwich Courier*, June 16, 1802.

24. Obituary, "Died Last Monday, after an illness of only three days," *State Gazette of South-Carolina* (Charleston, SC), June 24, 1790, 2.

25. Herbert A. Johnson, "The Constitutional Thought of William Johnson," *South Carolina Historical Magazine* 89, no. 3 (1988): 132–45.

26. "Sketch of the Samuel Townsend Family," Raynham Hall Museum, https://raynham hallmuseum.org/history/the-townsends.

27. "At Albany on Wednesday evening," *Spectator* (New York, NY), April 3, 1811, 2.

28. Estate book of Solomon Townsend, Collection of the Friends of Raynham Hall Museum.

29. Typescript of "From my Aunt Sarah T. 1842" from the notebook of Dr. Peter Townsend, Collection of the Friends of Raynham Hall Museum.

30. Harry Macy Jr., "Robert Townsend Jr., of New York City," *New York Genealogical and Biographical Record* 126 (1995): 108–11.

31. Letters, Robert Townsend to Solomon Townsend II, July 21 and July 26, 1833, Collection of the Friends of Raynham Hall Museum.

32. Solomon Townsend, Record Book of His Anchor Shop in Ferry Street, NYC 1795–1806, Townsend Family Papers, New-York Historical Society.

33. John Cox Jr., ed., *Oyster Bay Town Records* (New York: Tobias A. Wright, 1916).

34. Account book of Robert Townsend, 1791–1827, East Hampton Library, Long Island Collection.

35. Richard Townsend's manumission of Harry, NY Slave Manumissions, May 28, 1818, https://slavemanumission.wordpress.com/ny-manumission-data.

# INDEX

Italicized page numbers indicate illustrations in insert section.